MINISTRY WITH THE AGING

MINISTRY
WITH THE
AGING

Edited by William M. Clements

1817

Harper & Row, Publishers, San Francisco
Cambridge, Hagerstown, New York, Philadelphia,
London, Mexico City, São Paulo, Sydney

FIRST EDITION

Designed by Jim Mennick

Library of Congress Cataloging in Publication Data

Main entry under title:
MINISTRY WITH THE AGING.

Includes index.
  1. Church work with the aged—Addresses, essays,
lectures. 2. Aged—Religious life—Addresses,
essays, lectures. 3. Pastoral theology—Addresses,
essays, lectures. I. Clements, William M.
BV4435.M56 1980   259'.3   80-7739
ISBN 0-06-061496-X

---

81 82 83 84 85 10 9 8 7 6 5 4 3 2 1

Contents

List of Contributors

JOHN C. BENNETT is President Emeritus of Union Theological Seminary in New York City. His unique blend of Christian ethics and social action continues to influence new generations of pastors and theologians. He is the author of *The Radical Imperative* and co-author of *U.S. Foreign Policy and Christian Ethics*.

ELBERT C. COLE, Senior Minister of the Central United Methodist Church in metropolitan Kansas City, Missouri, is also Executive Director of the Shepherd's Center, a significant and innovative ecumenical development in the ministry with aging people.

JAMES W. EWING is the first Executive Director of the American Association of Pastoral Counselors. In this capacity his influence and leadership are being felt in many denominations and local parishes. Prior to this, he was Professor of Pastoral Care at Eden Theological Seminary in St. Louis, Missouri.

MARTIN J. HEINECKEN, a theologian and Professor Emeritus at the Lutheran Theological Seminary in Philadelphia, Pennsylvania, has in recent years written on behalf of the emerging ministry with the aging in his denomination, the Lutheran Church in America. He is the co-author of *The Church's Ministry with Older Adults: A Theological Basis.*

URBAN T. HOLMES, III, is Dean and Professor of Theology and Culture at the School of Theology of the University of the South, Sewanee, Tennessee. One of his special interests is Christian spirituality, and he is the widely appreciated author of *The Priest in Community, The Future Shape of Ministry, Ministry and Imagination,* and other books.

MELVIN A. KIMBLE is Professor of Pastoral Theology and Ministry at Luther-Northwestern Theological Seminaries, St. Paul, Minnesota. He developed one of the trend-setting courses to be offered to seminarians and laity in the area of religion and aging.

ROLF P. KNIERIM is Professor of Old Testament at the School of Theology at Claremont and the Claremont Graduate School in California. His creative scholarship has successfully challenged and engaged students in both Europe and America. He is the author of *Die Hauptbegriffe für Sünde im Alten Testament.*

JEAN B. LAPORTE, Professor in the Department of Theology at the University of Notre Dame, South Bend, Indiana, is widely acknowledged for his ability to relate the history and thought of the early Christian Church to contemporary religious life. He is the author of *La Doctrine Eucharistique chèz Philan d'Alexandrie.*

MARTIN E. MARTY is Fairfax M. Cone Distinguished Service Professor at the University of Chicago. One of his specialties is American religious history of the 20th century, and he is a widely read commentator on the contemporary religious scene in the United States. He is the author of *Baptism, Good News in the Early Church, A Nation of Behavers, Righteous Empire,* and other books.

DONALD E. MILLER is Professor of Christian Education and Ethics at Bethany Theological Seminary in Oak Brook, Illinois. His book, *The Wing-Footed Wanderer: Conscience and Transcendence,* is influential among a wide readership.

ALLEN J. MOORE, author of *The Young Adult Generation,* is Professor of Religion and Personality and Education at the School of Theology at Claremont and the Claremont Graduate School in

California. He has also served as the Dean of Summer Studies at the School of Theology, involving scholars and students from many cultures in creative dialogue.

GEORGE PATERSON, Associate Professor in both the School of Religion and the College of Medicine at the University of Iowa, is also Associate Director of Pastoral Services within the largest university-owned teaching hospital in the United States. He has authored *Helping Your Handicapped Child* and *The Cardiac Patient.*

BARBARA PAYNE is the Director of the Gerontology Department at Georgia State University in Atlanta, where she also teaches in the Sociology Department. She is the co-author of the often quoted book *Love in the Later Years* and the author of *Meaning and Measurement of Commitment to the Church.*

ANN BELFORD ULANOV, a Diplomate of the American Association of Pastoral Counselors and a Jungian Analyst, is Professor of Psychiatry and Religion at Union Theological Seminary in New York City. She is the author of *The Feminine in Jungian Psychology* and co-author of *Religion and the Unconscious.*

EVELYN EATON WHITEHEAD, whose specialty is developmental psychology and adult development and aging, is a consultant in education and ministry through Whitehead Associates in South Bend, Indiana. She is co-author of *Christian Life Patterns* and *Method in Ministry.*

JAMES D. WHITEHEAD, a historian of religion based in South Bend, Indiana, is a consultant in education and ministry through Whitehead Associates. He is the co-author of *Christian Life Patterns* and *Method in Ministry.*

WILLIAM M. CLEMENTS is Associate Professor and Pastoral Counselor in the Department of Family Practice of the College of Medicine at the University of Iowa. A gerontologist, he is the author of *Care and Counseling of the Aging.*

Preface

The writing of this book has involved the cooperation and hard work of people scattered across the United States. Their link with each other has been their desire to help create a genuinely useful and informative volume on religion and aging. The contributing authors have graciously worked for the good of the total book by gauging the length of their own chapters and by avoiding unnecessary overlaps. The authors have displayed amazing patience, on one hand, and have worked vigorously to meet deadlines, on the other. They have made my job as editor pleasantly growthful and challenging.

Other people have also been helpful along the way. Dr. David Moss of the Center for Religion and Psychotherapy in Chicago provided wise counsel at an early stage of development; Professor James Spalding of the School of Religion at the University of Iowa and Professor Allen Moore of the School of Theology and the Claremont Graduate School each made unique and penetrating suggestions for the design of the volume; Peggy Rakel of Iowa City provided valuable input into the arrangement of chapters through questions which helped clarify and crystallize the format. I am very appreciative of their encouragement and significant investment of time and energy, without which *Ministry with the Aging* would never have developed.

Unfortunately, during a portion of the preparation of this collaborative effort, illness kept me away from my desk. During my absence, Claudia Richards continued to work diligently and cheerfully on the typing and many other details of production such a collaborative effort always entails. There are few pages within *Ministry with the Aging* that have not benefited from the skill and care of Betty Clements, whose involvement in this project exceeded the bounds of her position as a research assistant and editor at the University of Iowa. My trust in her has certainly resulted in a much better book, as well as in a deeper understanding of love and hope.

1

Introduction: The New Context for Ministry with the Aging

William M. Clements

A ministry with the aging is hardly new in the life of the church. Even during the early formative centuries of Christianity elderly people were an integral part of the church community, involved in many aspects of the church's life, including its ministry. Since those early days, we can discern the presence, activity, and thought of older people in each age of the church's history, if we look below the surface. In historical accounts commonly available, the age of participants when significant events took place has been largely irrelevant to the matters at hand. Age has tended to be ignored as less significant than other qualities when the processes of historical distillation took place. For example, the fact that John Wesley was eighty-one when he reluctantly decided to ordain missionaries for America was neither important nor amazing. Today, however, we note (with some surprise, it seems) that Pope John XXIII was seventy-eight when he called Vatican Council II!

Perhaps the apparent inattentiveness to age in earlier periods of history will reveal more clearly certain central values and attitudes if we contrast it to the manner in which our own time deals with age. In the more distant past, chronological age was rarely considered a dominant issue in either the ascendancy or decline of people or of their ideas. Great age led neither to undue veneration nor to institutional marginalization. Perhaps life was experienced with more continuity across the decades, with fewer arbitrary distinctions between young adulthood, middle age, and old age. No stage or age of the life cycle was set apart for special treatment or scrutiny.

If this perspective is correct, then to single out for discussion one period of life, such as old age, is somewhat risky. The discussion might, for example, create an atmosphere in which the aged are seen as somehow being basically different from people at other points in the life cycle. The church's reluctance to enter the discussion about aging and the aged in recent times may stem from such concerns. Another risk is that the aged, when thus categorized, are excluded from the discussion and become dehumanized as needy objects.

An even greater hazard, however, is remaining silent. Such a silence by the church could result in a further erosion of the view that all of human life, regardless of age, is of supreme value and worthy of dignity and respect. Shifts in cultural values might then be expressed within the church in the further marginalization of the elderly, who, as a result, might become even less integrally related to ministry. The editor and contributors to this book are aware of these and other risks. The intent of this book is to pay particular attention to the process of aging without needlessly setting the aged even further apart through either idealization or trivialization.

If becoming aged in earlier periods of history did not exclude one from participation in ministry, what is the rationale for a book such as this? The question is particularly probing, because you will not find in these pages a call for a radical new form of ministry whose outlines have never appeared before. Instead, the quality called forth in this ministry with the aging reflects the best of previous experience and thought. In this sense, at least, it is not new and untried. What is undeniably novel is the *context* within which designs for this ministry emerge. Ministry with the aging today, in the next decade, and beyond will be significantly different because of the context within which it is found, not because of the principles on which it is based.

Other contributors outline the current situation of the aged in our society, to which the church is struggling to respond with an effective ministry. Briefly, however, it might be helpful to contrast certain aspects of the situation with those of previous years. For this purpose, I compare the year 1900 to the year 1976—the last year for which population figures are readily available. (Interestingly enough, this time period corresponds roughly with the life span of many elderly people in our society.)

Suppose we create for the purpose of illustration a congregation of 500 people who exactly duplicate the age distribution in the United States in 1900. You can see from Figure 1 that this congregation includes 119 children under ten years of age, 102 older children and adolescents, and so forth across the life span. About 47 of the people are fifty-five years of age or above; only 21 being over sixty-five.

Suppose that you suddenly find yourself transported to the year 1976 and the congregation of 500 members still duplicates the age distribution in the United States. This time, however, three-quarters of a century have passed. From Figure 1, you can see that this mythical congregation now includes a markedly different age distribution, with 76 children under ten years of age (a 36 percent decrease), 95 older children and adolescents, and so forth across the life span. About 100 of the people are fifty-five years of age or above, with 54 being over sixty-five. Within a period of seventy-six years, there has been an increase of 257 percent in the number of persons over sixty-five in this "typical" congregation.

Stop and consider for a moment what these changes mean in the life of the congregation—in the lives of families and individuals. How many fewer infant baptisms were there in 1976 than in 1900? How many fewer youths in confirmation classes? What about marriages and funerals?

In standard tables of vital statistics, deaths are usually reported as a number per 100,000 of population for each age (death rate). Figure 2 presents the *percentage* of deaths that would have occurred within each age group in the "typical" congregation in 1900 and 1976—not

Figure 1. AGE DISTRIBUTION FOR A TYPICAL CONGREGATION
OF 500 INDIVIDUALS

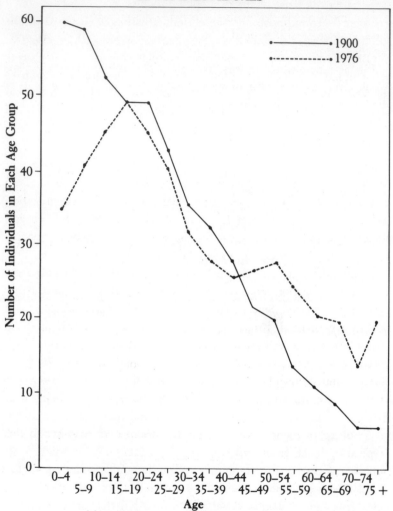

Data derived from U.S. Bureau of the Census, *Census of Population: 1970*, vol. 1, *Characteristics of the Population*, Part 1, United States Summary—Section 1: Table 51, "Single Years of Age: 1880 to 1970," and Table 53, "Age by Race and Sex: 1900 to 1970" (Washington, D.C.: U.S. Government Printing Office, 1973); and *Current Population Reports*, Series P-25, no. 800, "Estimates of the Population of the United States, by Age, Sex, and Race: 1976 to 1978": Table 2, "Estimates of the Resident Population of the United States by Age, Sex, and Race: July 1, 1976, to 1978" (Washington, D.C.: U.S. Government Printing Office, 1979).

the actual number of people who would have died. In 1900, then, 24.7 percent of the deaths in the congregation would involve infants; 11.4 percent, children aged one to four; and 5.2 percent, children aged five to fourteen.

Of the funerals held in this "typical" parish, a total of 41.3 percent would involve the deaths of young people (less than fifteen years of age). In contrast, only 19.8 percent of the funerals would involve people over age sixty-five.

The experience of the "typical" congregation in 1976 would be remarkably different. Here 2.5 percent of the deaths would involve infants; .45 percent, children aged one to four; and .67 percent, children aged five to fourteen. Now, a total of only 3.62 percent of the funerals would involve the deaths of youngsters less than fifteen years old, representing a 91 percent decrease since 1900 in the number of funerals for this age group in the parish. However, 64.9 percent of the funerals in 1976 would involve the deaths of people over age sixty-five, an increase of 328 percent since 1900.

When we compare the two ends of the life cycle—youth and old age—we see a dramatic reversal between 1900 and 1976 in the number of funerals that would have occurred in a "typical" congregation. In 1900, twice as many funerals would have involved youngsters as old people, while in 1976 for every child's funeral you would expect eighteen funerals for old people. Over three-quarters of a century, more people are now dying later in life; or, put another way, more people are living longer.

Statistical projections of "expectation of life," or years of life remaining, for each age group can help us get a better grasp on what "living longer" means for the church. You can see from a glance at Figure 3 that there has been a slight but significant increase in the years of life remaining for people above fifty-five years of age. For example, a white male fifty-five years of age in 1900 could count on 17.42 more years of life. In contrast, a white male at the same age in 1976 could count on 20.5 more years, a difference of slightly more than 3 years. The difference in expectation of life at age eighty is only 1.5 years, however.

Figure 2. DISTRIBUTION OF DEATHS DURING A YEAR'S PERIOD
OF TIME: COMPARISON BY AGE GROUP OF THOSE WHO DIED
IN 1900 AND 1976

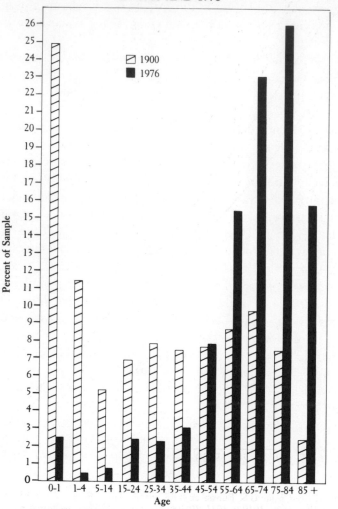

Data derived from U.S. Bureau of the Census, *Historical Statistics of the United States, Colonial Times to 1970, Bicentennial Edition, Part 2,* Series B 181–192, "Death Rate, by Age and Sex: 1900 to 1970" (Washington, D.C.: U.S. Government Printing Office, 1975); and *Statistical Abstract of the United States: 1978* (99th edition), no. 102, "Deaths and Death Rates by Sex, Race, and Age, 1940 to 1976" (Washington, D.C.: U.S. Government Printing Office, 1978).

Figure 3. EXPECTATION OF LIFE FOR WHITE MALES AT SELECTED AGES IN 1900 AND 1976

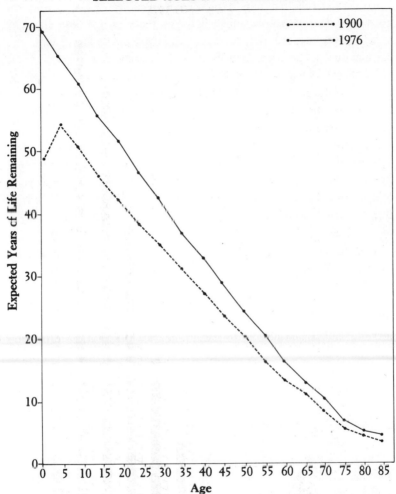

Data derived from U.S. Bureau of the Census, *United States Life Tables: 1929 to 1931, 1920 to 1929, 1919 to 1921, 1909 to 1911, 1901 to 1910, 1900 to 1902*, VIII–A, "Life Tables for White Males in the Original Registration States: 1900 to 1902" (Washington, D.C.: U.S. Government Printing Office, 1936); and *Statistical Abstract of the United States: 1978* (99th ed.), no. 100, "Expectation of Life and Mortality Rates, by Race, Age, and Sex: 1976" (Washington, D.C.: U.S. Government Printing Office, 1978).

You will recall that our "typical" congregation of 500 people for 1900 included 47 people above fifty-five years of age, and that the congregation for 1976 included over 100 people above fifty-five. Rough calculations for the purpose of illustration indicate that in 1900 people older than fifty-five in this congregation could, as a group, count on over 583 years of life remaining. The same rough calculations indicate that in 1976 people in the congregation above age fifty-five could count on almost 1,400 years of life remaining. Keep in mind that the 1976 group includes more than twice as many people as the 1900 group. The significant thing, however, from the standpoint of ministry is that in 1976 people older than fifty-five would, as a group, live 816 years longer than those in 1900. These 800-plus additional years will be lived by people who, by and large, are more vigorous, better educated, more affluent, and more mobile than their counterparts in 1900.

The trends illustrated by the two imaginary "typical" congregations lead to the conclusion that ministry with the aging in the 1980s and beyond will take place in a radically new context. This context, when taken in its entirety, is different from anything in the previous experience of the church and constitutes a challenge for the church on several fronts. It prompts us to reexamine those foundations for action and reflection that are crucial for the emergence of new designs for ministry. At the same time, this new context presents an opportunity for the flowering of the best new designs that are emerging. The challenge and the opportunity represent a potential renaissance in which ministry that is firmly rooted in the rich soil of tradition reaches out to a changing world in new and creative ways.

With this new context in mind, I turn to some of the key concepts underlying this volume. First of all, the model of ministry developed in these chapters is broad in scope. Unifying the discussion, in all of its rich diversity, is the concept that ministry belongs to all the people of God and is not an exclusive domain of any portion of the Christian community. In distinction from those emphases that tend to identify ministry almost exclusively with sacramental and pastoral responsibilities, a ministry with the aging is understood here as present among all believers. Ordained and lay, young and old, all people can be involved in this ministry of Christ.

Such a view implies that in actual experience ministry is not easily dichotomized. When we make this attempt by dividing it between "here" and "not there," between giving and receiving, doing and being, youth and adulthood, or between the middle years and old age, something vital is lost in the process. Within the community of believers, or within any one person's life, ministry does not accurately correspond to a chronological understanding of the life span, present at one stage and absent at another.

Much more is involved in the evolution of ministry than chronology, even though it is tempting to accept the sweeping generalizations within our culture that would have us uncritically focus on the middle years as a time of *doing* ministry, and on the years of youth and old age as a time of *needing* ministry. Such unexamined cultural assumptions probably obscure more reality than they enlighten. What is often lost in such a fragmented model of ministry is the subtle interplay in life between distance and nearness, light and darkness, earth and sky, that informs the horizon of human existence and meaning.

Even as the concept of ministry here is broad enough to span a lifetime, so also does the concept of aging reach beyond one tiny part of that lifetime. You will find here a focus on the *process* of aging, or *becoming old*. Aging as a process is not restricted to the last decades of life, although in this time period it becomes most obvious. To be aging is almost synonymous with being alive. It is closely related to our human finitude and points as a constant reminder to the limited amount of time available for living within the life cycle.

To be aging, and to be aware of one's participation in the process, can have enormous implications for the paths of meaning that lead to the horizon of human destiny and existence. Such self-awareness of aging may mean that crossing the mythical threshold into old age need come as no surprise, may be anticipated and planned for—perhaps even welcomed. To be aging implies a larger and longer process than mere membership in a chronological category of late adulthood called "the aged." The foundations, challenges, and designs for ministry discussed in these pages involve more of the life span than the aged, although they are certainly relevant to this time of life. To discover once again our unique vocation as Christians, this time within the context of an aging church whose membership is increasingly becoming older, can add new depth and breadth to understanding and participation in ministry.

We have viewed thus far both ministry and aging as broad categories of inclusion, with *ministry* including not only the ordained but also all Christians, and *aging* including people past the first decade of life, a much larger group than just the aged. But what are the characteristics of the relationships between ministry and aging? How do they relate to each other? Probably the most distinguishing quality of the relationship between ministry and aging is communicated through the word *with*. *Ministry* with *the Aging* implies that ministry occurs among people who are in a dynamic and evolving relationship together. There is a communal quality to the word *with* that is absent from words such as *to* or *for*. This ministry is shared among the aging.

You find affirmed here an almost obvious yet neglected truth—that people of all ages can think and plan, can give of themselves, and can receive graciously within a context of human relationships that may well include great diversities of age, strengths, and needs. You will, I hope, discern some realities that are relevant for your own personal life and ministry, as well as for the communities within which you live and move.

FOUNDATIONS

The first section of this volume consists of foundations for ministry with the aging. The goal here is to make available important information that otherwise might not be as readily accessible as our pressing needs sometimes require. Each chapter presents informatively and creatively findings distilled by an eminent scholar who has chosen only the most relevant issues for discussion.

Foundation chapters look in two directions. First, they illuminate the sustaining roots within our own rich tradition. From these roots, an emergent ministry with the aging can draw nourishment and support. Second, they provide a strong factual basis for a deeper appreciation of the presence and role of aging people within contemporary religious institutions. Taken together, these foundations help to provide a uniquely Christian perspective on aging that can help to clarify and sharpen a ministry of action and reflection.

In his chapter, "Age and Aging in the Old Testament," Rolf Knierim points out the generally positive attitude toward old people expressed throughout the broad span of the biblical period. Unveiled before us is an acute awareness of the painful realities of aging. Yet there is also a wisdom that can come with age, enabling acceptance of pain and recognition of the joy of God's love. From the earliest times, there is a strong feeling of satisfaction at having lived. Generally speaking, in the Old Testament aging is weighed in the balance and not found wanting.

Continuing the biblical perspective, Jean Laporte's discussion of "The Elderly in the Life and Thought of the Early Church" makes it clear that, in keeping with its heritage, the Early Church tried to recognize and benefit from the wisdom of its aged. Of particular significance to us is the apparently successful attempt of the Early Church to institutionalize this special wisdom, not only in the traditional councils of "elders" but also in the congregations of widows. We note with interest the burgeoning of urban poverty, especially that of elderly widows, that was part of the Early Church milieu. To be a widow may have been to be sad, lonely, and poor, but the church tried to mitigate the situation by recognizing within the state of widowhood something of value.

But what about the aged in our own time, in America? Martin Marty attempts to understand and illuminate the current situation in his chapter, "Cultural Antecedents to Contemporary American Attitudes toward Aging." The key question is, When did the aged become a "class" and (hence) a *problem?* Period by historical period, we see the "problem" developing. If we are indeed heading out in a new direction, as many believe, understanding the past, or how we got to where we are, may give us a clue to understanding the future.

Marty indicates that there can really be no clear-cut "history of the aged" in our society. Similarly, Martin Heinecken feels that there can really be no "theology of aging." At the same time, it is important to look at basic Christian theological concepts and affirmations in the light of the situation of the aged. "Christian Theology and Aging: Basic Affirmations" reviews the concepts of love and justice and relates them to aging. As our experience as a people and as a church continues to change, we can hope for creative new additions to our theology; in the meantime, the basic affirmations are there and need to be reflected on, to be reaffirmed, before we break new ground.

We might also suggest that we need not so much to find new forms of worship for a "new day" as to understand what worship means. In "Worship and the Aging: Memory and Repentance," Urban Holmes reminds us that "worship is an act grounded in memory" and that "the church cannot create memories for people deprived of the opportunity to build them over the years." The symbols with which the ritual of worship, the liturgy, is filled depend on memories—more than that, on memories of value, memories that call us to repentance. Old people, in whom memories are so strong, still have the potential—as they did in years gone by—to be "more honest" than the young, to face without fear the deepest questions of life (represented by the symbols we revere), to worship truly, to become wise. They cannot do this in a vacuum, however. The church must "take the past seriously" and must value the process of building memories of value in its people.

CHALLENGES

What are some of the challenges we face in a society that is rapidly becoming older and older? The second section of this volume addresses this question. Again, eminent scholars share with us thoughtful analyses of their particular areas of expertise.

These chapters clarify the issues and lend a Christian perspective to tasks that can seem overwhelming. Problems of adjustment, adaptation, and ethical judgment are closely related to the changes we are experiencing as an aging population and touch virtually all aspects of our lives. A religious view of these issues cannot make the difficult easy, the unpleasant pleasant, or the bitter sweet. We can, however, give ourselves some direction as we move ahead within our traditions;

we can discern something of value within the challenges that confront our society and personhood.

Perhaps the greatest challenge of aging is not the threat of time on our hands, of poverty, or of ill health; it is rather to face that which we fear most, to come to grips with the basic questions of life. Ann Belford Ulanov asks, "What is our end? To what goal are we moving? What purpose guides us? When we come to an end, at what end shall we have arrived?" Ulanov's chapter, "Aging: On the Way to One's End," examines aging from the point of view of depth psychology. We get a look at what aging really means deep inside our minds and hearts—the poverty of spirit that sometimes has to be faced, the richness and creativity that can be discovered. Ulanov points out that awareness of aging at any age gives us a precious opportunity to understand life, to see what really matters, to know the strength of the human spirit, to accept the love and grace of God.

Surely another great challenge of aging is *retirement*. We sense ambivalence in ourselves and in society as we face this tremendously significant event. In their discussion of "Retirement," Evelyn and James Whitehead review its social tasks (for example, financial adjustment) and its psychological tasks (for example, reexamining personal identity). They suggest defining retirement as a "life passage" and remind us of the important social and psychological functions of religious and cultural "rites of passage." If we see retirement as a religious event (as birth, marriage, and death are religious events), we can bring to it the Christian tradition's heritage of religious value and meaning. The church can recognize that the love of God does not depend on what we produce and can celebrate "grace-filled uselessness" and the "testimony of a lifetime of faith."

John Bennett's presentation of "Ethical Aspects of Aging in America" confronts us with the moral responsibility of society for the elderly and the mutual obligation of children and parents. Bennett illuminates some of the ethical questions that must be faced, thrashed out, and resolved as church and society attempt to deal responsibly with the problems of an ever-aging population: forced retirement versus freedom of choice, continuing responsibilities for elderly citizens, "the right to die," and "death with dignity." Of particular importance is the discussion of the ethics of *terminal suicide* (suicide of the terminally ill). In the face of the almost overwhelming obligation to prolong life, can individual decisions to stop that process be made responsibly? The question is still open, as the legalistic secular ethical tradition moves toward greater harmony with a humanized ethic of love and justice, the heart of the Judeo-Christian tradition.

Bennett points out the injustices of *ageism*, a way of thinking and acting that has much in common with sexism and racism. Stereotypes of the aged are being shattered right and left with the availability of accurate information from the social sciences. When sociologists turn their attention to religious behavior, the result is no different. In "Religion and the Elderly in Today's World," Barbara Payne reviews a number of studies of religious participation and attitudes of the elderly. It appears, for example, that church attendance figures are not the reliable indicators they were once thought to be. Moreover, long-held assumptions about the significantly positive function of religion in adjustment to old age have yet to be tested systematically. Payne summarizes the institutional and clerical responses of the church to the elderly and suggests some future directions from a sociological point of view.

Like attitudes toward the aged and like ideas about them, traditional "normative" views of families and family relations are being challenged on all fronts. A general reexamination of these theories, coupled with increasing interest in the elderly, has led to greater attention to the familial lives of older people. Allen Moore, in his chapter on "The Family Relations of Older People," explores the need for a new, dynamic definition of the family based on interaction. Christian education, for example, has been characterized by a life-stage approach that has emphasized age segregation and neglected the family as a whole. The roles of all family members—including the old, the retired, the never-married, the childless, and so on—need to be recognized as worthwhile. It may be that the church can come to a new appreciation of the biblical tradition that valued the older family member as bearer of wisdom and culture, and of the Early Church practice in which the shared life together emphasized a commonality of faith.

DESIGNS

The third division of this volume is concerned with practical applications, action approaches, getting up and going with something that has to be done. Contributors to this section write from their own experience, offering some reflection on these experiences, but primarily describing what has been done and what can be done.

We might compare the church at this point to an old person who has moved through various stages of the life cycle (birth, youthful exuberance that envisions never-ending growth, productivity, a gradual slowing down, and so forth). This old person (church) has come to a point where a "life review" is needed—a reevaluation of life and purpose through reminiscence. The old person spends some time remembering, evaluating the present in the light of life experiences, gathering strength for the future by reaching back to the roots. When these things have been done, the old person can be revitalized and can move forward into a new creativity.

The first chapter in this last section, James Ewing's "Adults with Parents in Crisis: A Personal Account," is indeed a deeply personal account of one pastor's experience not as a pastor but as the son of aged parents. Many of us have faced or will face the pain of realizing our parents' frailty, with all the agonizingly difficult decisions that accompany that realization. In Ewing's account, we can recognize ourselves, yet objectively we can see what must be done. More than that, we can see that the help offered by (and accepted from) pastor, congregation, and friends was what was needed and was truly helpful. Too often we as pastors, neighbors, or friends feel there is nothing we can do—that "just caring" is a poor substitute for "real action." Ministers and ministering congregations will find that while these difficult times with aged parents may not become the rule, neither will they be the exception. We need to be ready to respond sensitively and sensibly.

Many ministers realize that they are not prepared to respond to their older parishioners as sensitively and as sensibly as they would wish. Melvin Kimble points out that clergy are likely to be no more knowledgeable about aging than others, yet they are uniquely placed in our society to be particularly effective with the aged. Ministers and others within the religious community who recognize these opportunities for service may want to learn more about aging and the aged. In "Education for Ministry with the Aged" Kimble provides guidelines for designing both self-enrichment and continuing education programs. Organizers of continuing education courses for ministers will want to pay particular attention to Kimble's experience. His suggestions are also valuable for people involved in planning training sessions and informational programs for laypeople in the local church. While his ideas will not make us "omniscient gerontological practitioners," they can help to increase our awareness of the process of aging and deepen our experience of growing old.

Death is increasingly a phenomenon of the aged, as the statistics that I cited earlier show. The dying tend more and more to be old, and the family members who must be comforted and helped through bereavement are aged spouses, aged siblings, or adult children. The facts and consequences of death must be dealt with regardless of any ethical questions involved ("the right to die," "terminal suicide," and so on), important as these may be. Dying people and their families will always be there to be cared for and about. Effective ministry with the aged must include an understanding of the process of dying, the effects of significant losses, the value of caring. George Paterson, out of his own experience and observation, also includes in "Death, Dying, and the Elderly" some specific ideas and suggestions on effective pastoral care for dying older persons and their families.

In order to develop a more effective ministry with older people, Christian education must reevaluate its definitions of family and must deemphasize the "normative" descriptions that have characterized it. Donald Miller's discussion of "Adult Religious Education and the Aging" takes this idea a bit further—how can Christian educators begin to develop new educational theories and programs to include and, more, to involve older persons meaningfully? Miller makes some specific suggestions and lays the groundwork of educational aims, theories, and strategies of learning on which to develop a new structure.

Several chapters in this book suggest or imply the importance of using both the spiritual and the practical experience of the elderly. We tend to think of this involvement as a goal to work toward, and for many of us it is. Yet the path is not uncharted. Even now there are notable pioneers in this area. In "Lay Ministries with Older Adults" Elbert Cole describes and discusses the remarkable program of the Shepherd's Center in Kansas City, Missouri. This outstandingly successful and ongoing concern involves older people in a wide variety of lay ministries. I hope that a day will come when we can view such involvement not with patronizing amazement, but as a matter of course.

I

FOUNDATIONS

2

Age and Aging in the Old Testament

Rolf Knierim

The biblical authors have not given us an explicit or systematic anthropological chapter on aging and old age. But they certainly had a concept of old age and aging, and they have given us a variety of perspectives throughout the Old Testament. This chapter highlights those perspectives. Space does not allow for the interpretation of, or even reference to, the some two hundred and fifty passages in the Old Testament that are concerned with old age. It is also unavoidable that our approach be phenomenological in nature. This is not self-evident, for the texts extend over nearly a millennium and reflect changing historical situations or, occasionally, different cultural influences. Nevertheless, the phenomenological approach is preferable, not only because the basis for a historical reconstruction is scarcely sufficient, but because aging and age are trans-historical and trans-cultural human phenomena.

Old Testament perspectives on age and aging cannot, of course, exclude the theological aspect. The Bible offers no secular anthropology. In other words, the theological aspect is not a rationalization added secondarily to a biblical anthropology that was abstracted from theology; it is intrinsic to the anthropology of the biblical generations.

THE BIOLOGICAL PERSPECTIVE

AGING AND THE TIME OF DEATH

The phenomena of aging and age appear basically as a part of the life of humans which begins with birth and ends with death. They belong to the total life span between the moment one comes from the ground (Gen. 2:7) and the moment one returns to the ground (Gen. 3:19). The Israelites had a word for "the span, time, duration of life": *heled* (Ps. 39:4; 89:47). This time of life is filled with "all the days of X," or "all the days that X lived" (Gen. 5:5; 35:28), or with "the years of X" (Gen. 23:1). This means that a person's age, namely the total number of days and years of life, becomes fixed upon death. Aging and old age appear as the last phase in the total span of life, that phase in which human life as such will finally become inescapably terminated—unless death strikes sooner.

This is important because it shows that while aging and old age can be a part of a person's total age, the total age of a person is not determined by nor necessarily inclusive of aging or old age. It is determined by the moment of death. Death, however, can come at any moment. All life is mortal, not only the life of old people. Child mortality *was* high during the biblical generations. Deadly diseases, accidents, killing, hunger, and war have belonged to the experience of every generation. Death was ever imminent, by no means reserved for old people only. When it came, it marked the end of the life span, and nobody could do anything about it: "Which of you by being anxious can add one cubit to his span of life?" (Matt. 6:27; Luke 12:25).

Therefore, if death can come at every age, the real danger for human life does not lie in aging and old age. It actually lies in premature death which cuts short the full age of humans. Aging and old age are not periods of transition between life and death, and not at all the first phase of death. They belong to life. In view of the ever present danger of death, however, they are not to be taken for granted either. But if age is granted, it is appreciated as a blessing, as a gift of life reaching its fullness despite the frailties of mortal life's last phase.

The bases for this interpretation are the biblical statements about the total age of persons at the time of their death. On the one hand, the Old Testament portrays extreme old age as a sign of life full of blessing and vitality. There are the mythical ages of the primeval Methuselahs in Genesis 5, who died in their 800s and 900s after having procreated children throughout their centuries! The fact that these numbers are mythological and thus contribute nothing to our statistical knowledge of the actual age of primeval humanity is hardly relevant in this context. More important is the view of the biblical genealogists themselves for whom these numbers meant human life in its fullness, specifically symbolized by an enormously high age. Our texts do say that those heroes finally died, but more important than that, the texts emphasize how long they had lived.

In the post-Noachian era, the descendants of Shem are less aged than the primeval people, and their ages decrease as the generations pass on: Shem lives 600 years; Shela, 433; Peleg, 239; and Terah, the father of Abraham, 205 (Gen. 11:10–25, 32). The even lower ages of the still "abnormally" old patriarchs and Israelites belong to the same category, although they represent a transition from a mythically perceived age to historical experience: Abraham 175 years (Gen. 25:7); Jacob 147 (Gen. 47:28); Aaron 123 (Num. 33:29); Moses 120 (Deut. 34:7); Joshua 110 (Josh. 24:29); and Judith 105 (Jth. 16:23).

These figures exceed by far what the biblical tradition also knows about the real age of humans and their decrepitude. But they are important because they indicate an awareness, an appreciation, on the part of the biblical authors, of old age as an intrinsic part of human life before the arrival of death. They express an understanding of the life span which includes an exceedingly long stretch of old age, keeping death away from life as long as humanly possible. Therefore, what counts more than all the problems with old age is that at the moment of death one can say: "they lived so many years"; and when noting the fact of death, one speaks about "the years of his life" (Gen. 47:28). This means that in the face of death, the Old Testament understands aging and old age basically as a marvel of a well-rounded, fulfilled life. Judith 16:22–23 says about Judith: "Many desired to marry her,

but she remained a widow all the days of her life after Manasseh
her husband died and was gathered to his people. She became more
and more famous, and grew old in her husband's house, until she
was one hundred and five years old. She set her maid free. She died
in Bethulia, and they buried her in the cave of her husband Manasseh."
Genesis 25:8 says: "Abraham breathed his last and died in a good
old age, an old man and full of years, and was gathered to his people."

However burdensome life may be—it is not only burdensome for
old people—it is still life vis à vis death. This fact counts more than
any problem humans may have with life itself. And this understanding
remained so uncontested that it became the basis for the depiction
of the eschatological time in which "no more shall there be in it
[i.e., the new heaven and earth] an infant that lives but a few days,
or an old man who does not fill out his days; for the child shall die
a hundred years old" (Isa. 65:20).

On the other hand, the biblical people knew that their own lives
were much shorter. According to Genesis 6:3, Yahweh declares that
human life shall be no more than "a hundred and twenty years."
Sirach 18:9 states: "The number of a man's days is great if he reaches
a hundred years." And Psalm 90:10 says: "The days of our life span
amount to seventy years, and in their full strength to eighty years."
An older average age would be much more desirable, but death seems
to be closing in on the human life span.

Nevertheless, even these ages seem extraordinary when compared
with the real life span of those generations, which we can deduce
from historical data. The royal chronologies, for example, confront
us with quite a different picture. From the fourteen kings of the Davidic
dynasty whose life spans are recorded, we learn that the average lifetime
of a king was about forty-four years. And the kings were the privileged.
What might the average age of the underprivileged have been?[1]

There is an obvious tension between what the biblical generations
perceived to be normal and what they perceived to be their own individual reality, as confirmed by our statistical data. Occasionally, the Old
Testament articulates the reason for this tension: "The fear of Yahweh
prolongs life, but the years of the wicked will be short" (Prov. 10:27;

cf. also 1 Sam. 2:32; Ps. 90:7–10; Gen. 3:17–19, 22). To be sure, nowhere is it said that death itself is the punishment for sin. But it is clear that God's justice over the vanity of human ambitions is revealed in the toil, trouble, and fruitlessness of labor during life, as well as in a shortened life span, i.e., premature death. In view of this understanding, aging and old age appear as an integral phase of a blessed and fulfilled life, whereas death cuts such fulfillment short. At this point, the Old Testament asserts the rightness, goodness, and promise of life in its full span and, consequently, claims aging and old age as the actualization of life's fullness. This claim is expressed in the formula: "He died old and full [i.e., satisfied] of days."

OLD AGE AS A PHASE IN THE TOTAL LIFE PROCESS

The biblical literature is aware of phases in life, or life cycles. The Hebrew word for these phases is *gîl*, circle of age (Dan. 1:10). Another indication of this awareness is given in the etymology and semantic range of the various words used for age and aging. Thus, the verb *zāqan* basically means "to be bearded" and, hence, to "be or grow old" as opposed to those without beard (Gen. 18:12–13; 19:31; etc.). Accordingly, the noun *zāqān* means "beard" on the chin (Lev. 19:27; 1 Sam. 17:35; etc.), whereas *zōqen* (Gen. 48:10) and *zĕqūnîm* (Gen. 21:2, 7; etc.) mean "old age," and *ziqnâ* means "the growing old" (Gen. 24:26; 1 Kings 11:4; etc.). Finally, *zāqēn* is the "one who bears a beard." This word occurs most frequently, and is used for the "old man" (Judg. 19:16–22; 1 Sam. 28:14), "man full of days" (Gen. 25:8; 35:29), and the "old father" (Gen. 44:22), as opposed to the young men (Gen. 19:4; Josh. 6:21; etc.). These males represent the totality of the elders, the special class of people admitted to the cult of handling judgment in the gate. It must be said, however, that a *zāqēn*, an elder, is not necessarily an old man; he is an adult and can, as such, also be old.

However, the *śēbâ*, the person with a "hoary head" or "gray hair," really is old (Judg. 8:32; Hos. 7:9; etc.). And the adjective *yāšēš* (2 Chron. 36:17) means "aged, decrepit," whereas the adjective *yāšîš* (Job 12:12; 15:10; etc.) means "aged, venerable."

In its terminology for old age and other age groups, the Old Testament would seem to find three different patterns to describe the phases of life. According to Deuteronomy 32:35; Psalm 148:12; and Ezekiel 9:6, there are three phases: children, young adults, and adults. According to Jeremiah 51:22, there are four: children, youth, the young married, and the elderly. And according to Jeremiah 6:11 there are five: small child, youth, man/woman, elderly, aged. A comparison indicates that the different patterns were apparently generated by different perspectives. In the three-phase pattern, aging and old age do not appear at all because the phases are seen from the perspective of adulthood rather than its prestages. Older people are not an extra category because they are already adults. In the four-phase pattern, however, the classification subdivides the adults into two generations, differentiating between the young married and the elderly. The reasons for this subdivision are probably biological (different degrees of vitality) and sociological (parents and grandparents). In the five-phase pattern, the adults are subdivided into three groups, which clearly indicates an awareness of typical differences in personal vitality and social role, as well as of changing stages in the process of aging itself.

AGING AND WEAKENING VITALITY

We have seen that the Bible claims aging and old age as a part of life, an indispensable phase that rounds out the "fullness of life." This does not mean, however, that the Bible is unaware of the distinctly adverse conditions to which aging people and the elderly are subjected. On the contrary, it is well aware of them, and addresses them from a variety of perspectives. There is a recognition of the weakening biological condition of aging and/or old people: The hair is getting gray (1 Sam. 12:2; Ps. 71:18); the strength is spent (Ps. 71:9); the eyesight is fading (Gen. 48:10; Tob. 14:2; however, cf. Deut. 34:7: Moses' "eye was not dim, nor his natural force abated"); the senses are failing (2 Sam. 19:35; Eccles. 12:1–5); the feet are sick (1 Kings 15:23); the body is cold and heavy (1 Kings 1:1–4; 1 Sam. 4:18); and women cannot conceive any longer (Gen. 18:13).

These conditions are not enjoyable at all. They are distressing, and the biblical authors express this distress despite their basic claim that aging and old age belong to life. Consider the exceedingly sensitive and artistic self-description of an old person in Barzillai's speech to David:

> How many years have I still to live, that I should go up with the king to Jerusalem? I am this day eighty years old; can I discern what is pleasant and what is not? Can your servant taste what he eats or what he drinks? Can I still listen to the voice of singing men and singing women? . . . Pray let your servant return, that I may die in my own city, near the grave of my father and my mother. [2 Sam. 19:34–37]

In another lucid expression of this distressing condition the preacher of Ecclesiastes calls the days of aging and old age "the evil days" and "the years . . . when you will say: I have no pleasure in them" (Eccles. 12:1). We have here a realistic acceptance of the unavoidable conditions of old age, including the fact that they are not enjoyable. Even so, the writer, with wry humor, describes the aged condition in marvellously metaphorical language:

> The day when the keepers of the house tremble, and the strong men are bent, and the grinders cease because they are few, and those that look through the windows are dimmed, and the doors on the street are shut . . . before the silver cord is snapped, or the golden bowl is broken, or the pitcher is broken at the fountain, or the wheel broken at the cistern, and the dust returns to the earth as it was and the spirit returns to God who gave it.[2] [Eccles. 12:1–7]

THE SOCIOLOGICAL PERSPECTIVE

AN INTEGRAL PART OF SOCIETY

It must be said that being or becoming old did not mean being phased out of the mainstream of Israel's society, or out of any ancient society for that matter.[3] Old people always remained an integral part of societal life, and that in a twofold sense: diachronically and synchronically. Diachronically, in a society that perceived one generation as deeply imbedded in the tradition constituted by all the generations, the old people specifically represented the linkage between the former and the younger generations, between past and future. They were the bearers of the living tradition. And synchronically, in a society which understood itself as a corporate entity, the older people were very much a part of all the other groups of each generation.[4]

The diminishing vitality of individuals did not result in their removal from the society into isolated retirement homes, for example. And it did not result in being removed from societal functions that were proportionate to the potential of an old person. The ongoing societal importance of the elderly was institutionally guaranteed by the fact that they always remained a part of their families and clans. It is mainly in this framework that they continued to function for the society. And above all, in this framework, the society supported them. The basis for this societal place of the elderly was the interdependence of the individuals in this group, and the interdependence of the generations in the ongoing process of life.

PROTECTION BY SOCIETY

Society's protection of the elderly begins with protection by the family, basically expressed in the fifth commandment of the Decalogue: "Honor your father and your mother" (Exod. 20:12; see also Deut. 5:16; and Lev. 19:3).[5] The fifth commandment stands in the center of a variety of references that in turn reflect an intensive concern for parents throughout the history of the Old Testament society. "Whoever strikes his father or his mother shall be put to death" (Exod. 21:15); "Cursed be he who dishonors his father or mother" (Deut. 27:16); "He who does violence to his father, and chases away his mother is a son who causes shame and brings reproach" (Prov. 19:26); "The eye that mocks a father and scorns to obey a mother will be picked out by the ravens of the valley and eaten by the vultures" (Prov. 30:17).

It is important for us to realize that all these references address adults. They refer to the treatment of old parents by their adult children. As such they differ from passages dealing with the education of youngsters by adults (Prov. 1:8), or with obedience of youngsters to adults (Deut. 22:18–21).

Of equal importance is the fact that concern for parents was considered so central that it became one of the ten injunctions when the Decalogue was composed as the most condensed summary of Israel's ethical and religious identity. It is generally assumed that the fifth commandment refers to an attitude of reverence and respect for parents, and such an attitude is certainly not excluded from its meaning. What is less known, however, is that this commandment refers primarily to the material support of old parents by their adult children. Thus, Joseph says to his brothers: "Make haste and go up to my father and say to him . . . you shall dwell in the land of Goshen, and you shall be near me . . . and there I will provide for you . . ." (Gen. 45:9–11).

From biblical and Ancient Near Eastern evidence we learn that parents reached the moment of retirement when they transferred, sometimes even by way of contract, their possessions to their sons, especially the oldest. In turn, sons then became responsible for the care of parents, including burial at the time of their deaths (Prov. 23:22; Tob. 4:3, 4; etc.). Hence, the command to honor father and mother must be understood holistically, in the sense of taking care of, supporting, protecting, and respecting parents as long as they live. It reflects a genuine form of social security in which the old parents remained part of their families, with dignity and material security.

No wonder, then, that in the society at large, old persons were held in great respect: "You shall rise up before the hoary/gray head, and honor the face of an old man" (Lev. 19:32). If, however, due honor is not granted an old person, God himself will become the refuge and protector, as in Psalm 71:9, a prayer of an old person: "Do not cast me off in the time of old age; forsake me not when my strength is spent."

INCAPACITATION

In Leviticus 27, we find a financial assessment of different age groups in the event someone is unable to do physical work in the sanctuary. Males up to five years old were assessed five shekels; those between five and twenty years, twenty shekels; those between twenty and sixty years, fifty shekels; but those more than sixty years of age had to pay only fifteen shekels. Their physical incapacity was recognized and they received a huge tax break. This classification also shows that age sixty was considered to be the legitimate age of retirement. In some layers of the tradition, public officials such as Moses, Joshua, and Samuel are depicted as retiring from public office due to old age (Deut. 1–32; Josh. 22–24; 1 Sam. 12). In such instances, the retiring official gave account of his conduct of office in a farewell speech. Retirement from office, however, meant neither death nor complete inactivity thereafter. Samuel must have remained publicly active in various ways throughout the rest of his life. We should assume similar conditions for royal officers, especially military personnel, and for priests, prophets, sages, and scribes.

CONTINUING ACTIVITIES

The Old Testament says that humans eat their bread in the sweat of their face until they die (of natural death in old age). Accordingly, Sirach 11:30 advises, "grow old in your work." Old people were certainly involved in some sort of work, predominantly agricultural, for as long as and wherever they were capable, but there were also specific tasks for them. We have already mentioned the ongoing activities of retired officials, probably similar to the types of activities they had undertaken before retirement. Of particular importance in this respect was Israel's institution of the elders. It is true that "the old man is not necessarily to be equated with the Elder who occupied an official position in biblical society,"[6] and not everything that is said about the elders in the biblical tradition reflects the activities of old people. Indeed, in most cases, elders cannot be positively identified with old people. This is particularly true when they appear as office holders into whose hands decisions about political, military, administrative, and judicial matters were placed. Nevertheless, the usage of the word zāqēn, meaning a title of office as well as age (Gen. 18:11–12; 24:1; etc.) does indicate that old people are not by definition excluded from the function of the elders.[7]

We can infer from our knowledge, especially about Israel's judicial system, that old men played a significant role as elders in the councils in the gates (Ruth 4:1–12), and also in the royal councils (1 Kings 12:6–11). "Old men" functioned as advisors to the king in the royal council, and they participated in the gate in the arbitration of litigations and the adjudication of crimes. They were the most experienced in custom and law, and had the indispensable background needed for wise and balanced judgment. They personified the living tradition. Thus, the affairs of the community were in the best hands "in the assembly of the elders" (Ps. 107:32; Job 29:8).

In most instances in which the biblical texts speak about women, they do not refer to age; therefore, this aspect can only be deduced from the contexts. Done properly, such a task would require a special analysis from text to text which cannot be carried out at this point. Nevertheless, as with the problem of the elders, some suggestions can be inferred. For example, the adult Micah's mother who devoted silver for an image cannot have been all too young (Judg. 17:1–4). Also, the mothers of kings played important advisory roles (2 Chron. 22:3). One may ask how old were the wise women who are mentioned in 2 Samuel 14:2; 20:16. Of Judith, it is said that she "became more and more famous, and grew old in her husband's house" (Jth. 16:23). These direct references are few, but should not prevent us from assuming that the biblical generations were aware of the role and importance of old women in their respective environments to a much greater extent than our literature reflects.

Finally, old people played a very important role when they came to exercise what we call their last will or testament. When people, particularly fathers, were about to die, they assembled their children, gave them final instructions, blessed them, and praised God. In a last testamentary activity, they "set their house in order" (2 Sam. 17:23; 2 Kings 20:1) and transferred not only their possessions but the totality of the heritage of their tradition on to the next generation. Genesis 47:29–49:33 concludes: "When Jacob finished charging his sons, he drew up his feet into the bed, and breathed his last, and was gathered to his people" (see also Tob. 14:3). This last activity of old, dying people represented an institutionalized form through which the transition of the generations was experienced and the tradition transmitted.

It was considered of such fundamental importance that an entire literary genre emerged from it in the Intertestamental Literature, the "testament," through which the old pass their instructions on to the young.[8]

THE PSYCHOLOGICAL PERSPECTIVE

FOOLISHNESS

The biblical tradition says that along with their physical deterioration, the elderly are also subject to declining mental alertness. They are not, by virtue of their age, protected from doing foolish things. The "men of Sodom, both young and old, all the people to the last man," assembled in front of Lot's house demanding that he turn his guests over to them for, presumably, sexual molestation (Gen. 19:4–5). The story of the succession to David's throne in 2 Samuel 9–1 Kings 1, is heavily concerned with a king, David, who due to his advancing age was increasingly unable to keep matters under control. In failing to decide on his successor, he created conditions for chaos in the royal family, for fratricide and bloody revolutions. Eli (1 Sam. 2:22), Samuel (1 Sam. 8:5), and Solomon (1 Kings 11:4) shared the same fate, and in each case the consequences were grave.

Furthermore, "the wicked live, reach old age, and grow mighty in power" (Job 21:7). Job is not exactly happy with the entrenched ideological positions of his old friends which prevent them from realizing they might be confronted with a problem situation that cannot be solved within traditional thought patterns and demands a new horizon of understanding. And God is on his side! He reprimands the old men saying: "You have not spoken of me what is right, as my servant Job has" (Job 42:7). Young Elihu is even less satisfied with their performances, including that of Job. After a long, reverent silence, and after the arguments of the old are exhausted, he angrily launches into his diatribe:

> I am young in years, and you are aged; therefore I was timid and afraid to declare my opinion to you. I said, let days speak, and many years teach wisdom. But it is the spirit in a man, the breath of the Almighty that makes him understand. It is not the old that are wise, nor the aged that

understand what is right. Therefore, I say "listen to me; let me also declare my opinion." [Job 32:6–10]

Elihu is correct, too, as is Job. In fact, the failure of the old men to act and speak rightly borders on the tragic, just as they try to muster all their wisdom. They just don't understand the world anymore, no matter how hard they try.

Only one thing must be added: Elihu himself does not produce the solution either. The young generation is correct when pointing out with keen discernment that age and wisdom are not automatic companions, and when claiming that "it is the spirit in a man," and, perhaps, also "the breath of the Almighty that makes him understand." Elihu's only—and decisive—mistake is to believe that the spirit, the breath of the Almighty, breathes in the stronger vitality of the young instead of in the many years of the old. Thus, when displaying his own "wisdom," he fails just as pitifully as his older partners.

WISDOM

With the inclusion of that side glance at the young generation, the Book of Job makes it clear that true wisdom, the "spirit" and "breath of the Almighty," is by definition embodied neither in the number of accumulated years nor in the impulsive vitality of youth. This insight means, however, that as they approach old age people are once more confronted with a new intellectual problem. They are challenged to open their minds, to reach out for the moment in which the vision of life, reality, and truth is not confined to the perspective of old age, but in which aging and old age are envisioned from the ever-widening perspective of all of life, reality, and truth. When that moment is encountered, the biological and sociological factors of aging and old age are no longer the experiential background which determines everything. Age is transcended. Then, the minds of the old will not forever rest, and rust, on the sum total of past life experiences, but rather their life experience will teach them to expect and look for experiences they have never had before.

When that happens, the elderly are truly touched by the breath of the Almighty. They will be creative and as young as the young. "The young men and the old shall be merry" (Jer. 31:13). The same spirit of the Lord will inspire the elderly as the young (Joel 2:28). The old people "bring forth fruit in old age, they are ever full of sap and green" (Ps. 92:14). Then, the elderly will be able to accept reality, accommodate themselves in the new situation, and say: "I am old" (Josh. 23:2; 1 Sam. 12:2). With such an acceptance, the old person remains in control of life by giving up what he or she can no longer be or do, and at the same time assuming a transformed role: the orderly transfer of office, the regulation of inheritance, the making of one's testament, the advice to the young. Then, they will give and share their own lives beneficially, for others. They will establish themselves once more as indispensable members in a society which would be deprived of much of its own blessing without them. And, in all this, their old age will be blessed and renewed, and never wasted (Gen. 18:11–14; Ps. 92:14–15; Sir. 46:9).

This is what the biblical tradition means when it speaks of the wisdom of old people. It is the wisdom grounded in the fear, i.e., the reverence, of the Lord (Deut. 30:20): "The fear of the Lord prolongs life, but the years of the wicked will be short" (Prov. 10:27; see also 1 Sam. 2:32; Jer. 28:16–17); and "How attractive is wisdom in the aged, and understanding and counsel in honorable men" (Sir. 25:5; see also 2 Macc. 6:18–27).

But beyond these references, we must also mention the presence of the teachers of wisdom themselves in the biblical tradition, and beyond them the countless number of mostly anonymous persons who were instrumental in the formation of the Bible throughout its oral and written stages. We have good reason to assume that the teachers of wisdom, those standing behind the Books of Proverbs and Ecclesiastes, were generally depicted as and called "fathers," and were not young men. They were old (at least older). If we perceive these books and their contents as the legacy of old people, we can get a taste of the importance old people had in their societies, of what they were capable of doing, and more importantly, of the enormous esteem that wisdom—by and large represented by the old people—had in the society. The phenomenon of this literature is unparalleled in its time. Its contents reveal an amazing degree of mental vitality, and to this day one who does not appreciate it is a fool in the biblical sense.

To look at the biblical canon from the perspective of the variety of its "authors" reveals something very interesting. There are the lawgivers, the historians and novelists, the priests, the prophets, the poets of the hymns, and the teachers of wisdom. And even though the sages represent the professional concern for wisdom reflected in the Wisdom Literature, all the authors of the Old Testament represent the wisdom that is the result of Israel's total intellectual effort: the expression of her fear and knowledge of God. In this literature the elderly have forever received their place in the chorus of the voices. Here, the biblical tradition honors the fact that the old are not forgotten, silenced, excluded from society, pushed into the ghetto, but rather that they belong to the family and their counsel is forever with us. Hence, their presence in forming the Bible is just as important as what the Bible tells us about them. And when we read their words, what Sirach says becomes true for us: "He who devotes himself to the study of the instruction of the Most High will seek the wisdom of all the ancients, and will be concerned with prophecies" (Sir. 39:1). If there is truth in what some of us believe, namely that the biblical literature as a whole breathes the breath of the Almighty, then it is also true that a large portion of this breath breathes in and through the mind of its old people. And as the breath of the Almighty touches us through their minds, they are ours, and we are theirs.

NOTES

1. See H. W. Wolff, *Anthropology of the Old Testament* (Philadelphia: Fortress Press, 1974), pp. 119–127.
2. The metaphor as a whole clearly refers to the physical decrepitude of old age. It probably functioned as a riddle, which may be why it is difficult, if not impossible, to identify exactly some of the expressions.
3. See L. W. Simmons, *The Role of the Aged in Primitive Society* (New Haven: Yale

University Press, 1945). However, the categories of interpretation employed by Simmons (and anthropologists or ethnographers) for "primitive" societies are not indiscriminately applicable for the historical societies of the Ancient Near East, including Israel.

4. The word "corporate" here means a perception according to which the societal body as a whole is the basic entity and individuals are members. "Corporate" does not connote the disappearance of the individual into a collectivistic anonymity. The corporate perception of society implies that individuality is gained and shaped in relation to the corpus of all, i.e., in individuals finding their place and function in, and relative to, the community. On this wider subject see, among others, H. W. Robinson, *Corporate Personality in Ancient Israel*, Facet Books, Biblical Series II (Philadelphia: Fortress Press, 1964); Walter Eichrodt, *Theology of the Old Testament*, vol. 2 (Philadelphia: Westminster Press, 1975), p. 231; and J. Pedersen, *Israel, Its Life and Culture*, vol. 1/2 (London: Oxford University Press, and Copenhagen: Branner og Korch, 1926), pp. 29–96.

5. For the following, see the excellent article by Rainer Albertz, "Hintergrund und Bedeutung des Elterngebots im Dekalog," *ZAW* 90 (1978): 348–374. See also Gerald J. Blidstein, *Honor Thy Father and Mother: Filial Responsibility in Jewish Law and Ethics* (New York: Ktav Publishing House, 1975).

6. S. H. Blank, "Age, Old," in *The Interpreter's Dictionary of the Bible*, vol. 1 (New York: Abingdon Press, 1962), p. 55.

7. In fact, about one third of the references for the word *zāqēn* in the Old Testament, some sixty, have the meaning "old" and not "elder"; see Conrad, "zāqen," *Theologisches Wörterbuch zum Alten Testament*, vol. 2 (Stuttgart: Verlag W. Kohlhammer GMBH, 1975), p. 639 ff.

8. On this aspect, see Eckhard von Nordheim, "Die Lehre der Alten (Das Testament als Literaturgattung im Alten Testament und im Alten Vorderen Orient)," (Ph.D. diss., Theological Faculty, University of Munich, 1973).

3

The Elderly in the Life and Thought of the Early Church

Jean Laporte

The Early Church (of the first through fifth centuries) not only provided the elderly with material assistance, but also offered them an important role in the community which raised them to an honorable status. The early writings of the Church identify several different categories of older people, although the largest number of references are to destitute widows, because they were registered and assisted by the Church.[1] The reasons, methods, and evolution of this material assistance deserve some clarification to account for the peculiar position of widows in the Early Church. The Early Christian emphasis on density of prayer and continence requires some explanation, as does the evolution of the institution of the widows in the Church, and the loss of its spiritual character during the Constantinian era.

In addition to assistance, the Early Church had certain ideals about its elderly which deserve treatment in some depth, not only for historical reasons but also for the Church of today to consider as it searches to define its relationship to the elderly. The respect accorded the elderly, their position as counselors, and their spiritual contri-

bution to the community suggest some interesting possibilities for the
Church today.

IDENTIFICATION OF THE ELDERLY

A few remarks are necessary in order to obtain a clear view of who
composed the category of the elderly in the Early Church as a whole
and in its parts. Because of the absence of modern medicine and hy-
giene, there were fewer old people in the Early Church than there
are today, and the average age of death was much younger. One was,
therefore, considered an old man or woman at a younger age than
today. According to Plato, the age of sixty is the time of old age,[2]
and this is the minimum age found in I Timothy for registered widows.
Philo of Alexandria also considered a man sixty years of age as old,[3]
and *Didascalia Apostolorum*, a Church Order of third-century Syria,
lowered the requirement of age for the widows from sixty to fifty.[4]
When we discuss the role of the elderly in the Early Church and
the relevance of a similar role for them in the Church of today, we
must remember these differences.

Until recent times men in Europe, especially in the Mediterranean
countries, married much younger women. For this reason there were
a large number of widows in the Early Church, many of whom were
poor. A widow's situation was not the same as that of a widower. If
her husband had not provided for her in his last will, and if she was
not taken care of by her family, she could very well become destitute
in the anonymous crowd of a large town. Because the Church took
care of these widows, and registered them on the roll of her charities,
references to widows multiply in early Christian writings. The cases
of young widows in need of assistance were also well known,[5] though
the sources have much less to say about widows who lived with their
families, and who were probably kept busy. Little is said about widowers,
who continued to enjoy their possessions without hindrance. Little
also is said of old married couples. Enough mention is made, however,
regarding the spiritual role of other categories of old people in the
Early Church to support a parallel with the widows.

ASSISTANCE TO THE ELDERLY

The Early Church found her duty to help the poor, particularly widows and orphans, written in Scripture (Deut. 10:18, 14:29, 24:17–22; Ps. 68:6; Isa. 1:17; see also Mark 12:42 and Luke 7:12, 18:3). At the end of the first century, Clement of Rome, in his Epistle to the Corinthians (chapters 3, 8, 15; see also Isa. 1:17), referred to Isaiah, who proclaimed the rights of widow and orphan, and declared that God listens to the lament of the poor. The Epistle of Barnabas (chapters 2 and 3), written in the beginning of the second century, referred particularly to Isaiah 58 for the priority of social justice and almsgiving over sacrifices and fasting. Not much later, Hermas combined fasting with almsgiving when he suggested that the saving made through fasting be given to widows or to the poor.[6] In the seventh century, *Testamentum Domini* acclaimed God as the Protector of widows and the Liberator of orphans.[7]

Charity to the poor and the care of widows and orphans was encouraged in the New Testament as well as in the Old: "The kind of religion which is without stain and fault in the sight of God our Father is this: to go to the help of orphans and widows in their distress and keep oneself untarnished by the world" (James 1:27). These duties are based more specifically in the Pastoral Epistles of the Pauline corpus, which are the basis of every subsequent Church Order. According to I Timothy:

> The status of widow is to be granted only to widows who are such in the full sense. But if a widow has children or grandchildren, then they should learn as their first duty to show loyalty to the family and to repay what they owe to their parents and grandparents: for this God approves. [I Tim. 5:3–4]

Of course, widows were to be taken care of by their children or relatives whenever possible, for the Church did not consider itself a system of social security, but rather felt its duty was to care only for those who were destitute.[8] This warning to children was not pointless since the condition of a widow in late Judaism could be miserable,[9] and poverty seems to have been the lot of many widows in the Greco-Roman world as well.[10] The very fact that these warnings exist indicates that in Christianity, as in Judaism and Hellenism, too often old widows were abandoned by their families, and the Church had to provide help.

The care for widows, orphans, and other poor people became one of the first duties of bishops and of their assistants, the deacons. At the beginning of the second century Ignatius of Antioch warned the bishop of Smyrna, "Widows must not be neglected. After the Lord, you must be their guardian."[11] This duty of the bishop is emphasized by every Christian writer from Justin in the middle of the second century, to Chrysostom in Antioch and Gregory in Rome at the end of Patristic times.[12] Justin provides the first mention of a collection on Sundays, the sum of which was deposited with the bishop to be distributed to the poor.[13] Tertullian mentions a monthly collection—to which the faithful freely contributed—which was used for the support of the poor, particularly in the "agapes," community meals to which old widows and other poor people were invited.[14]

Didascalia Apostolorum, dating from the third century, gives the best representation of the job of the bishop and deacons in their assistance to widows and the poor: "Let him be merciful and gracious and full of love . . . and let his hand be open to give; and let him love the orphans with the widows, and be a lover of the poor and of strangers."[15] Later Church Orders such as the *Apostolic Church Order*, the *Statutes of the Apostles, Apostolic Constitutions*, and *Testamentum Domini*, manifest the same interest in widows.[16] The number of assisted widows and other poor people increased in the large urban communities of the Christian Empire. During the last persecutions, the Roman deacon and martyr St. Lawrence took care of 1300 of them,[17] and Chrysostom mentions 3000 virgins and widows at the end of the fourth century in Antioch.[18]

Large numbers of people, particularly the old, lived in extreme poverty and suffered the moral degradation that resulted from it. Chrysostom gives a very dark picture of the situation of widows supported by the Church, and of the difficult task of the priest put in charge of them:

> Careful scrutiny is needed, when they have to be enrolled, for infinite mischief has been caused by putting them on the list without due discrimination. For they have ruined households, and severed marriages, and have often been detected in thieving, and pilfering and unseemly deeds of that kind. . . . [Among other qualities such as freedom from the love of money, and skillfulness in the management of property, the superintendent of the widows should possess the quality of forbearance.] For widows are a class who, both on account of their poverty, their age, and their natural disposition, indulge in unlimited freedom of speech; and they make an unseasonable clamor and idle complaints and lamentations concerning things which they ought contently to accept. Now the superintendent should endure all these things in a generous spirit, and not be provoked either by their unreasonable annoyance or their unreasonable complaints. For this class of persons deserve to be pitied for their misfortunes, not to be insulted; and to trample upon their calamities, and add the pain of insult to that which poverty brings, would be an act of extreme brutality.[19]

Christian charity tried to answer the needs of the poor and the sick in many different places. A *diakonia,* or service of charity, was organized in churches of average importance, and many monastic *diako-niai* were also founded. In the cities, hospitals were built for the sick and for elderly people who needed to be nursed. They were gathered together for greater efficiency.[20] In *Didascalia* and other early documents, deacons and deaconesses are shown to have cared for the sick among the poor. The lives of Eastern monks reveal many instances of monastic charities, and of guest-houses and hospitals built in connection with monasteries. Rich donors, even Empress Eudoxia and Emperor Justinian, built hospitals which were managed by monks. In the West we do not see such foundations, except in Rome and in a few large cities. Generally, cities were medium-size, and there, as well as in rural areas, nobody would remain unknown and abandoned. Apparently the distributions of the Church to widows and the needy, together with private charities, seem to have been sufficient, and the social functions of the deacons gradually disappeared because they were no longer necessary.

IDEALS OFFERED TO THE ELDERLY IN THE EARLY CHURCH

Early Christianity paid marks of respect to the elderly and ascribed to them a significant spiritual role. In the writings of the Early Church, the elderly appear as the wise counselors of the young, with emphasis on Christian ideals of prayer, fasting, and continence. These ideals, which had been to some extent the privilege of the elderly, particularly of the widows, later on became monopolized by virginity and monasticism.

RESPECT FOR THE ELDERLY

The dignity which is the privilege of the elderly is first evidenced in special marks of respect. Plato states the foundation and the rule of this respect:

> Seniority is held in highest consideration alike by gods and by men who intend a long and happy life. Hence the public assault of a younger man on his senior is a shameful spectacle and abominable in the eye of heaven. If the younger man is struck by the elder, the seemly course is ever that he should meekly give place to his anger, and thus lay up a capital of the same consideration for his own old age. Hence our rule shall run thus. All shall show their reverence for their seniors in act and speech.[21]

In the Old Testament we find the same teaching: for example, "You shall rise in the presence of gray hairs, give honour to the aged, and fear your God" (Lev. 19:32). Paul gave similar advice to Timothy: "Never be harsh with an elder; appeal to him as if he were your father. Treat . . . the older women as mothers" (I Tim. 5:1–2). Timothy is exhorted to "honour the widows" in a way which can be paralleled with I Peter 2:17, "Honour the king," and with the precept of the Decalogue, "Honour your father and mother."[22] In the same spirit, according to liturgical books, a candidate for baptism was tested on this matter: "Has he honoured the widows?"[23]

The same marks of respect and the same warnings occur in other early writings. According to Athenagoras, the second century Christians treat the elderly as if they were their own father and mother, while Tatian defends Christian old women against the mockeries of the Greeks.[24] Clement of Rome sees a disregard for the respect due to the elderly as the cause of disorder in society, particularly in the Church of Corinth; he exhorts rebellious members to submit to the elders or presbyters, and to accept their correction (Corinthians 20 and 56). The Church Orders ascribe to the "Widows of the Church," and to other old women, a place of their own in church, and add that the young must give up their seat if an old man or woman enters when the church is full.[25]

Finally, the importance of the elderly in the Early Church is in itself a mark of respect. Early Christian writings show that the elderly were the top of the pyramid of Christian society. Although age itself had a certain dignity, this dignity and respect were not only a mere matter of years.

COUNSELORS AND HEALERS

New Testament discussions of the behavior and responsibilities of older men and women, and of widows in particular, require from them a high level of Christian perfection: personal, familial, and ecclesial. Those who fulfilled these requirements were certainly good guides, counselors, and, eventually, physicians of souls. Older women were told, for example, that "they must set a high standard, and school the younger women to be loving wives and mothers, temperate, chaste, and kind, busy at home, respecting the authority of their husbands" (Titus 2:4–5).

At the end of the second century Tertullian and Clement of Alexandria mention old men and women, not simply widows, in their role as counselors and healers of souls. In criticizing a bishop who accepted a young virgin into the midst of widows, Tertullian enlarges on the role of widows as counselors:

[The seat of widows is one] to which not merely "single-husbanded"—that is, married women—are at length elected, but "mothers" to boot, yes, and "educators of children;" in order . . . that their experimental training in all the affections may, on the one hand, have rendered them capable of readily aiding all others with counsel and comfort, and that, on the other, they may none the less have travelled down the whole course of probation whereby a female can be tested.[26]

Tertullian mentions the widows, together with priests and deacons, as those who enjoy special consideration in the Church. The same holy people—priests, deacons, widows—listen to the confession of a repenting sinner: they represent Christ, since the Church is Christ, and for this reason the pentitent begs them to intercede for him.[27]

In one of his sermons, Clement of Alexandria advises a rich man, poor in spiritual goods, to look for new friends who can help him by their prayers and intercessions:

Collect for yourself an unarmed, unwarlike, bloodless, passionless, stainless host, pious old men, orphans dear to God, widows armed with meekness, men adorned with love. Obtain with your money such guards, for body and soul, for whose sake a sinking ship is made buoyant, when steered by the prayers of the saints alone; and disease at its height is subdued, put to flight by the laying on of the hands; and the attack of robbers [devils] is disarmed, spoiled by pious prayers.[28]

Deep concern for the spiritual needs of others, and prayers of intercession dealing with problems of individual life were possible in the rather small communities of that time. In the same sermon, Clement lists these spiritual ministries of holy lay people:

Intercession for the pardon of sins; comforting the sick; weeping and groaning in sympathy for you to the Lord of all; teaching you some of the things useful for salvation; admonishing with confidence; counseling with kindness; and all can love truly without guile, without fear, without flattery, without pretence.[29]

INTENSITY OF SPIRITUAL LIFE

These spiritual ministries, especially counseling, do not belong to the elderly exclusively, but they do seem to be the natural fruit of

Christian life reaching its maturity. The connection of these ministries with old age, however, indicates that there are other reasons for which the elderly seem to be privileged in this regard. First, in so far as they are free from domestic duties, they can spend more time on prayer and in church.[30] They seem to make up the majority of the community who attend worship in week days.[31] We have seen that they are the "holy ones" mentioned by Tertullian, and the genuine friends and healers mentioned by Clement of Alexandria, who are always available when a weaker brother, even a fallen one, needs help.

Tertullian outlines the spiritual advantages of widowhood in his *Exhortation to Chastity*. After proving that a widower should not remarry because his present situation is the will of God, thus a second marriage would basically be an adultery, Tertullian gives an enthusiastic description of the new life awaiting the man in his holy widowhood:

> Happy man! You have released your debtor; sustain the loss. What if you come to feel that what we have called a loss is a gain? For continence will be a mean whereby you will traffic in a mighty substance of sanctity: by parsimony of the flesh you will gain the Spirit. For let us ponder over your conscience itself, to see how different a man feels himself when he chances to be deprived of his wife. He savours spiritually. If he is making prayer to the Lord, he is near heaven. If he is bending over the Scriptures, he is "wholly in them." If he is singing a psalm, he satisfies himself. If he is adjuring a demon, he is confident in himself.[32]

Interestingly, Tertullian only opposes a return to the flesh; he suggests to his widower the idea of taking with him some pious old widow:

> Then take some spiritual wife. Take to yourself from among the widows one fair in faith, dowered with poverty, sealed with age. You will thus make a good marriage. A plurality of such wives is pleasing to God.[33]

Most of our evidence about the place of elderly widows in the Early Church is related to the case of those widows who, because they were old and destitute, were materially supported by the Church. Since they were without family and lonely, they had plenty of leisure time which they could devote to God. Paul writes that the status of "widow of the Church" is to be granted to "one who is alone in the world, has her hope on God, and regularly attends the meeting for prayer and worship night and day" (1 Tim. 5:5). This style of life combines in Patristic literature with the description of Anna, who became the paradigm of Christian widows:

> There was a prophetess, Anna, the daughter of Phanuel, of the tribe of Asher. She was a very old woman, who had lived seven years with her husband after she was first married, and then alone as a widow to the age of eighty-four. She never left the temple, but worshiped day and night, fasting and praying. [Luke 2:36]

Here we find a "single-husbanded" widow, who was faithful to her spiritual life in widowhood and who spent all her time worshiping in the temple. She lived a life of prayer, fasting, and continence. Her quality as a prophetess manifests a charismatic aspect of her life.[34]

CONTINENCE AND CONSECRATION

The key to understanding the ideals offered to the elderly by the Early Church lies in the association of continence, fasting, and prayer— or the renunciation of the flesh for the sake of spiritual life. Athenagoras, Tertullian, Clement of Alexandria and others are proud of many old couples who turn to a life of continence.[35] There were many men and women of the Early Church who took up the ideals of continence at their baptism (as adults) and grew old like "the eunuch for the sake of the Kingdom of God." For instance, in his treatise *To his wife*, Tertullian writes,

> How many are there who from the moment of their baptism set the seal [of virginity] upon their flesh? How many, again, who by equal mutual consent cancel the debt of matrimony—voluntary eunuchs for the sake of their desire after the celestial kingdom! But if, while the marriage-tie is still intact, abstinence is endured, how much more when it has been undone [by death]![36]

Continence, however ideal, is not essential to contemplative life and to the exercise of charism. According to *Didascalia Apostolorum*, those who perform their duties of conjugal life are not empty of the

Holy Spirit, and must continue to pray and to receive the Eucharist.[37] Even according to Tertullian, a married couple can combine a high degree of active and contemplative life.[38] However, as we have mentioned, the interdiction of second marriage imposed on the "widows of the Church"—who are registered, or appointed, or even ordained—shows that a second marriage would for them be a grievous sin and a desecration, almost an adultery.

In the second century, Polycarp of Smyrna referred to the widows as the "altar of God";[39] *Didascalia Apostolorum*, in the third century, gives six references to this image. The altar of god—widows and orphans who eat the fruit of alms—should not be desecrated by offerings coming from sinners, especially from those who are guilty of social injustice.[40] The image of the altar attests to the consecration of the widow to God. This consecration cannot be compared to a marriage to Christ as in the case of consecrated virginity, because a widow expects to join her husband again in heaven in a spiritual union.[41] Even mystical images must fit the propriety of human situations. According to Augustine, though, the holy widow represents the praying Church, which is the Body or Bride of Christ.[42]

CHARISMATIC ASPECTS

The *Apostolic Tradition* by Hippolytus of Rome, reflecting a situation at the end of the second century, states that widows are appointed not to a liturgical ministry but to prayer, which is the duty of all.[43] This duty of prayer is imposed on them as a special role in the community, "Widows and virgins shall fast often and pray on behalf of the Church," and in Tertullian and in Clement of Alexandria, we see the widows attending to evening prayers.[44]

In *Didascalia* we find an extensive description of the good widow and the bad widow, which provides clues about the life of prayer of the widows and the recognition of their charismatic gifts. A good widow should not run from house to house in order to get money, or to gossip; she should not answer questions which are above her reach; she should not communicate with apostates and sinners in spite of their generous gifts in money:

Let a widow know that she is the altar of God. . . . A widow who wishes to please God sits at home and meditates upon the Lord day and night, and without ceasing at all times offers intercession and prays with purity before the Lord; and she receives what ever she asks, because her whole mind is set upon this. . . . But you, O widow who are without discipline, see your fellow widows or your brethren in sickness, and have no care to fast and pray over your members, and to lay hand upon them and to visit them, but feign yourself to be not in health, or not in leisure.[45]

Because the prayer of a widow has more weight before God than the prayer of other Christians, money is given to the bishop for widows, or directly to widows, in order to obtain a favor from God through their intercession. The widow is told the name of the donor so she might intercede for him or her by name. Their particular power of intercession can be explained by their situation as widows, since God listens to the prayer of the widow and orphan; but it comes also from the way of life of a good widow, a life of fasting, prayer, and continence. In the case of a good widow, we can truly speak of a spiritual gift, of a charism. This charism is put to the service of the community through prayer and laying on of hands. Its efficacy does not have to be proved other than by the fact that when someone is sick the faithful are eager to exchange their material gifts for these spiritual gifts in giving alms to the widows.

The charism of healing is not the only spiritual gift of the widows. The life of a good widow is similarly connected to a kind of charism of prophecy, reminiscent of the biblical Anna, as in the case of the three appointed widows of the *Apostolic Church Order:*

Three widows shall be appointed: two, who persevere in prayer because of all those who are in temptations and for revelations and instructions concerning what is required, but one who, abiding with those who are tried by sickness, is of good service, watchful, informing the priest of what is necessary.[46]

The first two widows exercise a charism, almost a ministry, of prophecy for the needs of individuals and of the community. The third widow is a kind of social worker and nurse for the sick, which would normally be the task of deaconesses. Apart from the case of this third widow, widows exercise no active ministry; their vocation is only to contemplative life. Through prayer, fasting, and continence they reach a great closeness to God, from whom they receive revelations and favors which benefit their community. Since their brethren expect to receive through their agency physical healing, spiritual counseling, revelations, and favors from God, the widows are regarded as being themselves spiritual or charismatic.[47]

DECAYING OF THE ORDER OF WIDOWS

Later writings, such as *Apostolic Constitutions,* mention nothing about the charismatic activities of widows, probably because an order of widows cannot be open to all and still remain a kind of religious order. The same feeling of secularization is apparent in Chrysostom's fourth-century description of the qualities required of the priest in charge of the widows—freedom from greed, forbearance, and long-sufferance.

Certainly there were good and holy widows in Antioch, Constantinople, and the other large cities of late antiquity, but there were many poor, and because of their large number, which led to anonymity and abandonment, individuals were inclined to lose their dignity. They often gave a show of their misery on the street in order to attract alms, and old women accepted jobs as sycophants or spies for a few pennies.

In the community, the virgins were ranked above the widows. Monastic groups were then carrying on the ideals which once were the privilege of the order of widows.[48] The emphasis was on consecrated virginity rather than on holy widowhood and on the question of the tolerance of second marriage. There had been a shift of interest from conjugal life and continence in marriage or widowhood to virginity, with greater worth ascribed to virginity.[49] In addition, monastic communities began to withdraw from the world into the desert or into convents within the towns. For this reason, and because they developed a spirituality of their own, they deprived the individual parish of the spiritual contribution of its contemplatives. Lost was the time when Christian communities were small enough to allow brotherly warnings, to share in material goods, and to keep their contemplatives.

VALIDITY FOR OUR TIMES OF THE EXPERIENCE
OF THE EARLY CHURCH

I have considered the attitude of the Early Church toward the elderly by examining the material assistance and respect given to them by the Church, and the counseling and spiritual contribution given by them to their community. The validity of the Early Christian experience for our own times can be considered under the same categories.

ASSISTANCE

Until recently the elderly were often able to provide financially for their own welfare, but inflation is now robbing them of their savings, and many can expect to end their days in real poverty. Just as in antiquity, and in spite of their traditions of charity, churches cannot assume the whole burden of assistance to the elderly. However, they can and must take care of exceptional cases of emergencies. For each particular case there can be no definite rules, since every Christian is in charge of the brother in need according to the principle of the Gospel: "Love your neighbor." If the community is very large, particularly in urban areas, charities should be coordinated through the social worker, whose occupation most closely approximates the ancient ministry of deacons and deaconesses. When they depend on the churches, these ministries might be integrated to clergy as they were in the Early Church; that is, such social workers might be given recognition, rank, and authority as helpers of the bishop.

RESPECT

Just as in antiquity, younger generations of our times should give the elderly respect and consideration, although it is perhaps more difficult today because of the increasing gap of needs between generations. An inquiry among the elderly would reveal priorities in detail. It would appear that the frustrations resulting from the modern development of bureaucracy are exceedingly painful and more humiliating for the elderly, who often can feel helpless and desperate when claiming their own rights.

COUNSELING

The world is changing so fast that the three generations—youth, adult, and elderly—differ deeply in their views regarding professional, pedagogical, and even moral matters. The ideals of righteousness, on which the happiness of older generations relied, may simply turn into an unjust condemnation of the young, who do not find the same help and stability in society. In so far as the pyramid of society remains in place, that is, in so far as the young, adults, and the elderly live together or see each other, counseling is possible. Of course, it can be appropriate and realistic only if it is cooperative and open-minded, and not understood as requiring mere obedience or passivity.

In the religious community itself, elderly men and women could more easily exercise their abilities as counselors, even as spiritual guides and conscience directors. They are all the more able to provide spiritual counseling as they are themselves advanced in wisdom—full of experience, considerate, and learned in the humanities and in religion.

We cannot doubt the high spiritual and moral value of the humanities. Many elderly men and women strongly regret that attending college was impossible during their youth. Presently universities, libraries, parishes, and organizations of continuing education for the elderly are trying to answer this need. The Early Church provided the elderly, and all those who regularly attended church, with a culture of its own, essentially biblical but permeated with Christian ideas through symbolism and liturgical use, which fulfilled for them the ancient ideals of the feast of every day.

SPIRITUAL CONTRIBUTION TO THE COMMUNITY

Churches today are still searching for a way to contribute to the elderly that is truly in the area of a church. Certainly churches can, and to some extent should, organize leisure activities for the elderly, but the feeling is that it is inadequate to merely offer entertainment and games. Therefore, going to the other extreme, preparation for death has seemed to be the alternative. For those elderly who are willing to put their remaining strength to the service of the community, the Church and the city have many jobs, especially if no money is claimed, and the area of charities is infinite. If these ideas are good, however, they are not perfectly satisfactory.

Perhaps the Early Church can provide the right answer to the question of the spiritual role of the elderly in the Church today. There is no evidence in the writings of the Early Church of a complex of death, or of any other special preparation of the elderly for death. For them, the earthly Church was part of the heavenly Church, or of Christ who is gloriously sitting on the right hand of the Father. But, unlike churches of today, which have dropped most of their weekly meetings of prayer, the Early Church encouraged prayer at home and meetings of prayer in the church. The prayer of praise and thanksgiving was in particularly high favor. The prayer of intercession was also practiced for the needs of all, and it was much more developed and diversified than today. The elderly were the basis of the community in these prayer meetings, possibly because the younger members were prevented from fully participating by the other duties of their active life. Therefore, just as in the Early Church, the service of prayer—if it existed and were appropriate—could be regularly attended by a group of elderly parishioners, and completed by the prayer of many others at home.[50]

Should we insist on this ancient association of prayer, fasting, and continence? These ideas seem to be antiquated, and no one yet has imagined that continence should be preached to the elderly! The Early Church actually considered the practice of continence for the sake of prayer as vocational.[51] Prayer, fasting, and continence must be understood in the context of the conversion from the flesh to the spirit which aims at a total dedication to God. The Early Church has a relatively negative position regarding second marriage, but regarded a first marriage as a blessing of God. There are different vocations in Christian life, however, and not all are to marriage. There are also, of course, failures in marriage. And the evolution of their spiritual life may lead certain men or women towards the practice of a kind of religious life. At this point, let us simply suggest that more opportunities be made for women after a divorce, or as widows, who in the maturity of age would like to live in a kind of community where they could find the advantage of both material and spiritual life. To some extent, the same is also true for men. Perhaps some religious orders could find in this direction a renewal of vitality which would not be too far from their caritative and contemplative destination.

NOTES

1. Concerning widows and more generally the ministry of women in the Early Church, including an excellent bibliography, see Roger Gryson, *The Ministry of Women in the Early Church* (Collegeville, Minnesota: Liturgical Press, 1976). Concerning service to the poor in the Early Church (*agapes, diakonia,* collects in the church, etc.), see A. Hamman, *Vie Liturgique et Sociale* (Tournai: Declee, 1978)
2. Plato, *Laws* 6. 759d (Bollingen Series LXXI, Pantheon Books).
3. Philo, *On the Creation*, trans. F. H. Colson and G. H. Whitaker, The Loeb Classical Library, vol. 1, pp. 103–105.
4. *Didascalia Apostolorum*, trans. R. Hugh Connolly (Oxford: Clarendon Press, 1929), p. 130.
5. Ibid., pp. 130–131.
6. *Shepherd of Hermas*, Similitude 5. 3.
7. *Testamentum Domini*, translated into English from the Syriac by James Cooper and A. J. Maclean (Edinburgh: T. T. Clark, 1902), chap. 32.
8. *Didascalia Apostolorum*, p. 34.
9. *Les institutions de Ancien Testament* 1. 5 (Paris: Le Cerf, 1957), p. 91.
10. *The Theodosian Code*, trans. C. Pharr (Princeton: Princeton University Press, 1952), note esp. 3. 8. 1–2.; 3. 12. 3.; 5. 1. 9.; 8. 17. 2. This legislation is late, and from Christian inspiration. We may presume the absence of such legislation before the fourth century, particularly for low social classes.
11. *Epistle to Polycarp* 4 (Ancient Christian Writers 1), p. 97.
12. See Gryson, *Ministry of Women*, chaps. 3 ff.
13. Justin, *Apology* 1. 67. 1–6. See also, Hamman, *Vie Liturgique*, pp. 251–291.
14. Tertullian, *Apologeticum* 39. 5–21; Clement of Alexandria, *Instructor* 2 (Ante-Nicene Fathers 2, p. 238). See also *Statutes of the Apostles*, in *Canones Ecclesiastici*, ed. and trans. Rev. G. Horner (London: Williams and Norgate, 1904), chap. 37; *Apostolic Tradition*, ed. G. Dix (London, S.P.C.K., 1968), p. 52.
15. *Didascalia Apostolorum*, p. 32.
16. *Apostolic Tradition* 11; *Apostolic Church Order*, trans. J. P. Arendzen, *Journal of Theological Studies* 3 (1902): 59–80; *Apostolic Constitutions* 3, 8. 25; *Testamentum Domini*, trans. J. Cooper and A. J. Maclean (Edinburgh, 1902).
17. Augustine, *Sermo* 102 (Migne, PL 38, 1388); Ambrose, *De officiis* 2. 140 (Migne, PL 16, 141).

18. Chrysostom, *On Matthew*, Homily 66. 3 (Nicene and Post-Nicene Fathers 10), p. 407.

19. Chrysostom, *On the Priesthood* 3. 16 (NPNF 9), p. 55.

20. Gregory Nazianzen, *On Basil* 25, 35, 62, 63 (Fathers of the Church 22). See also A. J. Festugiere, *Les Moines d'Orient*, vol. II/I (Paris: Le Cerf, 1962–64), p. 107; III/II, p. 36, 42–43, 63, 107.

21. Plato, *Laws* 9. 879c. See also Cicero, *De officiis* 1. 34. 122.

22. C. Spicq, *Les Epitres Patorales* (Paris: Etudes Bibliques, 1960), pp. 524–40.

23. *Apostolic Tradition* 20; *Statutes of the Apostles* 34.

24. Athenagoras, *A Plea for the Christians* 32 (ANF 2), p. 146; Tatian, *Address to the Greeks* 32–33.

25. *Didascalia Apostolorum*, pp. 119–124; *Statutes of the Apostles* 52; *Testamentum Domini* 4.

26. Tertullian, *On the Veiling of the Virgins* 9 (ANF 4), p. 33.

27. Tertullian, *On Monogamy* 11 (ANF 4), p. 67; *On Penitence* 9–10 (ACW 28), p. 32.

28. Clement of Alexandria, *Who Is the Rich Man That Shall be Saved* (Migne, PG 9, p. 640c–d; ANF 2, p. 601).

29. Ibid., 35 (ANF 2, pp. 601, 640d–f41 a).

30. I Cor. 7; Tertullian, *To His Wife* 1. 6–7 (ANF 4), p. 42–43 and *Exhortation to Chastity* 10 (ANF 4), p. 55.

31. Tertullian, *On Penitence* 9.

32. Tertullian, *Exhortation to Chastity* 10 (ANF 4), pp. 55–56.

33. Ibid., 12 (ANF 4), p. 56; also Tertullian, *On Monogamy* 16 (ANF 4), p. 72.

34. Tertullian, *Against the Psychic* 7–8; Origen, *Commentary on I Corinthians* 14:34–35; see Gryson, *Ministry of Women*, p. 28; *Apostolic Constitutions* 3. 1. (ANF 7), p. 427; Augustine, *In Psalmos* 131:23.

35. *A Plea for the Christians* 33 (ANF 3), p. 146; Tertullian, *To His Wife* 1.6 and *Against Marcion* 6.61; Clement, *Stromaton* 3.1 (LCC 2), p. 40.

36. Tertullian, *To His Wife* 1. 6 (ANF 4), p. 42.

37. *Didascalia Apostolorum*, pp. 242, 244, 254; *Statutes of the Apostles* 48.

38. Tertullian, *To His Wife* 2. 4–5.

39. Polycarp, *Philadelphians* 4; Tertullian, *To His Wife* 1. 7 (ANF 4), p. 43; *Didascalia Apostolorum*, pp. 88, 133, 134, 143, 156.

40. *Didascalia Apostolorum*, pp. 156–160; see also *Apostolic Constitutions* 4.

41. For instance, see Tertullian, *On Monogamy* 10 (ANF 4), pp. 66–67.

42. Augustine, *In Psalmos* 131:23.

43. *Apostolic Tradition* 11; *Didascalia Apostolorum* p. 133; *Statutes of the Apostles* 36.

44. *Apostolic Tradition* 25 and 27; Clement of Alexandria, *Instructor* 2. 1 (ANF 4), pp. 239–41, 248–49; Tertullian, *Apologeticum* 39; *Statutes of the Apostles* 36–38.

45. *Didascalia Apostolorum*, pp. 133, 140.

46. *Apostolic Church Order* 21; also in *Statutes of the Apostles* 18.

47. See Gryson, *Ministry of Women*, pp. 39–40.

48. Ibid., pp. 58–61. See also R. Metz, *La consecration des vierges dans l'Eglise romaine* (Paris: Presses Universitaires ete France, 1954).

49. Note Jovinian, who denied that virginity was a higher state than marriage, and the subsequent controversy in which his views were attacked by Jerome (*Adversus Jovinianum*, A.D. 392) and Augustine (*De bono conjugali* and *De sancta virginitate*, A.D. 401).

50. Tertullian, *Apologeticum* 39. 5–20 (a description of a meeting of this type, the *Agape*).

51. I Corinthians 7:7. Also Tertullian, *Exhortation to Chastity* 8.

4

Cultural Antecedents to Contemporary American Attitudes toward Aging

Martin E. Marty

It is difficult to describe the cultural antecedents of contemporary American attitudes toward the aged because it is so hard to discern what those attitudes are now. The aged—those over sixty-five years old—make up eleven percent of the population. They are themselves Americans, and presumably they have different attitudes toward themselves than many teenagers have toward them. For those under sixty-five, the aged may be subjects of rage, resentment, care, admiration, and love, which is only to begin citing a range of the spectrum of attitudes. But after surveying the literature, politics, and lore of and about the aged, one common denominator emerges. In contemporary America, older people are almost always lumped together and classified as a *problem.*

THE AGED AS A PROBLEM

Those who have any familiarity at all with historical records about the aged in earlier America—say, from 1492 until almost 1892—almost never see age–specific references about old people being a problem. How the problem came to be discerned or invented, whether the process was gradual or sudden, and whether certain events or persons produced the change in attitudes is a subject that merits inquiry. Attention to the problem of "the problem of the aged" may do as much as any other historical examination to illuminate present-day discontents and throw light on issues having to do with understanding and action in the future.

In earlier America, aged people were often problems to themselves and those around them. But in later America, the aged became a problem as a class. Today, whether or not an older person is making a contribution to the rest of society, in growing old—infirm or not— he or she automatically joins a caste that is described as a problem. There are no exemptions. As if by divine election or computerized, calculated necessity, everyone eventually becomes a part of the caste, just as people who are born retarded, or of a minority, or handicapped are categorized into problem zones by the larger society which surrounds them.

In the past, the aged still had an advantage over those who were trapped in some other stages of life—they were at least recognized as persons. According to widespread and well-confirmed opinions, child-hood was invented—which means it was discovered *and* made up— only in recent times, a process which has, in fact, been chronicled.[1] Awareness of this late discovery comes as a revelation to all those who had believed that because there were always so many children around, everyone knew what they were. Actually, mature people had thought of them as miniature adults. Because most people did not survive into their sixties in colonial and early national America, the young outnumbered the aged. Yet children were somehow less familiar to society than were the aged, who could, after all, speak up for themselves and who left records of individual achievement.

It cannot be said that during the seventeenth through the nineteenth centuries younger Americans were always insensitive to the presence of aged people. Old people lived in closer proximity to the young than they might today, and children then stood a better chance of being with grandparents, and even seeing them die, than they do now. In the somewhat simpler existence of colonial America, the aged were more integrated into family, church, and community life. This made it possible for those close to such persons to deal with the needs of each, within the context of family and community possibilities. Few people advocated isolating the aged or categorizing them as a problem group. They were free to be sages, counselors, curmudgeons, or even irrelevancies. But each won his or her own status, be it good or bad, by personal achievement, not automatically by longevity.

One element in the debate about the change in attitude which led to the aged being regarded as a problem has to do with a larger controversy among historians. On the one hand are those who speak of an unfolding process. W. Andrew Achenbaum, who wrote *Old Age in the New Land,* is most eloquent at defending this approach.² On the other hand are those in the camp of David Hackett Fischer, whose *Growing Old in America* stresses a rather sudden break in continuities and a "two-stage" theory of development.³

To the lay person the differences are not drastic or even important at first glance. If one posits beginning and ending points, there will be many agreements about these terminals. There is not even controversy about everything that occurred between the points. The issue is evolution versus revolution, development versus breach. Perhaps it would be well to picture Achenbaum's understanding along the lines of the science films we saw in high school. These motion pictures followed the growth of a seedling through its mature stages, condensing six weeks of life into two minutes of speeded-up film. All is a visible and gradual process. On the other hand, the "break" theory would be more like the kind of change of which we speak when, having been out of touch with a child through puberty, we again see this child-turned-adult and are moved to gasp about the "suddenness" of growing up. When do quantitative changes pile up enough to be regarded as qualitative? Achenbaum probably has the best of the argument. But, time-pacing aside, the question remains: "What did happen?"

To say that the idea and the issues of modernization contributed to understanding the aged as a problem is to approach a field of great complexity. Many sociologists have such a long view of history that they telescope a century or two and speak, as international economist Walt Rostow did of the Industrial Revolution, of a sudden "take-off." Historians, however, are wary: *was* there an "industrial revolution?" Did not the phenomena it describes reach back to Greek science, medieval technology, and population trends that were long developing? Some want to say there was nothing but process, never a revolution. Into this E. J. Hobsbawm has brought a dose of reality:

> Some time in the 1780s, and for the first time in human history, the shackles were taken off the productive power of human societies, which henceforth became capable of the constant, rapid, and up to the present limitless multi-plication of men, goods, and services. This is now technically known to the economists as the "take-off into self-sustained growth."[4]

We shall not, say the "process" people, be able to pinpoint a precise moment of "take-off" for the passage of aging problems into the problem of the aged. The process is too long, the variables are too many. We wake up somewhere around the turn of the twentieth century with a vastly different situation in hand than the one that prevailed at the turns into each of the three centuries that preceded it. Something happened along the way, and this something is still unfolding.

It is in this context that aspects of modernization theory are appropriate. For example, the attempt to understand the aged has naturally isolated them for comparative study because there are evidences that a situation comparable to that of earlier America still prevails in "non-modern" societies. For some years now, efforts have been made to view modernity as a tradition in an effort to overcome the provincialism which sees western ideas of development as being unique. The trends may indeed apply more aptly to technology; nevertheless, they may prove useful in examining issues of the discovery and hardening of age lines, the disruption of multigenerational families, and other features that separate the aged in America as a problem from the role of aged people in, say, Bangladesh or Sicily.

At the heart of any such modernizing process is the concept of what we might call an increasing "chopping up," sundering, making divisions and distinctions as history moves on. One of the more provocative analyses of the process comes from critic John Murray Cuddihy. In *The Ordeal of Civility* he reveals his impatience with the "secularized Calvinist" scholars of northwest Europe and Anglo-America. In "the eye of the hurricane" as it were, they serenely analyze change while others are the victims of it. He attacks a school of theory that includes Max Weber and Talcott Parsons, the latter of whom displayed "all but sovereign indifference to the high cost of . . . [the] 'passing of traditional society,' . . . this 'passage from home'. . . ." Still, Cuddihy pays respect to the theory. Modernization concentrates on:

> The differentiation of home from job; differentiation of the culture system from the personality and social systems; . . . differentiation of fact from value, of theory from praxis; differentiation of art from belief.
> Differentiation is the cutting edge of the modernization process, sundering cruelly what tradition had joined. . . . Differentiation slices through ancient primordial ties and identities, leaving crisis and 'wholeness hunger' in its wake. Differentiation divorces ends from means . . . nuclear from extended families.[5]

At the last line especially, students of aging perk up, since it mentions the family. Unfortunately for those who want clean breaks between historical periods, the extended family had begun to be cut into by many processes in Europe long before the migration into America. Recent studies have also shown that because of constant internal migrations, Americans in colonial times were not so settled down in a web of kin that extended both through time (the generations) and space (the neighborhood and region) as had been thought. Nevertheless, colonial America did not have the network of institutions—such as the Social Security system begun in the 1930s—which made feasible breaking up the extended family on generational lines and, along with it, changing the location and care of the aged to places physically removed from the following generation. Early national America had not yet arranged for a legal and economic basis to segregate the aged. No such system helped people plan for, and indeed forced, retirement at a certain period, thus helping form the group that becomes a "problem."

What is different about the more remote past and the recent past is that modernity has meant, along with the chopping up and sundering, a growth of choice. This growth represents the compensatory side of the modernization process. If it causes psychic damage because it cuts primordial ties, like those between generations, it also enlarges the range of possibilities. Only a romantic bias pictures pre-modern arrangements, in which grandmother lived on in infirmity through decades—possibly destroying her children and grandchildren even as they caused her great injury—as being superior in every respect to all modern possibilities. Even the most jaundiced social critic is likely to come away from retirement centers with a sense that many aged, and thus problematic, people are actually living reasonably fulfilled lives. They say they enjoy themselves. And so do their descendants who are "free" of them, and free to pick occasions for being together with them. Modernization takes with one hand and gives with another. Is life better or worse for the change? Would people, if they could, repeal the sundering process and give up choice? It is more important to notice differences in the situations than to concentrate *a priori* on which is "better" or "worse."

Rather than point to a two-stage set of epochs divided by a single breach, we shall watch an unfolding, much like the one in that science film about a growing plant. Yet there is in that film, as in our view, a moment when leaves spread and the whole organism changes shape. This unfolding carries us through a number of phases or stages in American life. It is necessary to deal with them in broad-brush fashion, with no effort being made to flesh out all details or shade in all colors. In each period, only certain aspects of the issue of the aged concern us.

PERIODS OF CHANGE

THE PRE-COLONIAL PERIOD—RUGGED INDIVIDUALISTS?

The growth of the Hispanic population in America is leading to fresh interest in the North American continent from 1492–1607, even though there have been such great breaches in continuity that it is not likely that attitudes from Spanish exploration days will haunt us or give us models for rescue. The *Conquistadores* were young men who brought with them young missionaries; they encountered young Native Americans, many of whom soon died off.

The lure of gold and of spreading the name of God meant haste, wastage of life, disaffiliation, and uprootage. At best only one note about the family, possibly a foreboding note, can be detected in precolonial writing in North America: there is a general absence of relationships. What chance do the aged have in such a picture?

> The notable lack for sixteenth-century America is the lack of personal relationships, familial and social. Families only rarely took part in the ventures. . . . Not only is there a lack of relationship between the sexes, but even between friend and friend, follower and leader. . . . The paradox stands that even in this era of high individualism, interest in individuality hardly appears.[6]

So much for any notion that America has "fallen" from a period of perfect social relations. Those lines sound like the complaints about "the organization man" and "the man in the gray flannel suit" of the corporate-suburban 1950s.

THE SEVENTEENTH CENTURY—NEW ENGLAND

The settlement of a land means something much different. When no type of familial relationship received much notice in the sixteenth century, the aged had to be nonexistent or at least simply overlooked. But when one settles a place, and consecrates it with intention, a new network of institutions and relations begins to develop. The cultural antecedents for the present-day notions that once there were "good old days" derive chiefly from seventeenth-century America.

Here again the picture is usually romanticized. The English settlers of Jamestown and a larger Virginia did not begin by creating such a network. They arrived in 1607, but no women came until 1619, and the issue of generationalism developed during the next forty years. The records give us almost nothing to go on, however. New Amsterdam was conceived more as a trading post than as a settlement. This meant that the fiscal adventurers had no great stake in what went on in the Dutch outpost, and the records are again meager. Backwoods colonial groups of continental provenance, because they often represented migrations of the persecuted in Europe, included aged people for whom there was care. But they do not come to mind when Americans of later periods ask what was going on.

For that, New England stands alone and supreme. When Americans today deal with the way images from colonial times might still serve as exemplars or blocks to understanding, they really mean not colonial America but New England. Try as one might to overcome old positive prejudices stamped on the mind by the articulate heirs of these settlers, and make whatever efforts one might to give equal time to the middle or southern colonies, the student of cycles of life, family structures, and attitudes toward the aged is drawn by the magnet of New England.

The reasons for this are fairly obvious. They do not all have to do with the transmission of culture through the publishing houses, textbook writing, and missionary ventures that issued later from literate New England. No, in their own time the New Englanders of Plymouth, Massachusetts Bay, New Haven, and Connecticut were uncommonly articulate and self-conscious. They had a sense of history, so they weighted their daily doings with a sense of portentousness and with an eye on posterity. A whole new historical and sociological industry has sprung up among people who are trying to see how the New England past haunts and shapes us today.

Thanks to well-kept records, archaeological remains, feminist interests in revisiting the past, and the new devices for measuring in history, demography and family existence are at the center of any number of studies of New England communities through more than one generation. Child nurture, social control, community cohesion, and the cycles of life through the period of dying are the preoccupations of people like John Demos, David Stannard, and Philip Greven. Their findings illuminate the attitudes that Americans today often unconsciously carry with them, thanks to pictures of the past they gained from folklore, the textbook tradition, or the mythology of the past portrayed in mass media.

John Demos in particular has written on the problem of old age in early New England.[7] He leads the group of scholars who have seen the importance of age as a determinant of historical experiences in that era. Demos has discovered materials for the colonial period which probably have their counterparts in other periods, but have not yet been studied by historians. He has found positive attitudes among New Englanders toward the aged, since they believed such people bore a likeness to God. The aged possessed special virtues, six of which the revered minister Cotton Mather urged upon his older church members: sobriety, gravity, temperance, orthodoxy, charity, and patience. From Demos and from demographic studies we can see how exchange of personal help and services crossed grandparent-grandchild lines. "While presumably enjoying their proximity to kin, elderly couples preferred to look after themselves," says Demos. Most of them evidently remained self-sufficient, he says, especially if both partners survived. Only a few had to appeal to public authority for relief. Retirement, while not a wholly unfamiliar idea, was not an automatic imposition on the unwilling. After age sixty most men evidently reduced their activities voluntarily.

On the basis of some evidence Demos speculates that the position of elderly people improved from mid-seventeenth century to mid-eighteenth. Yet, worse times were ahead—what David Hackett Fischer called a "revolution in age relations." Nineteenth-century "Young America" would be less and less inclined to acknowledge the claims of age. Increasing uprootedness and efficiency would make it more convenient for a bustling nation to overlook the once-honored aged.

THE ENLIGHTENMENT—EVERYONE'S ANCESTORS

A third period that colors the later American cultural attitude is that of the Enlightenment. Whether or not America had an Enlightenment to match the one in Europe, and whether or not its traces were imported, it must be said that beginning in the late 1750s and running until the turn of the century, a new *Zeitgeist* developed. This was a crucial period, for during it the colonists established independence and constituted a new society. The founders were people of intellect and stature. They were articulate, and their inquisitive minds showed them to be concerned with the biological and psychological processes associated with family stages and aging. Even more than the early New Englanders, they have become "everyone's ancestors." Though those who were best poised to speak for posterity were male, white, and well-off, young people in slums, "ethnic" immigrants, and blacks were later acculturated into their world. Their ideology was fused with public institutions. It had and still has a privileged position in the schools.

These Enlightment thinkers, people like Thomas Jefferson and Thomas Paine, James Madison and Benjamin Franklin, were chiefly deists and moralists. Curious about science and nature, they experimented with social relations and were self-conscious about what they catalogued and chronicled. They lived less under a sense of fate and more with one of intervention than did the theistic colonial New Englanders. Here was a new age of human mastery and dominion. Inevitably the Enlightened began to isolate the aged for special scrutiny.

The fact that some of them lived so long—Thomas Jefferson and John Adams died in 1826; Benjamin Franklin lived into his eighties; and Charles Carroll of Carrollton lived to age 95—meant that this extraordinarily gifted set of oldsters was given an opportunity to reflect on their own aging and pass on their ideas. What is remarkable among them is how few were inspired to isolate the problems of the aged. Few were stirred when the rare exceptions among them, like Thomas Paine in 1797 or Alexander Everett in 1823 (well into the next period of history), proposed pensions to be funded nationally in order to support the indigent elderly.[8]

THE NATIONAL PERIOD—RIGHTEOUS EMPIRE

The next period of cultural antecedency—the National Period— ran specifically from the turn of the century to the Civil War, and was the most explicitly religious. This was a time when white Protestants set out to create a civilization which Robert Handy calls a *Christian America* and I have seen as a *Righteous Empire*.[9] After the Enlightenment period, the churches moved out of latency into a time of new cultural aggression. Their instrument for coming to dominance was the conversion process of carefully cultivated revivals. Their product was the voluntary spirit which accentuated choice. The result of their strivings was the denominational pattern of competitive church life.

If the story ended there, it would have little bearing in a sequence of cultural antecedencies that left their mark on later and even non-Protestant America. But these churches, no longer established by law and yet privileged in society, had to legitimate themselves to the society. They did so through their moralistic and reformist concerns. If that makes them sound exploitative and calculating, it should also be said that the revivalists often were motivated by humanitarian concerns as well.[10] Their scope was limited, in that they did not consistently question the basic economic pattern of American life. In the South they could not speak up against slavery. But within that circumscription they were tireless in addressing new areas of human need that sought the redress the churches could bring.

The result was an Anglo-American nexus that historian Charles I. Foster has referred to as an "Errand of Mercy." Spilling over from the revivalist Protestantism to an interdenominational basis often motivated by lay energies, there was born the complex of voluntary associations which later America takes for granted in its secularized forms. Yet even 150 years later, religion continues to play a part in this "voluntaryistic" pattern. About half of all charitable dollars and half of the accountable charitable hours that are voluntarily donated are still channeled through religious institutions.

More than they knew, the people of the "errand of mercy" were participating in modernizing processes, for they were among the early pre-professional specialists on the American scene. With great ingenuity they located problem areas, began to develop expertise in dealing with them, and became accomplished at raising funds and propagandizing. By about 1837, the interdenominational wholism of the efforts had broken down and denominationalism chopped up their efforts, but the benevolent evangelicals themselves had begun the sundering through overspecialization. After they had dealt with orphans, prostitutes, drinkers, warmakers, and slaveholders, they became precise enough to form American urban branches of societies that did nothing, for example, but provide trusses for the ruptured poor. In such specialization, age too would soon become a target.

Charles I. Foster has collected the names of scores of the societies these humanitarians developed.[11] They founded such groups as American Female Guardian Society, Connecticut Society for the Suppression of Vice and the Promotion of Good Morals, Penitent Females' Refuge, and Philadelphia Society for the Encouragement of Faithful Domestics. Foster's long list indicates that slaveholders, the deaf and dumb, women, warmakers, alcohol users, seamen, the poor, Sabbath-breakers, the vicious, the illiterate, infants, poor widows, domestics, tobacco smokers, prostitutes, prisoners, half orphans, Jews, and destitute children were all "problems." But in five pages of one-line listings, there is only one reference to age, the Association for the Relief of Respectable, Aged, Indigent Females.

The most comprehensive books on social attitudes in the Protestant benevolent empire are silent on the subject of age because there is so much about which to be silent, for good and bad reasons. John R. Bodo has traced attitudes from 1812–1848 among people he calls "theocrats."[12] These were the Protestant leaders who, after the separation of church and state, continued to act as if they could still legislate for the whole country. Bodo finds these evangelicals to be dealing with issues like the Sabbath, immigrants, Indians, blacks and slavery, public schools, temperance, and "the West." But if anyone over fifty existed as a possible subject of organized concern, it did not turn up in his researches.

Similarly, Charles C. Cole, Jr., observed the northern evangelists, the religious tone-setters for the country between 1820–1860.[13] His list of concerns was essentially the same as that which Bodo turned up, though he also found an ever-increasing interest in nationalism. Since he dealt with the North alone, he also isolated the issue of slavery. The figures with whom Cole dealt—Lyman Beecher, Horace Bushnell, the brothers Arthur and Lewis Tappan, and others—were obsessed with moral reform. Although their catalogues of interest were quite comprehensive, the aged did not show up in them. Whether this is a mark of the evangelists' oversight, or a tribute to the way families then took care of their own aged, it does reveal a vastly different America. In a time when poverty was widespread and many of the poor were aged, no one found reason to isolate the aged as a problem. This is another sign that in an organized sense Americans have had little experience with the aged as a specific population sector. Or is it a sign that we have fallen from the day when the problems we now consider age-specific could still have been blended into other problems like those of being female, respectable, and poor?

Between the era when Protestants had the field almost to themselves and the late nineteenth century with its Social Gospel, revivalists moved toward a new stage of programmatic social reform. They became particularly conscious of the problem of poverty, even if at that time many of them joined evangelist Edward Norris Kirk in believing that poverty was the result of personal factors such as "improvidence, intemperance, and discouragement."[14] Becoming old was then, as now, a way of becoming poor, but the language and program of the evangelical humanitarian movement had little room for that topic.

1860–1917—THE TAKE-OFF

To those who take the modernization thesis through a two-stage development, the period between the Civil War and the First World War is the era of the great take-off, or the great coming-apart. Until that time the extended family prevailed everywhere. The aged "lived upstairs," the children paid obeisance and listened to them, society regarded them as sage counselors. And then, in this view, came all the "-ation" processes: immigration, urbanization, modernization, secularization, differentiation. As a result the aged were pushed aside. They became a problem and were treated as a specialty; the spirit of efficiency put them aside; they were forced into retirement. Society developed special homes where the aged could be hidden from view. They had to begin to learn to die in isolation.

Like so many other mythological pictures and stereotypes, the pictures I have drawn do render some processes in bold outline. Once again, "something" was happening. To engage in a revisionism that sweeps these processes aside is as destructive to understanding cultural antecedencies as it is to accept them all at face value and then fail to perceive the subtleties of process and the exceptions along the way.

The Social Gospel is the best known of all the church-based efforts to transform society. It flourished from late in the nineteenth century into World War I, appealing to the liberal Protestant, though it also had Roman Catholic counterparts. In the schemes of Walter Rauschenbusch, Washington Gladden, Robert Herron, and a number of social-minded and sometimes socialist Christians, the industrial order was the new element in life that needed "Christianization." By organizing energies for specific tasks this movement, like all such movements, neglected other tasks. While concentrating on the laborers and indus-trial poor, Rauschenbusch and his colleagues had blind spots concerning the problems of race relations and the subjection of emancipated blacks.

What is often overlooked is that in the decades when the poor were being discovered everywhere else, they rarely showed up on the Social Gospel screen. A concern for the durability of the family grew, but the Catholic and Protestant clergy were at no point pathfinders in seeking out the aged for care and concern. Divorce was a greater threat to family serenity; and without the family there could not have been care for the unmentioned aged.[15]

While the churches did eventually come to have homes for the aged, the ideology of social welfare for the aged had then passed into the hands of those who established settlement houses, who professional-ized urban care on secular terms. Unmarried mothers were then a much more attractive topic than were the aged poor or ill.[16]

More resistant to secular impulses were the conservative evangelicals, whose work in the slums has been a neglected story until Norris Magnu-son recently set it forth.[17] His study of the years 1865–1920 is a broad and careful scrutiny of rescue homes for women, the problems of unem-ployment, prison philanthropy, health care, and shelter provision among "holiness" people. Here, as always, if the aged belonged to any of these classes they were automatically and quietly included in concern, but they did not yet form a category like "fallen women" or "drinkers" or "the rich."

The problem historians have in dealing with the late nineteenth century is its complex of "turning-points," which taken together create what is as much a blur as a breach. Among the many changes was what is coming to be seen as a "professional revolution." In this period, according to the researches of historians who bring many ideologies (including Marxist outlooks) to their inquiries, middle-class privileged people who had been victims of differentiation processes then became agents of them. They developed formal disciplines in the academy and saw to it that they had credentialing processes that would assure their place in a meritocracy. They developed jargon and argot to use for demarcating who was "in" and who was "out." Many of them were liberated from the wholistic and still repressive small town life in which religion had served as the connecting tissue. They were secular professionals.[18]

In our context, while looking for fields to cover and areas in which to dominate as well as to serve, the new professionals found social work. And social work soon divided into specialties, one of which was the care of the aged. This was not the prime issue: the immigrant had priority in the settlement house and the delinquent child had been discovered. But care of the aged came into a new and separate stage. If there is any period in which one can speak of the aged being located as a problem, this is it.[19]

BETWEEN THE WARS—THE NEW DEAL

The penultimate period of cultural antecedency is an extension of the earlier one, but it issued in a new basis for dealing with the problem of the aged. If the process of seeing the aged as a problem is long and subtle and has few landmarks, passage of Social Security legislation in the 1930s stands out as a major development. The Depression had caused severe poverty in a society made more aware of social problems by two generations of agitators and social workers. In addition, many of the aged in a more educated America began to develop increasingly articulate voices along with the arts of self-representation. Citizens made a basic move. They institutionalized age and formalized the retirement process by creating the Social Security system. There was nothing subtle about the positive and negative effects of this change. It gave legal and economic legitimacy to patterns that had long been developing. Latter-day Americans can only with great empathy and historical imagination conceive of the country before Social Security.

While Catholicism, like Protestantism, established homes for the care of the aged, it too was rather passive in the realm of social programs and ideology. As late as the New Deal, according to the best study of those years, Catholic Social Action concentrated on labor, industrial democracy, child labor, and such issues, while dealing only marginally with the aged as a cohort needing special attention—this in the very decade in which the Social Security legislation was passed.[20] Catholic leaders did find good precedent for the Social Security Bill of 1935 in the encyclicals of Pius XI and Leo XIII. Even Catholic editors of major independent Catholic magazines who first opposed the bill came to regard it as one of the better measures of the New Deal. Father John A. Ryan, the most notable Catholic activist of the period, was even consulted on drafting the bill. His associate, John A. Lapp, thought it "by far the greatest achievement of the present administration—or of any administration in half a century," but here as elsewhere the initiative did not come from churchly diagnosticians or agitators.[21]

The Protestant leaders in the New Deal era, headed by Reinhold Niebuhr, continued to concentrate on labor as the new social zone. Of course, they supported Social Security legislation, but to my knowledge they did not position themselves so that those who discerned the problem of the aged in new ways would turn to them for leadership. We may hypothesize that since care of the aged was an area in which the churches were coming to have some expertise—as they did not in representing labor—they took the problems of the aged for granted in the political and social realms, and did not recognize specialization as significant in dealing with them. It is almost as if the aged and their special gifts and liabilities did not exist.

The most extensive canvas of the social functions of the church, a 569-page textbook that gathers up evidence in all areas, devotes only two pages at most to philanthropy or social concern in relation to aging and the old.[22] The author, David O. Moberg, cites studies which point to the "secularization of social welfare." In 1903, for example, fully one-third of the benevolent institutions were church-related, but in a study of thirty-four urban areas in 1940, 96% of all funds for relief and family welfare and 90% for health and welfare came from public funds. There were 2,783 Protestant, Catholic, and Jewish agencies in those cities and 18% of them were homes for the aged. But the initiative for care had slipped from the churches.

THE AGE OF RETIREMENT

The most recent period—can one speak of antecedency when one is in the midst of it—may be thought of as one which concentrates on "entitlement." It follows from the logic of the two periods before it. Daniel Bell has spoken of the way the various groups in society now feel that they are "entitled" to security, health, some measure of goods, respect, and the like.[23] In a welfare state the poor, the intellectually endowed, the unemployed, women, racial minorities, those deprived in youth, those disadvantaged by having served in the military regard themselves as somehow entitled to the benefits of an affluent society.

There seems to be no "going back," no relying again on the extended family as a care system. No going back to a wholistic outlook of that independence from the federal system seems likely. The rhetoric of antibureaucracy and opposition to Washington is widespread, for entitlement paradoxically has a populist sound, but reliance on federal economic patterns is as strong as ever. Meanwhile mass communication media and mass higher education have led to an increase of skills in generating advocacies. In such a pattern, the aged inevitably have become a part of entitlement and are their own advocates. During the 1960s they seemed to be suffering setbacks in the youth culture, when the indicators of what was important in life led them to be physically shelved, but in the 1970s they began to recover a place. This was the era of the Gray Panthers, a voluntary group, and the National Institute on Aging, created by Congress in 1974.

The aged may have carried with them into "their" era many of the problems inherited from economic and cultural antecedents. According to many critics, they were also bearers of a new cultural malaise that went with longevity and age-segregation: economic hardship in times of inflation, neglect by their children and grandchildren, dying in isolation from family contexts, anomie, boredom, not to mention their physical and medical needs. The aged and their advocates were both specialists and the subjects of specialization; they were sundered and chopped off in the modernizing process. But modernity has also brought them choice, with all its terrors and delights.

NEW DIRECTIONS

Try as I may to deal with process, to minimize modernization, to see tradition in modernity and modernity in tradition, nuclearity in old extended families and extension in modern nuclearity, I find that the period between the Civil War and the First World War is somehow a hinge period. Something decisive occurred. Not everything was a turning point or a take-off, but there were decisive shifts in the outlook of Americans, shifts with which their heirs a century later are still living, even as they try to understand the changes—and themselves.

Looking to the future, it is hard to say what effect the sheer increase in the number of aged persons will have on the group's status as a problem "class." Neither can we predict what will be the results of the growing demands of entitlement, of society's examination by specialists, and of the choices modernity has brought us. It may well be that our own time will prove to be another hinge period.

NOTES

1. Philippe Aries, *Centuries of Childhood: A Social History of Family Life* (New York: Knopf, 1962).
2. W. Andrew Achenbaum, *Old Age in the New Land: The American Experience Since 1790* (Baltimore: The Johns Hopkins University Press, 1979).
3. David Hackett Fischer, *Growing Old in America* (New York: Oxford University Press, 1977).
4. E. J. Hobsbawm, *The Age of Revolution* (Cleveland: World, 1962), pp. 28–29.

5. John Murray Cuddihy: *The Ordeal of Civility: Freud, Marx, Levi-Strauss, and the Jewish Struggle with Modernity* (New York: Basic, 1974), pp. 9–10.
6. Evelyn Page, *American Genesis: Pre-colonial Writing in the North* (Boston: Gambit, 1973), pp. 243–44.
7. John Demos, "Old Age in Early New England," in *Aging, Death, and the Completion of Being*, ed. David D. Van Tassel (Philadelphia: University of Pennsylvania Press, 1979), pp. 115, 139, 158. See also John Demos, *A Little Commonwealth: Family Life in Plymouth Colony* (New York: Oxford University Press, 1970); Edmund S. Morgan, *The Puritan Family: Religion and Domestic Relations in Seventeenth-Century New England* (New York: Harper & Row, 1966); Philip Greven, *The Protestant Temperament: Patterns of Child-Rearing, Religious Experience, and the Self in Early America* (New York: Knopf, 1977); David E. Stannard, *The Puritan Way of Death: A Study in Religion, Culture, and Social Change* (New York: Oxford University Press, 1977).
8. Achenbaum, *Old Age in the New Land*, p. 83.
9. Robert T. Handy, *A Christian America: Protestant Hopes and Historical Realities* (New York: Oxford University Press, 1971); Martin E. Marty, *Righteous Empire: The Protestant Experience in America* (New York: Dial, 1970).
10. See Lois W. Banner, "Religious Benevolence as Social Control: A Critique of an Interpretation," in *Religion in American History: Interpretive Essays*, ed. John W. Mulder and John F. Wilson (Englewood Cliffs, N.J.: Prentice-Hall, 1978), p. 218.
11. Charles I. Foster, *Errand of Mercy: The Evangelical United Front, 1790–1837* (Chapel Hill: The University of North Carolina Press, 1960), pp. 275–279.
12. John R. Bodo, *The Protestant Clergy and Public Issues, 1812–1848* (Princeton: Princeton University Press, 1954).
13. Charles C. Cole, Jr., *The Social Ideas of the Northern Evangelists, 1826–1860* (New York: Columbia University Press, 1954).
14. Quoted in Timothy Smith, *Revivalism and Social Reform in Mid-Nineteenth-Century America* (Nashville: Abingdon, 1957), pp. 163–177.
15. See, for example, Francis P. Weisenburger, *Triumph of Faith: Contributions of the Church to American Life, 1865–1900* (Richmond: William Byrd Press, 1962), especially chap. 6, "Family and Sex Relationships," p. 98.
16. Weisenburger, *Triumph of Faith*, chap. 11, "The Outreach of Benevolence," p. 197.
17. Norris Magnuson, *Salvation in the Slums: Evangelical Social Work, 1865–1920* (Metuchen, N.J.: The Scarecrow Press, 1977).
18. For an example of this literature, see Burton Bledstein, *The Culture of Professionalism: The Middle Class and the Development of Higher Education in America* (New York: Norton, 1976).
19. Achenbaum, *Old Age in the New Land*, pt. 3, is an important contribution to the discussion of the late nineteenth century and the age of Social Security. His researches obviously have an important influence on my choice to isolate the issue of the aged as a problem.
20. David J. O'Brien, *American Catholics and Social Reform: The New Deal Years* (New York: Oxford University Press, 1968).

21. O'Brien, *American Catholics and Social Reform*, pp. 54–55.
22. David O. Moberg, *The Church as a Social Institution: The Sociology of American Religion* (Englewood Cliffs, N.J.: Prentice-Hall, 1962), p. 151.
23. Daniel Bell, *The Cultural Contradictions of Capitalism* (New York: Basic Books, 1976), pp. 232–236.

5

Christian Theology and Aging: Basic Affirmations

Martin J. Heinecke

In any attempt to examine the various perspectives Christianity brings to aging, the theological perspective must be a significant consideration. From various religious points of view particular responses, both theoretical and practical, are elicited by the process of aging and the situation of the aged. It is my conviction, however, that there can be no separate "theology of aging," set apart from the theological orientation as a whole. Rather, the basic Christian theological affirmations are to be applied to the specific questions that arise in connection with aging and the aged. The task of the theologian is to address the Christian Gospel to the contemporary situation on the basis of the biblical witness and how that witness has fared through the years.[1]

CHRISTIAN THEOLOGICAL PERSPECTIVE AND HUMAN INSIGHT

In a theological examination of the contemporary situation, it is imperative that the contemporary state of human insights and discoveries be taken into account, in this case with respect to the aging process and the aged. For this descriptive task the theologian must rely on the observations of those who are expert in this field (gerontologists, anthropologists, psychologists, psychotherapists, sociologists, physicians, etc.). These experts rely on careful methods of observation and experiment, aimed at analysis and control. Their efforts are guided by what Paul Tillich calls technical or controlling reason.[2] It is because human beings are created "in the image of God" that they have the capacity to exercise such control within the limits of their finitude.

ULTIMATE QUESTIONS

Christian theology remains convinced, however, that the basic question of human existence itself, including the fundamental questions of human nature and destiny, are not matters of human discovery and control. These questions (e.g., "Why is there *something* and not *nothing?*"; "Who am *I?*"; "Why am I here?"; etc.) are not answerable with the power of "reasoning," nor are they discoverable by scientific methodology. The ultimate questions are answered only by a "revelation," which comes to us from outside our own "existence." The answers "are *spoken to* human existence from beyond it. Otherwise they could not be answers, for the question is human existence itself."[3]

This orientation presupposes that the entire human race is in a fallen (broken, estranged) state and, therefore, does not "know" the true heart of the "Lord God," the creator and sustainer of being. In Søren Kierkegaard's terms, humanity is "forsaken of the hidden immanence of the Eternal."[4] We human beings are derived beings, thus unless the relationship to the Creator to whom we owe our being is right, our relationship to ourselves and to each other and the created world cannot be right either.

This is our bondage in sin which necessitates not just an enlightenment of the intellect but a radical transformation of our lives, which the biblical witness speaks of as a rebirth (John 3:1–21). This is why the Christian Gospel of God's act in Jesus, the Christ, must be proclaimed as news by living witnesses who have themselves experienced that transformation. Someone must come running with the news of a once-and-for-all victory won over powers too great for us (sin and death), so that individuals may share in the fruits of that victory.

QUESTIONS OF AGING

Questions, or problems, of aging are inseparable from the questions of ultimate concern—from the appraisal of selfhood and purpose in life and finitude, through the various stages of growth and decline to certain death—so it will make a crucial difference how these questions are answered. The general attitude of a culture toward its aged is determined by its predominant view of human life, its values and its destiny. Hitler and his associates could ruthlessly exterminate all—including the aged—whom they saw as no longer contributing to the well-being of those of the right "blood and soil." A youth-minded culture that fears old age and despises the "old codgers" and "old crones" reveals its basic beliefs and values as surely as does a culture which worships its ancestors and is largely tied to its past. The way one comes to terms with death makes a difference, whether in Stoic resignation to extinction, or in fear of a future judgment, or in the sure hope of "the resurrection of the dead" (1 Cor. 15).[5]

Obviously there are many ways of arriving at a humane appraisal of the aging process and of old age. There are many different bases for asserting the dignity, worth, and rights, as well as the responsibilities, of individuals, including the aged. Today there is a veritable spate of literature and films written by people of all kinds of religious beliefs and nonbeliefs, all pleading the cause of the aged in much the same way: they ask not only for justice but for love, and appeal to the aged themselves to "raise their consciousness" and to continue to make constructive contributions to society. From the Christian point of view these humanistic efforts occur because human beings, created in God's image, are capable of attaining a high degree of what is called "civil righteousness," which builds a greater degree of human community within the limitations of our finitude and sinfulness.

All the Christian theologian can do, therefore, is to set forth the distinctively Christian basis on which the problems and opportunities connected with aging are to be considered. The actual goals of such a Christian perspective may not differ from those for which all persons of good will strive, so there will be vast areas of cooperation. But not only of cooperation. There must be a constant creative dialogue among all those who deal with human problems, from whatever perspective, so that they can learn from each other.

The Christian revelation has no monopoly on truth. In matters which we as human beings can discover for ourselves, the Christian Church must simply acknowledge what has been discovered and found to be so. This is, however, what the Church has in large measure failed to do. It has exceeded its sphere of competency, just as the natural sciences have often exceeded theirs.[6]

There are some who wish to call scientific advances "redemptive" in as much as they free us from ignorance and superstition, and enlarge our freedom and capacity for living. True as this is, such advances are not in the strict sense "redemptive" in as much as they have an equal potential for evil as for good, so dramatically evidenced by the issues surrounding the use of nuclear energy.

This double-edged potential applies also to the increase of the human life span and the ameliorization of the deterioration that accompanies aging. Does a longer and healthier life necessarily mean a better life? The biblical witness, with its stark realism about the evil of which human nature in its finite freedom is capable, must counteract all utopian dreams. At the same time the biblical belief in "the resurrection of the dead" and the coming of "a new heaven and a new earth" (Rev. 21), as history moves toward both its end in time *(finis)* and its goal *(telos),* raises hope for hitherto undreamed of possibilities for good in this life.[7]

While it is impossible to examine the whole range of Christian doctrine as it affects the aging, certain basic affirmations which are particularly relevant need to be recognized and applied to the special circumstances of aging.

THE FUNDAMENTAL AFFIRMATION OF GOD'S UNCONDITIONAL LOVE

At the heart of the Christian Gospel is the affirmation of God's unconditional love. This is the "revelation" that has to be "spoken to" human existence from beyond it. It was not only "spoken" but "lived" in Jesus, the Christ, the Word become flesh (John 1).

The apostle John writes "God is love" (1 John 4:8). This is the only time in the biblical witness that the categorical assertion is made that God's very being *is* love. The remainder of the biblical witness is in terms of what God *does*. God is what he does. So John goes right on to say: "In this the love of God was made manifest among us, that he sent his only Son into the world, so that we might live through him" (1 John 4:9).

Furthermore, John says: "We love, because God first loved us" (1 John 4:19). This is not a command nor is it an exhortation, but it is an indicative. It asserts that all acts of human love have their source and well-spring in God's prior acts of love. So John also asserts that just as God's love manifests itself in its actions toward men, so human love, which has its source in God, manifests itself through love of other human beings. "If anyone says, *I love God* and hates his brother, he is a liar; for he who does not love his brother whom he has seen cannot love God whom he has not seen. And this commandment we have from him, 'That he who loves God should love his brother also' " (1 John 4:20–21). The only way then to show love is by loving other human beings.

But all these assertions do not really communicate anything specific unless there is agreement upon the meaning of the word "love." In the English language the word "love" is notoriously a "weasel word," which we use indiscriminately. We "love" everything from peanuts to baseball to a Bach cantata to our children, our spouses, our neighbors and friends, and finally God himself. The only things we do not "love" are our enemies and those who have nothing to offer us.

EROS

The ancient Greeks were more discriminating. They had three words for love. The first is *eros*, which we usually associate with sexual love but which the Greeks used in a much more inclusive and yet very specific sense. *Eros* is the love that seeks and derives satisfaction from the object of its love. In Greek myth Eros is the child of Plenty and Poverty, to show that the poverty of one is satisfied by the plenty of another person or thing.[8] The beloved is loved for the sake of the satisfaction given.

Such love as *eros* is essential to human existence. No human being is self-sufficient; we are all in want. We are not gods or goddesses that we can live by ourselves on our own pedestals served by and accepting the worship of others. We are all created in interdependency. We should think of *eros*, therefore, on the highest possible level. We legitimately reach out for satisfaction in all kinds of things and persons— in food, drink, sex, music, and the arts. In fact, *eros* is the drive behind all learning, all creative activity, all striving for excellence.

But we can also see that such love could destroy the beloved if it exists only for the sake of the satisfaction rendered. It is true, for example, that we cannot sustain our lives and satisfy our biological needs except at the expense of the plants and animals we devour. But if there is not beyond this need a concern for the plants and animals *for their own sake*, then the planet will be ruthlessly plundered. If there is love only for the sake of the satisfaction derived, what happens to the love-relationship if the other person is no longer able, or does not want, to give the desired satisfaction. How easily love then turns into hatred. It is easy to love the beautiful bride or the handsome bridegroom, but what happens when time takes its toll, when the hair and teeth fall out and the strong young body becomes flabby? What happens if the friend turns enemy? What happens when God hides his face and does not satisfy our desires?

It is at this point that our "sinfulness" must be taken into account. We, in our self-centeredness seek ourselves in all we encounter and in all we do. In the nature of our interdependency this is self-destructive behavior. If we plunder the planet, we destroy ourselves. If we use and exploit a fellow human being for personal satisfaction, we destroy the other person and eventually ourselves. The I-Thou relationship becomes an I-It relationship in which the other person is manipulated and used like a "thing."[9]

AGAPE

Hence love as *eros* needs to be combined with, and actually overruled by, the love which the New Testament calls *agape*.[10] *Agape* is altogether for the sake of the beloved. It is self-giving, self-sacrificing love which "seeks not its own" (1 Cor. 13:5). It is love for the unlovable, the unworthy, and even the enemy who not only has nothing to offer but actually seeks to do harm.[11]

Such is the unconditional love of God to all his creatures, not one of whom is expendable. This is the love of God as manifested first in the covenant with Israel, and then uniquely in the life, suffering and death of Jesus, the Christ who "came not to be served but to serve, and to give his life as a ransom for many" (Matt. 20:28; see also Phil. 2:4–11). So God is, as Martin Luther said, "ein feuriger Abgrund der Liebe" (a fiery abyss of love). Luther used the analogy of the sun which freely sends forth its light and energy and gets nothing for its shining, but is in fact burning itself out for others. God's self-giving love, however, nevers burns itself out. It never fails (1 Cor. 13:8). It is suffering and victorious love.[12]

Specifically then, it is this love, *agape*, which is to be born anew in the Christian each day and which is to be dominant in the Christian's life. It is no trick to love the lovable, the children who pull at our heart strings and all the "beautiful people" who give us satisfaction and fulfill our lives. The test is when people actually have nothing to give in return, when they are only a burden. "A new commandment I give to you," Jesus said, "that you love one another, even as I have loved you" (John 13:34).

Because *agape* is a love that seeks no reward (return), it is a paradox. If this totally self-giving love is interpreted as meaning self-destruction, however, the paradox is completely misunderstood. The paradox of *agape* is like the "hedonistic paradox." If you make pleasure your conscious aim, you will never find it. Pleasure is the by-product of some engrossment. So, deliberately to seek self-fulfillment is self-defeating. Self-fulfillment is the gift that comes with self-giving, as every "lover" knows.[13]

FILIA

There is a third word for love, namely *filia*, the love of friendship. When two people, for whatever reason, take particular delight in each other, they experience *filia*. It may be that they are alike and have common interests or it may be that they are quite unlike but complement each other and so are knit as one. Here we have a combination of *eros* and *agape*—each seeks the good of the other and is faithful and true, while at the same time they have delight and satisfaction in each other.[14] "Greater love," Jesus said, "hath no man than that he lay down his life for his friend" (John 15:14).

THE AGED AND THE ATTITUDE OF LOVE

Significant implications for the attitude of the aged toward themselves, and of others to them, are apparent in the subtle interplay of *eros*, *agape*, and *filia*. The aged should be loved for the sake of the rich satisfaction they give to others, filling the want of others out of their plenty *(eros)*. Their wisdom, their experience, their patience born out of years of self-giving constitute an inestimable treasure. It is one of the tragedies of our culture that with the loss of the extended family so many people are deprived of this treasure trove. The same is true in public life and in employment where the aged are too readily discarded and hid away—out of sight, out of mind. Our culture is too often blind to the beauty of old age—wrinkles, white hair, halting gait, cracked voice, trembling hands, and all—that deserves better than the designation of "old crone" or "old codger." Out of sheer self-interest society should give the aged their proper place.

On the other hand, there is no question that the aged can become a burden with no longer anything to offer, requiring nothing so much as "tender, loving care."[15] We have too often yielded to the temptation to unload them or to neglect them, as past and present history so abundantly prove. It is then that *agape* must rule, even when they are not the kindly, gentle, loving beings we want them to be but instead veritable demons of irritability, obstinacy, and querulous self-centeredness. No matter how helpless or senile, wheel-chair patients cannot be run through the showers as though you were running dirty platters through the dish-washer; and they cannot be kept under constant sedation, just to keep them out of your hair. And when meals-

mission

on-wheels are brought to a lonely person who wants nothing so much as to have you stay and talk or listen, this is when Christ-like love is needed.

As for *filia*, what could be quite as wonderful as a friendship between youth and age where each serves and is served by the other and two souls are knit as one.

ASSURANCE OF GOD'S LOVE

There are many factors that enter into the opinion which people have of themselves as they grow older. To one who has lost all self-esteem it is far too glib simply to say, "Never mind, God loves you." Nevertheless, the Christian Church has no alternative except to offer that assurance again and again through its ministry of Word and Sacraments. "When my father and mother forsake me, then the Lord will take me up" (Ps. 27:10; see also Rom. 8:31–37). In the final analysis a person's real worth depends upon the fact that there is a God to whom each person is equally precious. This is why the Christian's baptism, assuring the individual of God's unconditional acceptance as an heir of salvation, is the bulwark of the Christian's life, freeing one from the burden of religiosity for work in the world (Matt. 11:28). Luther spoke of the Christian life as a constant return to baptism. Whenever doubts and tribulations come upon us, as they inevitably will, there is the reminder, "I have been baptized."

But baptism has another lifelong significance that those who are old sometimes forget: the necessity of daily rebirth to newness of life. The old Adam in us is a mighty good swimmer and must be drowned by daily sorrow and repentance, and a new man come forth daily who will live before God in righteousness and purity.[16]

Luther made a distinction between *securitas* (security) and *certitudo* (certainty or, better, confidence). In this world of our finite freedom, security is something we never have, in spite of all our desperate efforts. Confidence, ever renewed in a word of promise by a God who keeps his covenant, is a different matter. For the Christian, the sacrament of the Lord's Supper with its repeated individual assurance, "given and shed for you," is the seal upon God's promise. This assurance puts the whole aging process—the various stages of growth from birth to old age and certain death—into a quite different perspective.

THE CHURCH AS A COMMUNITY OF CARING

All the Church's assurances of God's love mean nothing if this love is not embodied in flesh and blood people who care. And if the Church is not a community of such caring love, it is not the Church of Jesus, the Christ. Unfortunately, we must face up to the miserable failure of the institution of the Church in this respect. In any case the true Church cannot be identified with any of its institutional manifestations. It is the "hidden" Church that cuts across the lines of all denominations which must be believed. We can put no boundary around where God is graciously active and his love embodied. It is a notorious truism there is often more actual love outside the Church as an institution than within it. Nevertheless, since the Church is constantly calling to repentance and rebirth and the grace of God is active there through Word and Sacrament, it is there that the prevailing "ageism" of our culture is to be counteracted. It is there that the needs of the aged, so far as the Church has the resources, are to be met in love. It is there that an act of "consciousness-raising," which so many need, is to be nurtured. It is there that the aged are to be aroused to use the vast power and political clout of their numbers in the cause of justice for themselves and others.

But obviously the Church can by no means meet all the needs of its own members, including those of its aged. Therefore, the Church must take up its task of advocacy on behalf of all those, specifically the aged, who in our society are the victims of injustice.

LOVE AND JUSTICE

As people are aroused to a sense of social responsibility for the plight of the aging, there is confusion from the failure to distinguish between justice and love. People are made into objects of charity when they are only asking for their just due, and there is scarcely anything more demeaning than that. On the one hand the state becomes a charitable institution; instead of furthering the general welfare with equal justice for all, it doles out largesse from funds which it has coerced people to pay in the name of benevolence. On the other hand the Church, instead of relying on gifts of love, virtually coerces people with the threat of punishment and the lure of reward. Thus law and gospel, justice and love, are confused, and the roles of church and state are often reversed. People are encouraged to bolster their self-esteem and feather their nest in heaven with grandiose gifts of benevolence, instead of shouldering a just burden of taxation which will guarantee to each member of society those basic requirements necessary for human life. Without exceeding its sphere of competency in economic matters, Christian theology has an essential contribution to make at this point. At the same time the Church must set its own house in order by convincing people that the way to show compassion and do justice in our society is by being willing to bear a sufficient and equitably distributed tax burden rather than by insisting on private benevolence.

THE RULE OF LOVE VERSUS THE RULE OF LAW

We have defined love, but what can we say about justice? Reams have been written and continue to be written about the nature of justice.[17] We cannot possibly settle the whole matter in a few sentences, but we can make some basic commonsense assertions.

Love is a matter of inner motivation and concern for the fellowman. No one can love in obedience to a command, nor can love ever be reduced to a set of rules. It must be free to do whatever the total situation demands, and so must take many forms. If everyone truly loved everyone else and were wise enough to know what is in the best interests of others, there would be no need for law in the sense of rules with sanctions and power to enforce them.

Law is necessary wherever people live together in this world, not only because of our ignorance and finitude, but also because of our sinfulness. Law is God's way of getting his will done in spite of our unwillingness to do it freely and without coercion. Therefore, Martin

Luther spoke of the law as "the left hand of God." It is the same God of love who with his right hand accepts and forgives unconditionally, who with left hand coerces for the common good.

This conception of law is the basis for the state as a God-given order of sinful reality. This is the meaning of Paul's statement in Romans 13. The power of the sword (or coercion) is given to those in authority to reward those who do good and to punish those who do wrong. A law which has no sanctions, which can simply be violated with complete impunity, and which carries no reward for its observance, is no law. It is only advice which a person may choose to follow or not.

TOWARD A DEFINITION OF JUSTICE

The purpose of the law is to enforce justice. But what is justice? Ask any child or any person on the street and you will get a ready answer. Whatever else justice may mean it first of all means fairness; it means giving to each our due, our fair share, what we have earned, what we deserve. Justice is blind, carefully balancing her scales without respect to persons. Justice does not mean treating everyone alike but rather treating them as equals—in so far as they are really equal— and then taking into account the differences.

Children do not mind rules that are justly enforced. They do not resent punishment if they think it is fair. What children resent is playing favorites, inequitable distribution, not allowing equal opportunity. What they resent is not being able to count on the actual meting out of a reward or punishment once it has been promised or threatened. They want to rely on the stability as well as on the fairness of the law; they don't want the rules changed in the middle of the game.

It is no different with adults, however unjust and unfair they themselves may be and however much their self-love may distort their discernment of what actually is fair. In a complex situation of conflicting claims it may be difficult to sort out what is just, but the goal is clear enough. Every citizen understands the words "Equal Justice for All" written above the entrance to the Supreme Court, and our gorge rises within us when we experience the blatant malfeasances of justice in our government, our courts, our economic system. What eats more into our vitals and destroys our very being more than an outraged sense of justice? What unjust tyrant has ever been secure on his throne against the rebellion of those whom he has wronged!

JUSTICE, LOVE, AND THE CHURCH

Laws and institutions cannot be loving, only just or unjust. In the realm of law and institutions love must take the form of justice. Only people themselves can be loving, going beyond justice with love. Love breaks through the order of justice and gives more than what is due and right. At the same time, motivated by love, we may discern more clearly what is just because self-interest does not cloud our vision. Self-centeredness, vengeance, greed, lust (all the seven deadly sins) are bound to distort the sense of justice: "You cannot fill the glass completely full unless you are willing to let it run over. You cannot even be just, if you are not determined to be loving."[18] You cannot boast of how loving you are when you are not just.

This close interrelationship of love and justice has enormous implications for the Church. Jesus' injunction to his followers to "love one another" (John 15:17) enjoins the Church as well and demands a commitment to the task of advocacy on behalf of all the unjustly treated, including the aged. This most particularly includes the indigent aged, of whom there are millions in this land of abundance. We are not concerned now about the spontaneous act of compassion. We are talking about the gross inequities, the brutal injustices of our fabulously wealthy society, which condemns millions—among them the aged—to poverty, through no fault of their own.

The Church must actively respond to the challenges of basic Christian theological affirmations as they relate to the questions and problems of aging. If the Church is truly to be an agent of God's grace, if it is to proclaim the good news of God's unconditional love and manifest itself as a caring community, then it must join together with all persons of good will to advocate justice for the elderly by means of just laws justly enforced.

The Lutheran Church in America, one of the large Protestant denominations and in some ways typical of others, has affirmed in its Statement on Human Rights:

> Older adults are entitled to respect, affection, and care from their children, to the opportunity to continue as participatory members of society, and should not be denied, because of circumstances beyond their control, adequate housing, sustenance, and health care.[19]

This is a realistic minimal goal, readily attainable by a shifting of priorities and elimination of waste, mismanagement, and fraud. But it will take a real, sacrificial effort motivated by love. In these efforts the growing number of the aged who still have their wits about them and unflagging zeal, may be expected to play a major role. In the words of Maggie Kuhn, that dynamic leader of the Gray Panthers:

> It might just be one of God's surprises for us, that he may use those closest to death—nearer to that other life—to show the Church how to break with self-centered purposes and goals and look to the good of all and serve that good.

NOTES

1. Paul Tillich, *Systematic Theology*, vol. 1 (Chicago: University of Chicago Press, 1951), especially pp. 34–68.
2. Tillich, *Systematic Theology*, p. 71.
3. Tillich, *Systematic Theology*, p. 64.
4. Søren Kierkegaard, *The Sickness Unto Death* (Princeton, N.J.: Princeton University Press, 1944).
5. Elisabeth Kubler-Ross, *On Death and Dying* (New York: Macmillan, 1976).
6. Martin J. Heinecken, *God in the Space Age* (Philadelphia: John C. Winston Co., 1959).
7. Reinhold Niebuhr, *The Nature and Destiny of Man*, 2 vols. (New York: Charles Scribner's Sons, 1941–1945); Jürgen Moltmann, *The Theology of Hope* (New York: Harper & Row, 1967).
8. Plato, *Symposium*, 1:200.
9. Martin Buber, *I and Thou* (New York: Scribners, 1958).
10. Anders Nygren, *Agape and Eros* (Philadelphia: Westminster, 1953); Nygren shows how the god-relation is determined by whichever is the "dominant motif," either *nomos* (the law): man gets what he deserves from a Law-giver; *eros:* man is attracted

by the magnetism of what God in his perfection has to offer (Aristotle's Unmoved Mover); or *agape:* sinful man is sought out by the outgoing love of God.

11. Matt. 5:43–48 (The Sermon on the Mount).

12. Søren Kierkegaard, *Works of Love* (Princeton, N.J.: Princeton University Press, 1946), p. 9.

13. For criticisms of this view of *agape* see: Martin Cyril D'Arcy, *The Mind and the Heart of Love, Lion and Unicorn* (New York: Henry Holt & Co., 1947).

14. St. Augustine, *Confessions* (New York: Sheed & Ward, 1943), pp. 68 ff., in praise of friendship.

15. Mary Adelaide Mendelson, *Tender Loving Greed* (New York: Knopf, 1974); a true life horror story that disembowels America's nursing home industry, exposing it as the nadir of human exploitation. An examination of some 200 nursing homes in 21 states.

16. Martin Luther, *Small Catechism on the Daily Significance of Baptism.*

17. For a recent discussion see: John Rawls, *A Theory of Justice* (Cambridge, Mass.: Harvard University Press, 1971).

18. Gustav Wingren, *Creation and Law* (Philadelphia: Muhlenberg, 1961); Karl H. Hertz, *Two Kingdoms and One World* (Minneapolis: Augsburg, 1976); Emil Brunner, *The Divine Imperative* (Philadelpia: Westminster, 1947).

19. "Aging and the Older Adult, A Social Statement," adopted by the Ninth Biennial Convention of the Lutheran Church in America, 1978.

6

Worship and Aging: Memory and Repentance

Urban T. Holmes

In 1935 my father took us to Europe for six months—my mother, my two sisters, and me. It was an irrational act. The Depression was very much with us and he had no money to spare. Already the intimations of the war to come were in many minds and as we toured the continent a certain inquietude prevailed—discernable even to a five-year-old boy. Someone asked my father why he chose to make the trip. I shall never forget his reply: "I want to make memories for my children."

He was a man of many memories, not all pleasant, but each enriched his life or gave him insight into the human condition. Not a memory was wasted. He could give his children no greater gift than the opportunity to gather memories that would enable us to experience life as he had, with the same play of light and shadow that reveals within the present a depth that comes only from recalling the past and that also gives birth to hope for the future.

What does this have to do with worship and aging? Worship is an act grounded in memory. To worship is, of course, to attribute

worth or value. Usually we would assume that to worship is to attribute
ultimate value to God. But behind that attribution of worth to God
is the memory that God has made us of value. The sense of worth
moves from ourselves to God and back. We recognize the value of
God as we perceive ourselves mirrored in God's creation. This is something of what it means for humankind to be "in the image of God"
(Gen. 2:3). A person with no memory is one who is incapable of
worship: lacking the sense of self-worth, one cannot attribute worth
to God. Perhaps that is a strong statement, but I will stand by it.
Worship is an action which finds expression in liturgy or ritual. A
ritual is a bundle of symbols in which a community of believers repeat-
edly participates. The original event that called the community into
being is made present in power. The symbols constitute our memory.
An example is the bread and wine in the Holy Eucharist, which we
take, bless, break, and eat in order to "proclaim the death of the
Lord," that event on Calvary that constituted the church "until he
comes" (I Cor. 11:26). The bread and wine are symbols, which when
taken, blessed, broken, and eaten, evoke with power the memory of
the church. They call forth the past into the present and give us
hope for the future.

Worship requires the accumulation of memories, as a house we live
in gradually becomes furnished with associations. It is not something
that the church can "invent" for those who are aging. It is meant to
be built within a lifetime, and the richer its evocation of the past
reaching back into our childhood, the greater is its ability to open to
us the possibilities of life now and in the future.

Gregory of Nyssa, the fourth century father of reflection upon the
life of Christian prayer, once wrote, "Already at birth we are driven
by the very nature of things toward our departure, for which we must
carefully prepare our hands, our feet, and the rest."[1] The purposeful
recognition of the "drivenness" of life requires intentionally building
a memory rich in symbolic meaning.

My purpose in this chapter is, therefore, not to prescribe ways in
which we can devise new liturgies for old people, by which they can
construct a world of meaning singularly appropriate for their stage in

life, but rather to urge to the church that a full and proper understanding of the tradition and its ritual expression will nourish hope for the future at all points in life, not only in the latter half of it. The church cannot create memories for people deprived of the opportunity to build them over the years. Meager and shallow worship for the aging is not a "gerontological problem," it is a human problem, and cannot be solved by liturgical gimmickry at the nursing home.

THE PHENOMENOLOGY OF WORSHIP

When we look at an act of worship, a liturgy, or ritual, we see immediately that it is integral to religion. Religion can be defined in several ways. It is the movement from chaos to cosmos, a sense of God's ordering of our experiences, which threaten to overwhelm us in disorder. Religion universally consists of community, creed, and cult. Community is our life together. Despite what A. N. Whitehead has said about religion being what we do with our solitude, religion is essentially collaborative. Creed is what we believe as a community. Cult is what we do to enact what we believe—or it is the enactment which gives rise to our belief. Cult or liturgy is the dramatic re-presentation of God's presence among humankind.

Schlomo Deshen, an Israeli anthropologist, describes religion as "a system of symbols that refers to problems of ultimate meaning and thereby formulates an existential order."[2] A religious community is constituted by the symbols it shares. For example, the Christian community is called into being by the death and resurrection of Jesus, embodied for us in the Cross. The community's creed is an exposition of its symbols and, as already noted, cult or ritual is a bundle of symbols in which we participate through a dramatic action. Our focus in worship in particular and in religion in general is upon those symbols. This is why all authentic Christian worship is related to the symbols of the death and resurrection of Jesus.

The aging are obviously fully aware of the "problem of ultimate meaning" caught up in the final question of death. Death confronts us with the threat of chaos. The symbols of our religious faith that would "formulate an existential order" are of central concern for them. It should be clear, therefore, why Deshen's definition and its relationship to the act of worship has particular relevance to the aging. For Christians the threat of death is overcome by the victory of resurrection, both made present in the liturgy of the church.

Robert Bellah, an American sociologist of religion, has made the point that at the heart of any person's meaning lies symbolic reality. He goes on to say that the lack of concern for the symbolic in American culture—which is so banal and unreflective as to think that rituals are "optional"—has resulted in the acute impoverishment of meaning in American life.[3] In a very real sense the elders of a community are the guardians of its symbolic reality. It may well be that a significant element in the isolation felt by the aging in our society is the low value our culture places upon symbolic reality. The isolation that comes from symbolism's decline presents us with both a problem for the aging in the church's worship and a dilemma for those who have lived in a land depleted of symbolic meaning.

But before we pursue the issue of worship for the aging in the face of our culture's symbolic retardation, we need to look still more closely at worship itself. M. D. Chenu, a scholar in liturgical studies, has been quoted as having said that good liturgy always borders on the vulgar. The word "vulgar" carries here the connotation of earthy, as opposed to "refined." Good liturgy, if vulgar, is full of ambiguities, risk, "numinousity," sensuality, discomfort, and excitement. It contains the totality of human experience and places it, open to the future, before God. I would describe such liturgy as *sensible:* capable of being apprehended by all the senses.

Poor liturgy is *sentimental.* I mean it evokes an uncomplicated, nonthreatening, safe feeling of a domesticated God. It is like a *placebo* or, even worse, a tranquilizer, that covers over the play of light and shadow that falls on every life. It is joy without terror, laughter without tears, and love without fear. Sentimental liturgy as opposed to sensible liturgy, attempts to tie everything up into a neat package, without any room for doubt, frustration, and suffering. As a consequence, a whole world within each of us is ignored or suppressed.

The symbols within liturgy depend upon our memory to generate their power. Sensible worship brings to consciousness an array of memories, which move beyond simple nostalgia. A true symbol of the kind that constitutes worship points beyond itself, not only denoting something—washing, healing, blessing—but also connoting that which is all but hidden. The "hiddenness" is not just buried in the past, but bears a promise of the future. There is again that play of light and shadow, which opens for us the possibility of giving meaning to our present experience, and hope for the future.

It is extremely important that we never forget sensible liturgy always has this future dimension. Indeed, liturgy depends upon the memory of the past, but it is a memory that bears a promise. When Joshua led the Israelites across the Jordan into the promised land, he had a cairn built of twelve stones from the riverbed. "These stones are to stand as a memorial among you," Joshua declared (Josh. 4:6). When the children ask what the stones mean they are not only to be told of what God did in the past, but they are to be reminded of his covenant for the future. In the same way, the Christian Eucharist is not only a remembrance of what Christ did for us on Calvary, but it is also an anticipation of that heavenly banquet which we shall eat and drink with him in eternal life.

Good liturgy has, therefore, a movement from out of the past through the present into the future. It embodies the undiscovered "more," at which true symbols always hint. Sensible worship is, never just an escape into the past, but always opens to the future. Liturgy provides guideposts for us as we move into the unknown, even into death.

AGING AND THE SYMBOLIC QUEST

Henri Nouwen in his book *Aging* writes, "There can hardly be a more alienated feeling than that which believes, 'I am who I was.' "[4] Our culture glorifies youth and subordinates "being" to "having." This works against the natural flow of the aging process, which should lead us inward to "be" where we may discover images of hope. I read recently a squib for a restaurant in a large city. The owners, according to the writer, "Love people of all ages and strive to make all people feel young." How perverse of the owners! Is it not a truer love to help people be who they *are*, rather than to insult them with the pretence that they can be something "better"? Yet this is what we do, often with the best of intentions.

When we reach the "noon of life," the movement is toward the "twilight"; there is a turning inward. Our consciousness naturally reflects upon who we are, and we search for a vision of what we might become. Most of us are familiar with the proclivity of old people to tell stories about the past. Such stories offer appropriate clues for what is yet to come. What a pity it is that so many of us are loath to "waste the time" to listen. I well remember the last time my father visited in my home. We took turns sitting with him in the living room listening. Now I wish I had had enough sense to have stayed longer and asked more questions. I need him to help me know who I am in order that I might become that person.

The story-telling of the aging is a source for an enriched memory and a stimulus for the imagination. William Lynch, a Jesuit theologian, has written that hope is born of imagination and imagination requires a continuity with the past.[5] There is no profit in being bitter about the past or longing for a fantasized potency lost in our despair over an unappreciated aging. The wisdom that graces the older person can be defined as the willingness to acknowledge what the past has made us and yet forgive the past that we might be open to the future. Hope, humor, and vision are three gifts of one who grows old not only gracefully, but with purpose.

Another way to say this is that as we grow older the *time* we have (or appear to have) diminishes, but the *space* of our world should expand. Death comes closer and we can no longer think in terms of time measured in many years ahead, but we can gain more freedom to explore the space of our inner world. This is one way to describe a "second childhood," which is a bit like Paul Ricoeur's "second naivete."[6] We move into what some have called a receptive mode of consciousness—as opposed to an action mode—where images and free association within space take precedence over temporal, logical thinking, with its desire for prediction and control. We become like the little child, not in the literal foolishness of pretending to be one, but in the graceful wisdom of one who has recovered the capacity of wonder and surprise.

There is in such wisdom a poverty of heart, a fruitful emptiness of cant, which, as Nouwen points out, "makes us relate to life as a gift to be shared."[7] In the receptive mode of consciousness we can be freed from egocentricity, from always worrying about our public image and the quantifiable success of our efforts. We have a tolerance for ambiguity and can accept possibility of achieving that affirmation of the unity of being which James Fowler describes as the sixth and final stage in the evolution of the person of faith.[8] The images I share here are spatial images, relatively unconcerned with the sequence of events. To share, to tolerate, to affirm, to be independent of the need to prove oneself—all these are the gifts of age and of the receptive mode of consciousness, as opposed to the action mode of systemic thought and institutional definition of the self.

The language of the receptive mode of consciousness is symbol and story. Barbara Myerhoff, an anthropologist at the University of Southern California, describes the ritual called the *Oneg Shabbat* (literally the "Delight of the Sabbath") in a Jewish center for the elderly. It is the one ritual left to these Jewish women in their eighties and nineties, mostly now without their husbands, and it is the climax of the week's activities. Each week one of the women is asked to light the candles, which brings in the Sabbath. It is a treasured responsibility, recalling for each childhood memories of her mother. Everything about the ritual is predictable, except who does the lighting. Myerhoff, in commenting on the significance of the *Oneg Shabbat* writes,

> Ritual is often a means for access to the past, by abrogating time and change, reasserting identity and continuing and recreating moods and feelings of prior experiences. In both religious and household rituals, Jews are able to establish temporary, profoundly emotional connections in terms of their broadest identity as an ancient people, and with their identities as individuals and as members of families.[9]

The celebration of the Sabbath is the anticipation of the Day of Yahweh. This ritual not only looks back for symbols of identity, it recalls the destiny of the chosen people of Yahweh. The Sabbath is the *last* day of the week—unlike Sunday for Christians—and the week is a paradigm of history. To remember the Sabbath is to look forward to the promise of that time when the saints shall be gathered in Jerusalem with Yahweh. The *Oneg Shabbat* looks forward to the Sabbath rest.

Worship is rooted in the receptive mode of human consciousness. If we understand the nature of such consciousness we will grasp the power of the archaic symbol and discover the center of meaning. The "archaic symbol" is that archetype or primordial image hallowed by centuries of reverent recollection (such as the Sabbath, the Cross, the sacred fire, the Kaaba, and the peace pipe) which constitutes in itself the reality of a religious community. Successful aging does not reject intellectual rigor, nor does it embrace sentimentality and nostalgia. It perceives that consciousness is more than logical thought, and that possibilities for a significant aging lie in an awareness of the archaic power of symbol and myth.

CULTURAL IMPOVERISHMENT

Our culture tends to place high values on prediction, control, and consumption. Our way of life depends upon our ability to predict how much of a commodity a given portion of the population will consume and to control the production of that commodity to maintain our economic system. The problem with such priorities is not that we hold them, but that we tend to exclude other values we desperately need for a healthy balance.

Recently I met a most remarkable person: a woman who is a teacher of young people, an analytical psychologist, and an astrologer. She had taught for years in a private secondary school in a suburb of Manhattan. Upon her retirement the students requested that she be invited to speak at their commencement. The board of trustees refused that request on the grounds that what she had to say would not be "appropriate." The board is made up of Wall Street types. I have met few wiser persons than this remarkable woman. Her wisdom, however, is of a kind that is a threat to anyone who has committed his integrity "lock, stock, and barrel" to a description of reality provided by a ticker tape.

The *illusion* of reality contained within such an outlook necessarily makes an idol of potency: Impotence is the greatest threat; the ultimate impotence is death! So certain questions catch in our throat as others are repeated again and again with less and less assurance as we grow older. We ask what is the data; not what does it mean; how much do we have, we inquire, and avoid asking how good is it; what is it, not why is it. Understanding, qualification, and purpose are the qualities of the wise person. But we have little use for wisdom. Our culture is grounded on "facts" of a kind that can be fed into a computer and used to predict consumption and production. It has been pointed out by students of the aging process that after age forty a person is less capable of managing facts—numbers, details, and formulas—and such a person is therefore less efficient. On the other hand, wisdom, the ability to see things in perspective and to make intuitive judgments, grows in us as we grow older. Yet wisdom is of little use to computers. In fact, in a computer world wisdom can be subversive. It calls into question the value of facts, which are unrelated to a life lived in the pursuit of meaning, meaningfulness, and truth. Our culture seems almost defensively to make an idol out of the less wise but seemingly more potent: the youth.

For the adolescent there are two major crises to be resolved: sexuality and vocation. Much of our society, even in maturity, assumes sexuality means a good orgasm. When that seems to fade its passage is lamented with an ever more frantic commitment to vocation or job with only periodic excursions—frequently frenetic, often nostalgic—in the quest of renewed sexual prowess. Such an understanding of sexuality is pathetically limited, to say the least. Similarly, finding identity in our job is disastrous. It binds us to a notion of self-worth related to our role and status within the various institutions of which we are a part, and carefully hides from us the real task of the second part of life: the inner quest.

All of us have seen people who have come to the age of retirement and literally pine away from a sense of losing self-worth. Our recent "solution" to this is to make it a federal crime to force someone to retire before seventy. As usual, we miss the point. The problem is our tendency to rely on attribution of value by the institution rather than to value the integrity of the inner life: to "do," to "be active" is good; simply to exist as oneself is unacceptable.

The American nuclear family, despite premature predictions of its demise, is very much with us. It is designed to support our kind of culture. Unfortunately, as we well know, it is only a two-generation family, incapable of absorbing the increasing proportion of elderly in our population. So old age becomes a "problem to be solved." In the act of making it a *technological issue*, we preclude the possibility of a realistic solution. There is no place for the aging in our society, not because the aging have no place, but because we have not only declared their place off-limits, we also suggest again and again that it is a non-place.

It is like the land of Narnia in C. S. Lewis' delightful children's books for adults. In *The Lion, the Witch, and the Wardrobe,* the children are assured that there is no such land, because if there were our society would be challenged.[10] The world of symbol and story is "childish" for our society because to take it seriously would render the illusions of contemporary reality self-evident. The aging, if you stop to think about it, pose a problem because they are subversive!

This attitude is related to the fact that our society is antiritualistic. Our social scientists have even reduced ritual to theories of institutional validation—we perform this or that rite to maintain equilibrium within the social system—and dismiss the possibility that liturgy has an effervescence that intimates more than the socially prescribed reality. On the whole, however, we do not even attempt to justify the existence of cultic activity. If we dismiss it as "primitive," on the assumption that to be primitive is to be less than an "up-to-date" human.

But the aging have something in common with primitive humanity, which the contemporary culture pretends does not exist. They have a common intentionality about life. Aging and its ultimate end in death is itself an acknowledged fact, not a fearful thing to be covered by the cosmetician's art, by the skill of the plastic surgeon, or, finally, by the mortician's gift of illusion. There is a certain fascination with death in sophisticated circles these days, but the horror of death is cloaked in speculative studies, such as Raymond Moody's optimistic little book, *Life After Life.*[11] I suspect that some of the bitterness of growing old in America lies in the lack of support the culture as a whole gives us as we face, with anything but joy, the reality of our own death.

However, the old Eskimo solution is no solution for us. To walk out on the ice, once one could no longer care for oneself, and to await death by freezing or a passing polar bear has a certain simple practicality to it. But it is the solution of a people with different cultural sensibilities—not that we should have romantic notions that anything but grim necessity required what was, at best, an unwelcomed state of affairs. Yet this practice was an acceptance of reality and supported by the ritual of the people who believed in the spirits that inhabited the bottom of the sea. Our own pretence that death never comes actually denies reality.

Our culture, with its abrogation of the primitive, has nothing to offer except ultimate despair, for death is given meaning only when it takes on a symbolic quality. What Masters and Johnson did with sex, reducing it to a predictable, controllable exercise, we do with death as well. We assume that if we know the physiology of death and the psychology of the dying, death will no longer be a problem—just as sexual dysfunction is solved technologically. It is no more comfort to me to discern with some accuracy the signs within myself of advancing old age than it is to note the difference between a clitoral and vaginal orgasm. They both reflect our one-dimensional, disenchanted, emotionally retarded culture's blindness to both mystery and the God who is the final cause of both orgasm and death.

Without meaning we have meaninglessness—an obvious fact which

appears to escape us much of the time. If aging is simply the decline
of my ability to contribute to a consumer society and death the awaited
end of my deepening misery at not being able to be "productive,"
then no amount of helpful hints for occupying my waning years is
going to cut through my deep-seated sense of despair.

Not even the "wisdom" of the kindly cynic will help overcome an
enveloping meaninglessness. In John Fowles' novel *Daniel Martin*, ad-
vertised as a "defense of humanism," the author describes the hero's
reaction to the priest arranging for the funeral of a friend who had
committed suicide. As the priest leaves, Daniel Martin laments having
to suffer through "ritual, in a world already stifled with it."[12] If we
allow the author to foist this banal observation off on us as "truth,"
then we deserve the despair that awaits not only him but all of us as
the "wisdom" of the Daniel Martins of this world fades before the
last great reality.

WORSHIP AND DREAD

Aging can be a dreadful thing; that is to say that the alternative
to despair is dread. Dread, as a necessary experience of spiritual growth
and aging, if done *sub specie eternatatis*, under the vision of God, is
an act of spiritual growth. Dread, as Thomas Merton has defined it,
is the emotion that accompanies the silent, listening, receptive passage
through good and evil.[13] One does not come to wholeness except
through experiencing death, the last great enemy of the good. If the
Cross means anything it means this.

But notice that dread is very different from despair. It is not a
resignation or surrender to meaninglessness. It is not the emotion of
some latter-day "pop" Stoic, engaging in self-euthanasia as the final
act of defiance before the meaninglessness of life. Dread is the emotion
of one who is aware of the meaning of existence, particularly the meaning of death. If one wishes to be whole one must wrestle with the
demons, including death.

In Carlos Castaneda's account of his apprenticeship to the Yaqui
shaman, don Juan, he asks don Juan if it is so terrible to be timid.

Don Juan answers, "If you are going to die there is no time for timidity. . . . Being timid prevents us from examining and exploiting our lot as men." Castaneda replies, "It is not natural to live with the constant idea of our death, don Juan."

Then don Juan says:

> Our death is waiting and this very act we're performing now may well be our last battle on earth . . . I call it a battle because it is a struggle. Most people move from act to act without any struggle or thought. A hunter, on the contrary, assesses every act; and since he has an intimate knowledge of his death, he proceeds judiciously, as if every act were his last battle. Only a fool would fail to notice the advantage a hunter has over his fellow men.[14]

For "hunter" read "the Christian seeking to own the faith," and we have here a Christian statement. The "struggle" of which don Juan speaks is one that is filled with dread, because the battle is the cosmic conflict between good and evil. As we grow older we cannot afford to be timid about this struggle.

The life of worship, pursued from the day we become a Christian at our baptism, is one in which the Cross, a dread symbol, stands at the center. The Cross never lets us escape the fact of death—the death of Jesus and our death. It may not be "natural" to live with the constant idea of death, but the Christian does. Consequently the realization of aging does not bring death as a novel notion. In abrogating timidity, death is a reality with which the Christian has lived an entire life of faith because of a life of worship.

I write of the Cross as a "dread symbol." The Cross is a symbol, as well as an actual instrument, of suffering and death. This stark fact must not be hidden for the Christian. Jürgen Moltmann, a contemporary theologian, has reminded us of the belief in Christian thinking that "by the aid of the *meditatio crucis* [contemplation of the cross], the soul returns to the darkness of its uncreated ground."[15] That is, we come face to face with God, the God who in Jesus suffered and died for us. In the contemplation of the suffering or passion of God we find what Moltmann calls "sympathetic union" with God, "sympathetic" in the etymological sense: "to suffer together."[16] By virtue of this "sympathy," the Cross is also a symbol of life. It is the awareness of death as evil that provokes the hope of life as the ultimate good.

Authentic Christian ritual is a constant play upon the theme of the Cross as both a source of destruction and as a means of new life. There is a sensible reality there, which when played out within the act of worship, touches our imagination as it calls on our memories to perceive the temporality of life and its future promise.

I think of a small, yet not inconsequential memory of my own. When I was a child it was the custom on Easter Sunday afternoon to have a children's service at which we presented our Lenten offering boxes and placed bundles of flowers on a cross—"flowering the cross" we called it—representing the triumph of Easter. This was followed by an Easter egg hunt. My "mite box" never seemed to be as heavy as others. My flowers seemed the most bedraggled, colorless, and wilted. The other children, with arrangements that all looked fresh from the florist's shop, made snide little comments, and boasted of their Lenten offerings. I never found the golden egg at the Easter egg hunt either. But strange as it may seem, I loved that service and our time together at the church on Easter Sunday afternoon. I can still smell the flowers and sense the thrill of the possibility that I might find the golden egg. It is the stuff of which, I truly believe, my later sense of vocation to the priesthood was made.

The point is that the "flowered" Cross and all that surrounded my childhood memory of Easter Sunday is to me a means of identifying *both* my struggle with a sense of low self-worth—an awareness which is very important for my own spiritual journey—and my expectation that within the church there is a hope for acceptance. I told this story in my seminary chapel in a Maundy Thursday sermon on the importance of remembering. The next week I found a "golden egg" in my chapel stall. Someone had understood and given me a lovely gift, which I shall add to my remembrance. It still gives me "goose bumps" to think that in the eyes of someone—maybe God himself—I am worth the golden egg.

There is a growing honesty in many aging people, born of a freedom from the practical demands of our technological society. There is very little they have to prove, since they are already acknowledged and acknowledge themselves. And what a power there is in this honesty. Old people, if we do not oppress them, can face the real questions that we, in our fear of dread, avoid. Free from the strivings of the ego, they can constitute a world of meaning, which is related to life as "being."

But let us not be romantic about this. The culture of the aging is as much a product of our entire life together as is the culture of the youth. A people reared to believe that ritual is pointless and that success is measured by the profit margin, are not going to become wise men and women—celebrating the symbols of faith before the fear of death—just because they have begun to slow down or have retired. This can only happen when the church takes the past seriously and starts to help us build memories when we are children.

Memories vary in value, of course, like anything else. Those which only call us into the past, and leave us weeping for days gone by, are of little worth. That "old time religion" can be a snare and illusion. Usually such memories lack the pain so characteristic of dread. They do not call us to repent.

Several years ago I returned to the house in Louisiana in which my family and I lived when my children were little. As I sat talking to the present occupants I began to hear—I mean that quite literally—the voice of my older daughter, who was then living in Wisconsin. The sound of this ten-year-old child's voice was unbearable! My wife tells me my countenance became ashen! I could only think of my insensitivity to her as a young priest "on the way up." I had no choice but to go to the phone and call my daughter and say to her, "Teresa, I want to be a better father to you now and in the future." It is a vow, evoked by a dread memory, that lives as much with me now as I write, as it did that afternoon. This is what I mean by a memory of value. I have always loved my daughter, but somehow that love has slowly become less "cluttered" with my own agenda.

This is something of what I think worship should be for the aging. The evocation of a memory that calls them to repentance, and consequently makes them a source of wisdom. The aging are to us a witness of a "cleaner" set of values, purged of the clutter of egocentric striving and open to the whisper of God calling us into being. It is a deeply satisfying prospect for which to long. I pray that it will happen to me and to us all.

NOTES

1. Gregory of Nyssa, *The Life of Moses*, trans. Everett Ferguson and Abraham J. Malherbe (New York: Paulist Press, 1978), p. 79.
2. Schlomo Deshen and Mosha Shokeid, *The Predicament of Homecoming: Cultural and Social Life of North African Immigrants in Israel* (Ithaca, New York: Cornell University Press, 1974), p. 156.
3. Robert N. Bellah, "Christianity and Symbolic Realism," *Journal for The Scientific Study of Religion* 9, no. 2 (Summer, 1970): 89–96.
4. Henri Nouwen and Walter J. Gaffney, *Aging* (Garden City, N.Y.: Doubleday & Co., 1974), p. 40.
5. William Lynch, *Images of Hope: Imagination as Healer of the Hopeless* (Baltimore: Helicon Press, 1965), pp. 243–250.
6. Paul Ricoeur, *The Symbolism of Evil*, trans. Emerson Buchanan (New York: Harper & Row, 1967), p. 351.
7. Nouwen, *Aging*, p. 101.
8. James Fowler and Sam Keen, *Life Maps: Conversations on the Journey of Faith* (Waco, Texas: Word Books, 1978), pp. 87–95.
9. Barbara Myerhoff, "The Older Woman as Androgyne," *Parabola* 3, no. 4 (Nov. 1978): 85.
10. C. S. Lewis, *The Lion, the Witch, and the Wardrobe* (New York: Macmillan, 1950).
11. Raymond A. Moody, Jr., *Life After Life* (Atlanta: Mockingbird Books, 1976).
12. John Fowles, *Daniel Martin* (Boston: Little, Brown & Co., 1977), p. 213.
13. Thomas Merton, *Contemplative Prayer* (Garden City, N.Y.: Image Books, 1969), p. 25.
14. Carlos Castaneda, *Journey to Ixtlan: The Lessons of Don Juan* (New York: Simon and Schuster, 1972), p. 112.
15. Jürgen Moltmann, *The Crucified God: The Cross of Christ as the Foundation and Criticism of Christian Theology*, trans. R. A. Wilson and John Bowden (New York: Harper & Row, 1974), p. 59.
16. Ibid., p. 272.

II

CHALLENGES

7

Aging: On the Way to One's End

Ann Belford Ulanov

"We who are old know that age is more than a disability. It is an intense and varied experience, almost beyond our capacity at times, but something to be carried high. If it is a long defeat, it is also a victory, meaningful for the initiates of time, if not for those who have come less far."[1]

These words of Florida Scott-Maxwell capture the essence of aging as a process no less complicated and mysterious in its psychology and spirituality than in its physiology. We cheat ourselves and our loved ones when we resort to over-simplified pictures of what it means to grow old. We reduce many levels to one; we flatten richly textured meanings into monotony; we squeeze out passion and excitement to focus on dread alone—the dread of illness, of infirmity, of isolation, of death.

No, aging means more than fear and infirmity and death. It touches all the large questions of life. What is our end? To what goal are we moving? What purpose guides us? When we come to an end, at what end shall we have arrived? Aging presses these questions upon us throughout our lives. Depth psychology makes that indisputably clear.

Unconscious fantasies and dreams indicate subliminal awareness of these end-questions throughout life, even from our earliest years.

What does aging look like from the perspective of unconscious mental process? Aging looks like a determined philosopher asking fundamental questions about the ends of life—its meaning, its purposes, its goals. Aging looks like a passionate psychologist insisting on making sense of all his patients.

Take for example the young woman who seeks therapy either to escape from, or finally turn and face, the menacing sense of emptiness that has dogged her for many years. Her earliest memory of this encroaching threat was at the age of six when her mother made her try on last year's summer clothes to see which ones still fit. She could no longer squeeze into her favorite playsuit, its stiff white material still vivid in her mind's eye with its red and blue rick-rack trim. She remembered registering intense shock, as if struck by a blow. She loved that playsuit and had attached herself to it. It was her favorite clothing, her favorite self! That it no longer fit, that she no longer fit, that things could go away like that, no more be part of herself, marked the terrible threat of passing time, even to a six-year-old. All things to which she attached herself could go away, then, no longer "fit" for her. The adult woman remembered that moment as her first unforgettable taste of mortality, of the tragic fact that loving something did not make it immune to time and change.

Other images of aging involve a similar sense of time passing, or worse, running out, to a beleaguered psyche. A late-middle-aged man suffering extreme anxiety at the thought of retirement, of "all that yawning unfilled up time" ready to swallow him, vacillated between compulsive readings of his projected income, in bed with the door closed and the blinds drawn, and total withdrawal into sleep. There, in bed, he hoped to escape the fearful future by abandoning the present, immersing himself in the past, reading trashy historical novels about people from other pasts. Working through his panic about retirement, and no longer holding down a job, he became acutely aware of the poverty of his life where so few of his energies were put to work. He projected onto future retirement a present emptiness that he tried to displace by frantic overworking. Retirement threatened the end of this defense, and as it came to an end, revealed to what purpose the defense had been employed: to protect him from what he felt to be an endless void. Facing the end of work meant facing the end of hiding from what he feared was a life devoid of purpose, without end. What he feared as an ending at last showed itself as a beginning. Finally, he had to take up the end-questions: Who was he apart from work? What was this feared void? Where was meaning to be found?

Images of passing time raise the fundamental questions of purposes in life—temporary purposes, final purposes. A woman entering meno-pause frankly confessed she wanted no part of it. She felt she would no longer be sexually attractive. She looked at her body with a critical eye, spying out evidence of aging as signs of ugliness. She feared being useless, dried up in some way even more inclusive than infertility. What surfaced in her meditations were intense feelings about her sexual experiences and her own identity as a woman. Was she more than a mother, which she soon could not ever become again? Was her identity as female dependent only on the ability to bear children? Did femininity only mean maternity for her? What other aspects of her femaleness needed to be lived? What freeing up from maternal qualities did her sexuality need? Had she lived her assertive energies enough? Had she defined her own authority? Had she developed ways to give to others in different modes from the supportive parent role? Had she left unlived large aspects of her own sexual satisfaction that she needed to face?

Women's sense of aging often reunites them with their bodies. A young woman married, divorced, now pursuing her own career, which was proving both successful and deeply satisfying to her, nonetheless feared a barrenness that she was projecting onto the old age to come: "What if I discover when I'm old and alone that this was all a mistake, and I should have settled for a husband and children?" She feels the finite scope of her resources of energy and time. Contrary to all the comforting propaganda of women's magazines, she feels she simply cannot "do everything." For her, now, it is a clear choice between career and family. Another young woman wonders if she should have children and fears that passing time, the running out of the biological

clock, will make her decision for her. By default, she will bear no
children because she waited too long, until she was too old even to
attempt it. A third woman debates whether to become pregnant again.
She knows this would be her last child because of her age, and that
fact confronts her with what maternity has meant to her. Why does
she want another child? To protect her daughter from the "only-child
syndrome"? Because it is now or never? Because it postpones other
questions about her identity, about her role in the world, giving her
excellent reasons for doing her work only halfheartedly? Vague fears
can be left vague for a few more years as she raises a preschooler.

Issues of pregnancy and birth raise basic questions about marriage.
Is it stable enough? Have the husband and wife become merely parents
together, somehow having lost each other as individuals who chose
to live in intimacy? The passing of time marked by the end of the
possibility of childbearing raises the end-questions: What really matters
to me? How do I contribute most to those around me? What is central
to life and do I get my teeth into it or run away from it?

Teeth turn up as a frequent unconscious image of aging in dreams.
Teeth fall out or break. The dreams point to the fear of losing one's
bite, of becoming feeble, of losing something irreplacable that cannot
grow again, of failure to take hold of life, to cite but a few patients'
associations. Thus the end-questions of purpose and meaning that aging
turns up require for their examination a determination, a willingness,
aggression to ask all the questions, pleasant and unpleasant, to hang
on, to bite, as symbolized by strong teeth in working order.

Still more vivid is the image of aging as time leaping out of contact,
of the frenzied feeling that one's unlived life will find no outlet, no
scope for expression, but simply remain trapped inside oneself, to be
carried into the grave. One woman in her fifties had turned her whole
life around, leaving an unsatisfactory marriage, closing a business that
had become a harrowing ordeal, striking out finally, at whatever cost,
to find and become what Winnicott calls the "true self."[2] In the
first years after her life-changing decision she succumbed many times
to feelings of despair in her search for a life of meaning. At times
she even gave up hope of finding a place in herself and in the world

where she could feel alive, real, connected to others. She feared she was dead already or would die' before she had lived.

Sometimes we want to avoid this task of finding truth, and wish only that our time would end. One ninety-year-old woman had longed for the release of death but dreamed of a life still to be lived: "I was visiting the house of the painter Orozco. He showed me the gallery of his paintings. There was one open space where nothing yet was hung, a space to be filled with a painting that was still to be completed."[3] On waking, the woman knew she was to do that painting. It was as if the dream were replying to the woman's longing for death with a flat "no"—there was life ahead to be lived, not just for the sake of her own self expression, but for the sake of others, for the painting would be hung in a gallery open to the public, displayed as a work of art along with the creations of a famous painter. Thus the significance of living all the life given us to live reaches beyond our own needs and our own small visions. Others need to see what we have made of human experience—how we have designed it and expressed it— for their own edification and to help create a human culture that sustains such experience.

PSYCHOLOGICAL THEORIES OF AGING

One emphasis in depth psychology that cuts across all schools of theory stresses aging as a product of what is stored up in youth.[4] Freud focused on the decisively formative influences of our first years of life, climaxing in the Oedipal drama. Later problems with sexual intimacy, with authority, with giving oneself to a life of value find their roots in unworked-through Oedipal conflicts. Erikson sketches the developmental stages of life, where what comes later is the cumulative product of earlier stages successfully negotiated. If we fail to achieve a basic trust in ourselves and others, we find it harder to achieve any reliable autonomy, for at any moment we fear that the self we seek to rely on may break down. If as elderly persons we look back on our lives with a sense of despair at having missed its meaning, that despair manifests itself in terms of concrete stages of missed identity, failures of intimacy, of stagnating instead of generating renewed interests in life as both it and we change. Winnicott sees adult disorders as rooted in early failures of innate maturational processes to unfold. These processes were hindered, Winnicott believes, because the environment demanded compliance with others' expectations instead of our own.

On the other hand, our old age can find us reaping the benefits of lives richly spent, not only in the storehouse of memories, but in the fruition of problems worked through, plans executed, meditations undertaken, suffering survived. Old age harvests the work of a lifetime, making available the fullness of a richly ploughed imagination and well-nourished mind, a body exercised and cared for. Even in suffering illness and infirmity, our engagement in life lived to the full sustains a life that is livable right up to the end, for its ends go on being met.

Who I am and who I have come to be are the result of who was with me when I was growing, whose influence molded the vision of life that took shape within me. This dependence of the self upon others is a frightful fact of human life, sometimes demonstrating with grim force how much we make or break for each other the possibility of being. Our nation's treatment of the aged underlines this interpersonal fact. Forced into retirement, confined by limited income and rising prices, treated as periphery, the aged citizen must achieve a spiritual autonomy of heroic proportions to assert the value and wisdom of his or her years.

To achieve that assertion of authority, to refuse to concede to a peripheral place in society, or accept merely marginal significance, an older person must depend on how he or she lived all through life. From this perspective, age is simply the consequence of what we have stored up in youth. If we spend a lifetime avoiding who we are, veering off from the central issues of finding and building our personal way of being, our personal ways of putting ourselves into the world; of facing the hard questions of injustice and suffering—or the sometimes harder ones of justice and pleasure—of facing the blasting challenges of really loving someone more than ourselves; of surviving failure and learning from it; of reaching to the center, always the center, seeing persons as uniquely themselves, not fully defined by class or economic level or education or talent, we reap the results in old age. We survive as unique persons who go on growing, experiencing, changing, and consolidating ourselves. Life continues to offer excitement. If we veered off then, now we find our days empty of any content. The only difference between then and now is that aging reduces the camouflage that hides the emptiness from us. Aging does not bring emptiness; it only increasingly reveals what is or is not there. If we fled from hard questions then, now we find ourselves overwhelmed with the problems of the world, with little hope in human ingenuity and goodness. We drift now because we never took much hold of our own center. Empty of purpose, we yield to nameless fears, to infectious diseases, or, in attempts to veer off still again, we settle down to routines of narrow scope, safe repetition, dull survival.

Attitudes that we formed in our earliest years come to the fore again in our late years. Perhaps it is the simplicity of early youth and old age that brings these attitudes into clearer focus. In both times our lives are relatively free from clutter and the tasks of surviving. We spend more time at home, more time alone, more time resting. There are spaces all through the day when reflection demands our attention. Our attitudes focus on feelings of struggle and persecution on the one hand, and of creative mixture and reparation on the other.[5]

Aging brings a weakening of energies, illness often enough, forgetfulness, restriction of movement, fear of death. Some of us feel done in by these events, as if assaulted, almost overcome, defeated. We experience aging as a malevolent process directed against us. As if especially singled out, we feel persecuted by the inevitable physiological processes and defend ourselves with elaborations on a persecutory motif. Thus the older person retreats into hypochondria, hedged round by an army of combative symptoms that ward off any simple meeting with another person or with their own actual inner selves. Life turns into a battlefield of oversimplified forces—good against evil—in which our persons exist as unwilling and loudly plaintive or silently martyred victims. This embattled attitude weaves fantasies around the given facts of aging, turning ordinary events that in fact happen to everyone into a special personal cross—a false cross—constructed just for our special misery.

Unfortunately, these fantasies possess the power to imbue us with the forbidding tonality of victimhood. Remember how it feels to be such a complainer? We come to believe fervently in our victimization and experience others as coldly indifferent or hostile to us. They in turn experience us as inaccessible, as entrenched behind a wall of aches and pains, repelling any person, any fact, any exchange, that does not directly concern our own suffering.

If, on the other hand, we are the ones trying to make contact with an aging relative or friend living the drama of victimhood, we must deal with the hostility they arouse in us when they refuse any comfort or intimacy we may be bringing them. They, who feel so persecuted by life, will in effect be persecuting us. They make us angry by rejecting anything that exists outside their self-enclosed preoccupation; they enrage us with their constantly telegraphed message: "You owe me!" But, worse still, the hostility they arouse in us evokes a hostile self-attack in us. We suffer guilt and self-reproach at our sense of being burdened by them, by their suffering, by their aging victimhood. After all, we lecture ourselves, we have health and they do not, we have better means to a good life than they, more mobility, more "something," even if only youth. They make us feel guilty for being ourselves and guilty for the anger that their self-centered manipulations of us provoke in us, guilty for the inevitable processes of aging. If we just loved them more, they somehow signal us, we could postpone death for them. For no matter what we do, we come away feeling it was never enough. Their attitude of persecution sets up its counterpart in us: we feel persecuted by their feeling persecuted, and round and round it goes in the vicious repetition of unhappy parody.

In sharp contrast, those who age with attitudes of creative mixture and reparation make us hopeful about the resources of the human spirit. Think of those older friends or relatives who continue to take what life offers them and reshape it into their personal styles of being, not denying hardship, but neither reducing it to some simple black-and-white scheme.[6] Instead, illness, chronic pain, even a major operation, can be endured and somehow found place for. These people see the possibilities of receiving help from medicine, from reading and reflection, and they welcome visits from friends as friends, not mere collaborators in misery or victimhood. Such people go on living, reaching out for what is available, thinking new ideas, exposing themselves to what is there—a new book, a new bird, a new sight or sound, a new way of sensing or feeling or understanding their worlds. Such persons long ago gave up the simplistic fantasy that one can get rid of all badness and hold onto only the good. They are tough-minded.[7] They consent to the mixture of good and bad that inevitably surrounds us all, making creative use of what is there, what is offered—in themselves, in the world around them—with less emphasis on or complaining about what has been taken away, lost, or denied. These are our wise old people to whom we must look for hope and strength, on whom we can gratefully lean, for they inspire a faith in being, a conviction that what we need will be provided. We recognize them as content, as gifted with the full acceptance of life, and therefore as wise.

Old wise men and women repair the damage done by depression, by pain, by ungratefulness, because they recognize the complex mixture of positive and negative, of good and bad, in themselves, in us, and in life, and they work with that full construction of reality. Thus the sharp unsentimental humor of an older friend who refuses easy answers or simplistic consolations, preferring to meditate on the mysteries of life and death. Thus the buoyancy of spirit that increases in some older persons, as if in direct proportion to the decrease in physical energy. They burn with life and come to treasure each moment.

Florida Scott Maxwell, who became a Jungian analyst at the age of fifty, wrote at the age of eighty-two:

> Age puzzles me. I thought it was a quiet time. My seventies were interesting, and fairly serene, but my eighties are passionate. I grow more intense as I age. To my own surprise I burst out with hot conviction. Only a few years ago I enjoyed tranquillity, now I am so disturbed by the outer world and by human quality in general, that I want to put things right as though I still owed a debt to life. I must calm down. I am far too frail to indulge in moral fervour.[8]

AGING AND CHRISTIAN FAITH

Christian faith concerns itself with living such moments of choice in life. Along with depth psychology, Christianity recognizes the stern fact that age is a product of youth. The generations of fathers sharpen the generations of children's teeth. We cannot escape the historicity or the finitude of our lives. The world we live in, the people who raised us, the values we were exposed to—all go to mold who we are. Thus one aspect of our faith focuses strongly on the injunction to be our neighbor's keeper, to manifest God's love and mercy in day-to-day dealings with other people, no matter how crass in nature. For in all our exchanges with others we either contribute to their possibility to be, or we attack that being; we help others produce justice or injustice.

The wherewithal to do such tasks arises from another source in our faith, that notion of the soul's life held in God's presence which reaches beyond time and yet comes to us only in the moments of time that we have fully lived. From this perspective, the processes of aging present quite a different picture from the usual discouraging one. They show an increasing liberation from distractions, allowing us to see through to the essential truth. The natural concerns with survival, security, and accomplishment of worldly position, fade with aging, are necessarily reduced in significance. We see as we get older that these things are not what matter, but that something less perishable, more irreplacable matters: the uniqueness of each human person. Christian faith talks about this as the life of the soul, the soul that lives outside of time and continues after time comes to an end. This, the soul's life, provides the terms of the end-questions.

Aging offers the advantage of seeing these questions clearly. Usually we avoid them by projecting onto time an indefinite number of years, stretching hazily into the uncertain future that will make up the "rest" of our life. But as we grow older we begin to discern the end-point of those years. Our projection comes loose from the time-process and we find all the energy that went into the projection, falling back upon us to stir up concern for the present moment, the quality of life as it is actually being lived, not the vague quantity of life that can somehow be imagined to stretch ahead. The question of how we are living now strikes to the center of our being as the essential questions: do we have a center? What is it? What really matters?

Our faith both confronts and comforts us at this point. The only questions that matter, our tradition tells us, are: What is the center of our lives? Does God occupy that place or does some idol? The comfort comes quickly after this challenge, for to ask those questions of the center is to live at the center, to want it, to seek it. We need not have the answers securely in hand, tied up tightly in maxims and proverbs. We need only want with heart and soul and strength and mind to open ourselves to that center, to find it, and to be found in it.

From the Judeo-Christian perspective, life is always *created* life, held in relationship to the creator God. Even death is subsumed within this relationship—as a mark of sin's denial of that relationship. To live in the kingdom of God is to live with full awareness that the relationship is the center-point, the end and beginning of life, and that we find our being as created being only in this relationship that surpasses death as we know it.

From the perspective of this centering of life we discover another view of aging. Not only is it a traveling toward a more simple life that gives us the opportunity to see through to the center of our lives; aging also no longer defines itself as a mere conclusion of youth, a consequence only of what went before to shape us. Aging now includes a break with the past, a break we initiate when we exercise our choice for a life lived from the center.

At any age we can ask what really matters in life, what is the central value around which life is gathered. The child who outgrew her playsuit tasted mortality and the transience of all things. Even at her young age she could already ask what might persist through time, prove incorruptible, to borrow the language of Scripture. The woman who wrestles over the problems occasioned by the end of her fertility knows something about the anguishing process of disidentification with her sense of being alive and real. For the capacity to bear life, however precious, is not the center of life. Even parenthood, one of life's great experiences, is not in itself the ultimate source of being and cannot provide the solace and strength of that source. What then can? a woman in such a position asks herself. Thus she embarks on the age-old journey of the soul, described in what some think of as outdated language as the sacrifice of the natural self to the spiritual self.

We do not need to wait until death looms to ask these questions. Our Christian heritage speaks of an ever-present zone of communication with a God who is outside time, who breaks into our chronology at all points and any moment when summoned. At any time in our lives, the determinative weight of history can be met with transcendent presence. Or put another way, at any juncture of our lives we can open ourselves to perceive through immediate events an eternal loving presence.

Psychologically, a corollary growth of consciousness accompanies this spiritual development.[9] Aging can mean acquiring consciousness and boldly moving out of our initial states of unconscious identity with instincts, parents, family, social group, or social norms. Consciousness induces a radical sense of our own "I-ness" in relation to other "I's." Radical because it breaks merely assumed connections and brings home to us an awareness of our own separateness and fragility. Like Pascal's thinking reed, we know, whatever the consequences, the precious gift of reflectiveness upon all that happens around us. We are open to receive from the world and from our own interior fantasies and dreams, a knowledge of personality that is being constructed within us.[10] And from that openness to our own inner development, we become aware of parallel interior experience in others. Thus the value of the person— that fragile, passing, endlessly vulnerable, but also unique self of each human being—takes center stage, as if its construction or failure to be constructed occupies a central place in existence, as surely it is meant to do.

The development of consciousness requires a constant attention to where the realm of choice intersects with necessity, choice not much supported by society and certainly not simply in a form supplied by our nature. Choice does not come to us easily or in unmistakable terms. If it did, it would not be choice but compulsion. Rewards for personality decisions chosen thoughtfully, carefully and well, are delivered late in life, most often posthumously. Like the spiritual life, the life of choice, which is the life of consciousness, depends on willingness to participate in life through unflinching, often daring reflection on what is happening to us, somehow making sense out of it, working on the problems that beset us more than solving them. Similarly, the life of the soul depends on the daring, conscious choice to respond to the God that seeks us; to turn inward to develop endurance to face the silence that awaits us there; to hear in daily events the mysterious voice of providence.

These choices find little support in worldly terms. Rarely do they bring fame or power or fortune. They offer no protection against the ravages of disease or accident. In religious terms, such choices have always been described as a kind of renunciation of the world, a breaking with the language and values of the world to point up our movement into another dimension.

Awareness of aging, at whatever age, gives us a chance for this kind of consciousness time and again. The choice for the moment, for the life lived from the center for its own sake instead of for immediate reward, for participation in the central relationships—these opportunities are abundantly available at any point in life. Here the values of personality and faith show forth. At any stage in our lives we can exercise such consciousness and the privilege of choice that goes with it. Illness, weakening energies, poverty, fatigue make no major difference. No matter how much time has gone by, or how ravaging it has been, this choice remains. Unlike the life of the body that cuts off possibilities as we age, the life of the soul increases its range at any and every age.

We are brought finally, then, to one of the great paradoxes of religious tradition. As one life goes, another begins. The new life of the soul, that startling rebirth that so often accompanies closeness to death, rises before us. Religion has often been caricatured as the escape hatch of the old hedging their bets, taking refuge from a terrible reality in the sweet illusion of an all-caring God. But aging can also be seen as a losing of stiffness, a movement away from that destructive inflexibility in which we avoid altogether the questions of life's meaning and do not permit ourselves to face life's centers. Aging brings home to us what we have done or failed to do with our lives, our creativity or our waste, our openness to or zealous hiding from what really matters. Precisely at that point, age cracks us open, sometimes for the first time, makes us aware of the center, makes us look for it and for relation to it. Aging does not mark an end but rather the beginning of making sense of the end-questions, so that life can have an end in every sense of the word.

NOTES

1. Florida Scott-Maxwell, *The Measure of My Days* (New York: Knopf, 1968), p. 5.
2. D. W. Winnicott, *Maturational Processes and the Facilitating Environment* (New York: International Universities Press, 1965), chap. 12.
3. Cited in Ann and Barry Ulanov, *Religion and the Unconscious* (Philadelphia: Westminster Press, 1975), chap. 11, n. 11, p. 278.
4. See, for example, Bernice L. Neugarten, "Time, Age, and the Life Cycle," in *The American Journal of Psychiatry* 136, no. 7 (July 1979): 887–894.
5. Melanie Klein, the late British psychoanalyst, formulated these attitudes as the "paranoid-schizoid position," and the "depressive position." See her papers, "A Contribution to the Psychogenesis of Manic-Depressive States," and "Mourning and Its Relation to Manic-Depressive States" in *Love, Guilt and Reparation and Other Works 1921–1945* (New York: Delacorte Press/Seymour Lawrence, 1975), and her paper "Notes on Some Schizoid Mechanisms" in *Envy and Gratitude and Other Works, 1946–1963* (New York: Delacorte Press/Seymour Lawrence, 1975). For discussion of the importance of these attitudes, see also Ulanov and Ulanov, *Religion and the Unconscious*, pp. 151–153.
6. See Klein's discussion of overcoming loneliness as a result of consenting to life's ambiguities and mixtures of good and evil in her paper "On the Sense of Loneliness," in *Envy and Gratitude.*
7. Freud has often been cited as a paragon of an attitude of tough realism. The following excerpt from his letter to Lou Andreas-Salome captures his unflinching perception of "bad" aspects of aging, yet shows he can nonetheless take in the daily "good" that life offers:

    My dear Lou,
        Do not fail to note the address; it indicates the most beautiful garden and the most charming house in which we have ever spent our summer holiday . . .

the year in its caprice has let us enjoy an uncannily beautiful but unfortunately somewhat premature spring. Here would be the right place—at least for a native of Vienna—"to die in beauty."

I cannot agree with the eulogy of old age to which you give expression in your kind letter . . . you adapt yourself so much better than I. But for that matter you are by no means so old and you do not get so angry. The suppressed rage exhausts one or what is still left over of one's former ego. And it is too late to create a new one at seventy-eight.

(*Letters*, ed. Ernst Pfeiffer, trans. Elaine and William Robson-Scott [New York: Harcourt, Brace Jovanovich, 1972], p. 202.)

8. Scott-Maxwell, *The Measure of My Days*, pp. 13–14.

9. See for example, C. G. Jung, "On the Symbolic Life," in *The Symbolic Life*, Collected Works, vol. 20, trans. R. F. C. Hull (Princeton: Princeton University Press, 1976), pp. 267–281. For a discussion of a variety of psychological theorists' views of our "inner world" see H. Guntrip, *Schizoid Phenomena, Object Relations and the Self* (New York: International Universities Press, 1969), pp. 404–426.

10. See for example, C. G. Jung, "The Stages of Life," in *The Structure and Dynamics of the Psyche*, Collected Works, vol. 8, trans. R. F. C. Hull (New York: Pantheon for Bollingen Foundation, 1960), pp. 393–94, 399, 402.

8

Retirement

Evelyn Eaton Whitehead
and James D. Whitehead

Americans have mixed feelings about retirement. The sense that retirement is a difficult, often negative experience seems widespread. Yet at the same time most of us would find it appealing to move away from the demands of a rigid work schedule or to leave a monotonous or physically taxing job. We are now passing laws to delay or do away with mandatory retirement, just when increasing numbers of workers express interest in retiring early.

Our ambivalence reflects, in part, our widely different experiences of retirement. Retiring as a widowed Chicano domestic worker in poor health is quite different from retiring as a corporate executive with a well-financed pension and stock options. The use of one word—retirement—to designate these and many other experiences seems to suggest that there is a single, common pattern that does or should describe what it is to be retired. But we know, of course, that this is not the case. Retirement is not a homogeneous experience. For each individual what it will mean to retire will be dramatically affected by health, family situation, interests and skills, gender and social class, and by the money on which one will live.

While these individual differences remain, there are similarities and trends that are important as well. There is evidence that through the 1950s and 1960s wage-earners and salaried workers who had the option to retire before age sixty-five were increasingly choosing to do so. In the 1970s the specter of continuing inflation slowed this trend. Workers began to delay their move to dependence on a fixed income, deciding instead to work a few years longer, especially if this increased the financial benefits available to them when they did retire. But there is not much evidence that most Americans want to continue into their senior years the patterns of work responsibility that characterize their mid-years.[1]

Retirement is the choice of most Americans. The resentment experienced and expressed about retirement tends to focus on factors that limit this choice—such as compulsory regulations that do not permit flexible response to the real requirements of the work place or to the preferences of older workers, and fixed limits in income that inhibit the choice of how one's post-retirement years will be lived.

REHEARSAL FOR RETIREMENT

Retirement does not catch us totally unaware. Persons approaching retirement today are the second generation to do so. Most of us have witnessed the event of retirement in our own parents' lives or at least in the lives of others in their generation. It has become a part of the normal expectable life-pattern of Americans, indeed, of most persons in industrialized nations. We share the cultural expectation that our own investment in work will change as we grow older, and that there will be some experience of retirement in our senior years. We may not look forward to it (though there is evidence that more and more of us view retirement positively); we may not plan well for it (though, here again, personal planning for retirement is on the increase); but it does not take us by surprise. Many of us, at least by the time we reach our own mid-years and often much earlier, begin to "rehearse" for retirement. The rehearsal may take many forms. A couple invests in property in the sun belt, looking forward to moving there after retirement. A wife daydreams about what it will be like to have her husband home and "underfoot" all day. A college professor plans to have time to complete a manuscript on which she has been working intermittently over the past ten years. A factory worker toys with the idea of starting a part-time electrical repair business out of his garage, planning to continue it as a supplementary source of income after retirement.

EMERGENCE OF THE YOUNG-OLD

Bernice Neugarten, a pioneering gerontologist at the University of Chicago, has pointed out one of the effects of current retirement trends in America.[2] There are increasing numbers of men and women who choose to retire in their late fifties and early sixties. Relatively healthy and relatively affluent, they remain vigorous participants in social and civic life well into their seventies. The attitudes and life-experiences of these "young-old" contradict the negative expectations of the retirement years as a time of disintegration and disengagement. They signal a life style that is likely to become more and more characteristic of retired Americans.

SOCIAL TASKS OF RETIREMENT

Retirement is not, in the experience of most Americans, an unwelcomed event. It is, however, a time of significant transition. It marks a movement from one adult way of life to another. For most of us, marriage had marked a significant change in our personal life style of early adulthood. The decision to marry and to marry *this* person affects how we see ourselves, how we relate to other people, how we use resources of time and money and talent. Retirement marks a similar transition in life style. The development of a post-retirement way of life that is personally appropriate and personally satisfying is a central task in mature adulthood.

FINANCIAL ADJUSTMENT

With few exceptions, retirement income is less than that of the immediate pre-retirement years. And while some work-related expenses may fall off, the overall effect of retirement is to reduce the money upon which one lives. For many persons in retirement it is not this initial reduction in income that is of most concern, but the threat that inflation will continue to erode the buying power of this relatively fixed amount.

USE OF TIME

The establishment of a satisfactory post-retirement life style will require decisions about using time. Should we resume a busy schedule in a second career or adopt a recreation-centered life style? Do we want to spend more time with our grandchildren or shall we assume a new set of responsibilities as community volunteers? These choices concerning the use of time will require personal flexibility as we adopt new roles (leisured senior citizen, civic volunteer, pastor *emeritus*) and adapt to changes in former relationships (now that I am retired, how do I relate to my spouse? to my former work colleagues? to my adult children and their families?).

LIVING ARRANGEMENTS

Retirement is often the occasion of a major decision about living arrangements. Should we keep the house or get a smaller apartment? Should we seek out a better climate or stay here where we have roots? Do we want to be closer to our married children or to strike out on our own? Should we move now to a retirement complex that has medical and other support services available in case we may need these as we grow older? Whatever the decision made concerning living arrangements, it will have significant effect on the development of a post-retirement life style.

PSYCHOLOGICAL TASKS OF RETIREMENT

Retirement is a social transition that has significant personal ramifications. Retirement invites a reassessment of life; it can provoke feelings of both accomplishment and loss; it can bring under review our sense of security and our understanding of what life means. The experience can challenge the way we see ourselves as well as the way we are seen by others.

IDENTIFICATION AS AN OLDER PERSON

Retirement marks the movement into mature age. To be retired is to be old, at least as society sees it. One of the challenges of the retirement experience is to come to terms with what it means to be identified as an older person.

Many retired persons have a healthy resistance to being identified as old. Our culture's stereotyped images of aging are sufficiently negative that few of us would want to be so described. Americans see the aged as sedentary, lonely, poor, helpless, and uninteresting.[3] Little wonder so many choose to place themselves outside that category! Most people over sixty-five testify that this description does not fit their own experience of growing older and being old. They report that, for them personally, life after retirement holds a mixture of possibility and problems, of satisfactions and disappointments, not unlike the patterns of life at other stages. But it is significant that older persons do not see their experience as a sign that the negative cultural stereotypes of aging are wrong. Instead they feel that they are the fortunate exceptions. True, their own lives continue to be interesting and useful and enjoyable, but they see "most old people" in the same negative light as do younger Americans.

Their resistance to seeing themselves as old may serve them well, in that it shows that they are unwilling to accept these negative images. But there are at least two less fortunate results. They are likely to resist associations with other retired people, who, after all, *are* "old" and therefore undesirable. This resistance will close many possibilities for developing new social ties with people of a similar age. The tendency toward isolation not only contributes to loneliness, it works against the sense of social cohesion and common purpose that can result in effective political action by older persons.

There is a second negative result of this reluctance among retired persons to identify themselves as old. The stereotypes of aging are not challenged and the inaccurate myths of the post-retirement years as a time of personal difficulty and dissatisfaction are perpetuated. We are all thereby deprived of a rich variety of models of mature age.

RE-EXAMINING PERSONAL IDENTITY AND MEANING

Adult life is a continuing process of development—taking on new tasks, letting go of previous responsibilities, and changing in response to the demands of ongoing relationships. Every major life event (marriage, parenthood, career movement, illness) requires such personal reorganization. The transition of retirement falls into this pattern. At retirement we will let go of some involvements of mid-life (the former daily work schedule and "on-the-job" responsibilities); we may keep some (continuing relationships with friends from the workplace) and modify others (using job skills in a volunteer capacity or in a part-time job). We will be asked to change—to "give up"—some aspects of who we have been and to take up new roles and relationships.

The transition of retirement can be more difficult than some earlier adult changes. At retirement what we are giving up (personal and social identity as a worker) is often much clearer than what it is we will gain (since our culture's images and expectations of post-retirement life are vague and often negative).

Even in its ambiguity, however, retirement can mark a movement into a new stage of personality expansion. The event of retirement and the personal changes and choices it provokes can raise the larger question of the meaning of our own lives. Now, with most of life behind us, we face the question of its significance. This can be an anxious question.

Moving into mature age we feel ourselves being removed from many of the sources to which we have customarily turned to find an answer. Frequently we may have looked to our productive involvement in the world or to social responsibilities for confirmation of our current value and long-term significance. But the changes of retirement—both those we choose and those that are forced—alter these sources of personal meaning. In aging, some forms of productivity may decrease or motivation in work may change. We may be required to retire or to shift work responsibilities. We may choose to do so for positive reasons (I want to spend my time differently) or negative (I experience declining vigor or poor health). We might see ourselves replaced by others—by persons who are younger rather than by persons more experienced. Does accumulated experience, then, that factor which is our particular advantage as we grow older, count for nothing?

These changes affect the meaning we derive from being a productive person. And our relationship to what we have produced also changes. The works of our hands are less under our control. Children and junior colleagues move out on their own. Pet projects are now being directed by others. The meaning we have achieved in what we have produced, while not denied, is nevertheless altered.

As the question of meaning comes to prominence in the mature years, it arouses a range of responses. Attitudes of self-acceptance, integrity, and wholeness struggle against a pervading sense of despair and disgust. Each of these is a possible response to the ambiguous evidence of life; each is a possible judgment of our own lives.

The psychological challenge of mature age, then, focuses upon evaluation of our own lives as either meaningful or absurd. The challenge is favorably resolved when affirmation outweighs despair. We move toward a basic appreciation of our life as having been good, appropriate, and of some value beyond ourselves. But the challenge of meaning in mature age is not always resolved successfully. As we face our own aging we may find it difficult to accept the shape and limits of our own lives. And we fear that death will come "too soon"—before we can make sense of life, before we can somehow endow it with significance.

Maturity in mature age does not do away with despair or with the fear of death. The strain between affirmation and doubt is not resolved. There remains a dynamic tension, but one in which—ultimately—meaning prevails.[4]

RETIREMENT AS A LIFE PASSAGE

Retirement, then, is an expectable social transition, one which has its own opportunities and tasks. It has become, to borrow a phrase from anthropology, one of the life passages of American culture. Significant life passages—such as puberty or marriage or parenthood—can be understood as transitions with three stages.[5] The first is an experience of being *separated* from a former state. Something is being taken away; we lose something of what we have been. The middle stage is an experience of being *in between*—we are no longer who we used to be, but have not yet reached a sense of what we are becoming. This can be a period of confusion and disorientation. The final stage of the passage is one of *resolution*. We know ourselves and are known by others in a new role in the community. Many cultures develop "rites of passage" to assist persons as they move through these critical phases of the major transitions of life.[6]

Retirement has only recently become one of the expectable life transitions of American culture. It can be instructive to explore these stages in the passage of retirement and to examine ways in which communities may assist in this important and expectable transition.

The separation stage of retirement occurs in the "retiring" of a person's social identity. For many decades we have been known (and have known ourselves) in part through what we do. We might be a salesman or a secretary or a lawyer. At retirement, this role in society, this social identity, is changed or even removed. We can expect some experience of threat and loss as we are separated from this role and its familiar signs of our worth.

In the middle stage of this passage one might experience disorientation and even anxiety. As we let go the signs of a former social identity, to what can one look forward? What kind of life is there after retirement? The third stage of the passage of retirement, that of resolution and reincorporation, occurs as the retired person finds a satisfying way to live this new experience and to contribute to the community. This resolution will include an ability to enjoy leisure without feeling guilty, to care for younger generations without meddling, and to find new indications of personal value and worth apart from social and economic productivity.

Such a successful resolution of this passage of retirement does not happen automatically or by magic. It depends intimately on the resources of the person retiring and on the responses of the person's loved ones and community. These responses can be thought of as the rites of passage for retirement. "Rites of passage" may conjure up images of tribal medicine men and esoteric ceremonies. But these rites can be understood more broadly as the efforts of a group to care for its members in certain key, potentially dangerous, moments in life.

Rites function to *protect* and to *predict.* They protect persons in transition by helping them to identify and acknowledge the danger of the passage. Our own passage is located within a larger history or myth which "makes sense" of these changes. Rites allow us to look into the eye of the danger, to "see through" it, instead of retreating or refusing to acknowledge our fears.

As rites protect, they also predict. With rites a community foresees a good outcome to the passage. In ritual stories and testimonies, we learn that others before us have survived the passage. Not only have they survived, they have grown and flourished. Ritual pre-dicts, that is, it prophesies to us (when we are too confused or frightened to see it for ourselves) that a new stage in life awaits us and that we are able to move toward this new life.

RETIREMENT AS A RELIGIOUS EVENT

If the humanist can see in retirement a critical human passage which demands rites to assist the transition, a Christian may see here a sacramental transition.[7] Such a transition appears to a believer as not only a time of danger, but also as a special opportunity for learning and growth—as a time of grace and the visitation of God. How can the Christian tradition bring its heritage of religious value and ritual to bear on this life passage? Let us consider some elements that might be included in religious rites of passage at retirement. In the initial stages of the transition the community of faith can provide opportunities for persons who are retiring (and their spouses) to acknowledge the changes they face and to talk about the distress they may experience. This may take the form of adult education programming, pre-retirement counseling, and prayer and support groups. These protective environments can encourage those retiring to share their expectations and apprehensions and thus to face the passage rather than to ignore or avoid it.

During the middle period of the transition, an initial distress or uneasiness may develop into a more sustained ambiguity. The lurking questions may surface: "Am I more than what I do; no longer able to identify myself with my job, who am I; do I have worth beyond what I have accomplished?" A religious community at this point can assist in recalling that separation from our former social identity and its signs of worth can have religious significance. This separation invites one to a level of self-acceptance that a busy, achievement-oriented adult life may well have obscured. Worth is, finally, not in productivity. Personal value is founded in something more basic than power or responsibility or salary. It rests on the rock of God's love. The cultural phenomenon of retirement can thus serve a religious function. Separating us from accumulated credentials and accustomed "proofs of merit," it invites us to acknowledge a value in life beyond and prior to human achievement.

Other questions and anxieties may arise in the heart of the passage. Retirement may seem to say that we are not good for anything anymore, that we are useless. At different points in our lives we find ourselves in "useless" time: periods of illness or recuperation, times of prayer or play or vacation—when we are not "earning our way." We may have felt uncomfortable in these nonproductive moments and resisted their apparent uselessness. Yet we have often recognized the importance of these periods, times that in their very emptiness create space for new insight, for deeper appreciation, for renewed commitment. Retirement invites us into a similar experience of being nonproductive. How are we to confront this challenge to our usefulness? How can the Church assist us?

In its ministry to retirement a Christian community will devise and celebrate ways in which its senior members can continue to contribute to the community of faith. But this ministry of inclusion must not overshadow an equally important and parallel ministry. At the heart of Christianity, as well as other religious traditions, is the celebration of *uselessness*. We are not sufficient to our own salvation; our lives—

our relationship with God—are a gift. We have not generated ourselves; we cannot, finally, justify ourselves.

This intuition of the gracefulness of life can have special significance for us at retirement. Christian rites of passage at retirement will announce to us all—in a special way to those of us moving through retirement—the good news of our uselessness. The aging person in the Christian community stands as a sign of what we have always believed, even if we have found it difficult to live: Christians are not justified or validated by their works or their achievements and credentials. Retirement can thus serve (ironically) a religious function in separating us from our roles and social identity. The Church assists us in embracing this event through an interpretation of its religious significance. I do not have to do *anything* to be loved by God, to be a part of this community of faith.

The Taoist tradition, of all the world's religious heritages, has most exuberantly celebrated such uselessness. Arguing that it is human interference in life that disrupts development, Chuang Tzu tells of certain trees whose gnarled features and uselessness provided them with extraordinary longevity and of the crippled person whose uselessness for war guaranteed him a lengthy life. Chuang Tzu concludes: "All men know the use of the useful, but nobody knows the use of the useless."[8]

A community will certainly provide roles and activities for its mature members, but not as ways for them to earn respect. The community will make use of the many talents of its seniors, but not to prove their continued usefulness. Through its creative ministry of rites of passage at retirement, the religious community will celebrate the special witness of this stage of life: an emptying out of credentials and a celebration of the grace-filled uselessness of the children of God.

THE MINISTRY OF MATURE CHRISTIANS

The religious community will provide opportunities for its retiring members to embrace both the threat and the special invitations of this life passage. It may also be expected to construct a rite of celebration which welcomes individuals out of this passage and into their new stage of maturity. Such a celebration—in the parish or the family or the support group—would highlight a new role, one not limited to economic productivity and social usefulness, but one which witnesses to the Christian's deepest relationship with God. This celebration will also acknowledge to the believing community the special contribution of its maturest members: their personal testimony to the meaningfulness of life.

Psychologists have alerted us to the process of life review through which older adults reflect on the positive and negative elements of their own lives as they seek a fuller appreciation of its uniqueness and meaning.[9] If this is a psychological task, it is also a religious one. In religious recollection *(anamnesis)* believers recover the meaning of the past for the present—in Jesus' life, but also in the "deposit of faith" which is their own life history. Religious communities can assist this psycho-religious task by supporting older persons in this effort at integration and by celebrating its fruits.

As such a life review is successfully achieved, the older person is delivered from an obsessive need to return to the past with either guilt or nostalgia. The past, one's personal history, can become a resource for the community—further witness to the goodness of life and to God's presence in it, even in the face of life's ambiguity and limits. Here the resolution of a psychological task (the challenge to come to terms with the meaning of our own life) becomes a public gift, a ministry to be given to the next generation of believers. Older adults can stand as signs that life taken as a whole has a meaning and a direction. Only they can show us that the wisdom of Christianity is adequate to the full report of a human life span. Perhaps here we touch something of the particular witness of *widows* in early Christianity and *sages* within the Asian religious traditions.

The religious rites of passage at retirement, therefore, must include not only the ministry of the community to its aging members, but also the recognition and celebration of the ministry of mature Christians: the testimony of a life of faith. In caring for mature Christians through the development of these rites, we assist them (and ourselves) to come to a better appreciation of how they in turn are to continue to care for the community.

NOTES

1. For an overview of current research evidence concerning retirement in the United States, see Dan Fritz, *The Changing Retirement Scene: A Challenge for Decision Makers* (Los Angeles, Calif.: University of Southern California Press, 1978).
2. Bernice L. Neugarten, "The Future and the Young-Old," *The Gerontologist* 15 (February, 1975): 4–9.
3. Louis Harris and Associates, *The Myth and Reality of Aging in America* (Washington, D.C.: National Council on the Aging, 1975), pp. 41–69. See also pp. 128–164 for a discussion of the discrepancy between this view and the acutal experience of older persons.
4. Erik Erikson explores this struggle for personal meaning in "Dr. Borg's Life-Cycle" in *Adulthood*, ed. Erik Erikson (New York: Norton, 1978), pp. 1–28.
5. Victor Turner's particular interest is the experience of liminality or marginality in such passages, which he sees as a potential experience of the sacred. See his *The Ritual Process: Structure and Anti-Structure* (New York: Cornell University Press, 1977) and "Passages, Margins, and Poverty: Religious Symbols of Communitas," *Worship* 46 (1972): 390–412, 482–494.
6. In the discussion of rites of passage, Turner and others are indebted to the work at the beginning of this century of Arnold van Gennep. See van Gennep, *Rites of Passage*, trans. Monika B. Vizedom and Gabrielle L. Caffe (Chicago: University of Chicago Press, 1960).
7. Christian sacraments of passage have focused especially on entry into life (Baptism), entry into adult commitment (Matrimony and Ordination), and entry into death (Extreme Unction or the rite of the sick). Retirement, as distinguished from illness or death, appears in our time as a new and significant passage to which a sacramental ministry might well respond. For an expanded consideration of such a sacramental ministry, see Evelyn Eaton Whitehead and James D. Whitehead, *Christian Life Patterns* (New York: Doubleday, 1979), especially "To Grow Old Among Christians," pp. 181–200.
8. See *The Complete Works of Chuang Tzu*, ed. Burton Watson (New York: Columbia University Press, 1968), p. 67.
9. Robert N. Butler, "The Life Review: An Interpretation of Reminiscence in the Aged," in *Middle Age and Aging*, ed. Bernice L. Neugarten (Chicago: University of Chicago Press, 1968), pp. 486–496.

9

Ethical Aspects of Aging in America

John C. Bennett

Before discussing ethical issues, society must move away from common yet inaccurate stereotypes about aging. Accurate judgments about what the elderly (persons over sixty-five years of age) can do and about what provisions society can make for them depend on this correction.

To speak in broad terms, what can be said about people between sixty-five and eighty is different from what can be said about those over eighty. In the thirty- to thirty-five-year age spread between sixty-five and ninety-five (and above), in addition to the enormous age differences the differences between individuals regardless of age are remarkable. I live in a retirement center and am impressed by the capacity for creative activity of many individuals in their late eighties, and sometimes into their nineties. Society's stereotypes of the elderly as people who are unhealthy, ingrown, inactive, out-of-date in their ideas, rigid, and vulnerable to "senility," often have the effect of self-fulfilling prophecies. When these stereotypes influence public policies or the policies within institutions for the elderly, they produce serious injustices.

Some observers use the word "ageism" to indicate parallels with "sexism" and "racism." There is, however, a difference: *anyone* who lives long enough, regardless of sex or race or any other social differentiation, will be vulnerable to this type of discrimination.[1]

THE MORAL RESPONSIBILITY OF SOCIETY

The injustice of the usual sterotypes of the elderly obscures their capacity for a meaningful, useful, and satisfying life. This, however, does not mean that they do not have special needs. Retirement, though it may not be tied so generally to age sixty-five, does inevitably mean that older people become dependent on provisions made by society as a whole. This includes their own savings, their contributions to Social Security, and private pension plans. Circumstances can easily force many elderly people to live in impoverished conditions. According to a recent estimate, six out of every ten older Americans are poor.[2] One aspect of their poverty is that, as Robert Butler has put it: "Many, I think most, elderly poor become poor after becoming old."[3] The contrast between so much conspicuous wealth and their fall into poverty, which is a psychological shock in old age, is a moral offense.

Moral offense though it be, the question often raised is, How can society afford to provide the material conditions for an externally good life for so many who are not economically productive? Does society have an obligation to do better than it is now doing for the elderly? Most readers of this book will readily answer "yes," but there is more to be said. One of the few published attempts to seek an answer to that question in ethical terms leads the author, Donald Marquis, to curious results. He has an intuitive conviction that society should have more beneficient policies in relation to the elderly, but he finds that the ethical systems with which he is familiar do not clearly confirm his intuition.[4]

I think we can make best moral sense of society's responsibility for the elderly by thinking of it as a matter of justice. Should we not think of justice as including provisions for the well-being of humanity at each stage of the life cycle? The test of the justice of institutions and policies should be their effect on all persons. The years of productivity create claims for producers in their years of retirement. But being human involves claims beyond what one has earned. Here justice is raised through love to higher levels of sensitivity and compassion.[5]

While society is not altogether consistent in its practice, there are many indications that we judge ourselves and our institutions by the degree to which provisions are made for the handicapped of all kinds. Christian ethics is clear about this; it puts emphasis on caring for those who, for whatever reasons, are in greatest need. Those who are guided by Christian ethics cannot evade the judgment in Jesus' story of the Last Judgment in Matthew 25, in the parable of the Good Samaritan, and in the pervasive emphasis in the Gospels on the moral claims of the poor.

There are two considerations which may enable productive people, who are most sure that they have earned their advantages, to accept their part in the support of the elderly.

The first is that the present producers will themselves become elderly and, as things go, will probably live even longer than those who are now elderly. This means all that they do to support better retirement incomes and better conditions of life for the elderly will create or maintain structures and policies from which they themselves will benefit in due time.

The second consideration is that younger producers in many cases have living parents and feel (or should feel) some responsibility for them now. Under present conditions this responsibility usually cannot be discharged by including parents in their own homes, as was so often done in the past. Moreover, it is better for parents not to be financially dependent on their children; the problem is too immense to be solved entirely through the private efforts of individual families. The great increase in the span of life and the staggering medical costs for the elderly aggravate the problem so much that for most people it can only be adequately dealt with through public planning on a national scale.

The Social Security system has been an enormous help to the elderly. Even so, a Social Security income—the only income that many elderly people have—does not generally keep people out of poverty. Unfortunately, Social Security exemplifies the familiar words taken out of context, "to everyone that hath shall be given": those who were in the lower income brackets as producers now receive miserably low incomes. The SSI (Supplementary Security Income) represents a move away from this principle, but there is clearly a need to increase income somehow so that all can live their last years above the poverty line.

The vulnerability of the aging to illness gives them an enormous stake in whatever new provisions are agreed upon to make medical care available to the whole population. Medicare was a very important breakthrough, however, the difference between the actual medical charges and the amount allowed by Medicare often results in a crushing burden for those who do not have other forms of health insurance.

Perhaps the greatest gap in current insurance provision for the elderly is the area of a catastrophic illness that extends far beyond the limits of Medicare. New alternatives, such as home care, should be studied, and new legislation should be enacted to correct inequities.

THE MUTUAL OBLIGATION OF CHILDREN AND PARENTS

Children generally recognize that they have a significant responsibility for their elderly parents. I have said that this usually takes a different form than it once did when parents could be expected to live with their children. That arrangement was more manageable when people lived on farms or in good-sized houses with a large number of children, and in a community where the parents had lived and found moral and social support from friends, other relatives, and activities in the community. It is now quite different. Children, often with both husband and wife employed outside the home, live in smaller houses or apartments in communities that are strange to their parents. Also, each generation needs and benefits from independence from the other. Living together can indeed create strains between two or three generations, so it is often best for them to live separately but near each other. This makes it possible for children to offer parents help as they need it, and allows them to continue contacts that express mutual love and provide mutual moral support. In particular cases, of course, the best solution to problems created by weakness or illness might be for parents to live with children, or in a nursing home.

It is fortunate for both parents and children when the former choose to enter a retirement community which has several levels of living and care, including a nursing unit. The value of this is that the parents take the initiative and that the nursing unit is a part of a larger community. Though this choice is becoming more and more common, it is usually too expensive to be the normal route.

When parents are in nursing homes—and this is true when they have put themselves there by way of a retirement community—children still have a responsibility to keep alert about the living conditions and the medical treatment which their parents receive. Here the knowledge that we have concerning the reversibility of many of the conditions that give rise to senility is most important. Does the nursing home work at such possibilities of reversal? Does it take the easy course of keeping patients too drugged? Does it provide space for privacy? Does it encourage contact with people outside? Does it allow patients to keep some of their prized possessions which can provide continuity with their past lives and help them to preserve their sense of identity? On matters of this kind children should be advocates for their parents.

Yet a large proportion of people in nursing homes have no children or close relatives who are near them. Therefore, churches or councils of churches and other voluntary agencies need to make it their responsibility to know about nursing homes in the community and to be advocates for patients who need such help.

When we consider the plight of the aging who are chronically ill or very old, there is nothing more important than keeping conditions in nursing homes under continual public scrutiny. No other country has such a large proportion of such institutions run for profit. Critics of this situation admit that many profit-making institutions are well administered—professionally and humanely—but there is a built-in conflict of interest between giving the best possible service to the residents and efforts to increase profits.[6] Competition often works well when people have the capacity to choose among hotels or airlines, for example.

But people in nursing homes usually have neither the strength nor the funds to choose. They may become so dependent on the institution that there is no alternative but to accept whatever exploitation they experience. People who are weak and vulnerable, who have no bargaining power and no defenders, are the most likely to be taken advantage of by those with power over their lives. There are few more destructive symptoms of the sin which is such a pervasive human condition.

There is widespread awareness of abuses in nursing homes; many laws have been passed to protect people against such abuse. But there seems to be great difficulty in enforcing them.[7] At any one time there are about 1,000,000 elderly persons in such institutions. There are also an uncounted number of the elderly in small boarding houses, single-occupancy apartment houses, or hotels who are neglected and in misery. Many of them live in sections of cities where they are afraid to go out because of the dangers of mugging or even sadistic violence. And far too often the elderly are risking their lives in fire traps. It is fitting that Robert Butler, in an important book on the elderly, *Why Survive?* entitled his first chapter, "The Tragedy of Old Age in America."

ENABLING FREEDOM OF CHOICE

The people who are classified as elderly include millions who are fully able to take advantage of great freedom of choice. Yet for many stereotyping seriously limits that freedom of choice. So does poverty. The choice between living independently, in one's own home or in a retirement community, and being institutionalized, is of decisive importance. Often a choice can be provided by social provisions for home-care.

One central area of decision is the choice between retiring and continuing to work at a job in which one has had experience and which has been very fulfilling. Forced retirement at sixty-five has long been accepted by business and many institutions, but today it is under serious question. Laws forbidding forced retirement before seventy have been enacted in several states, and a federal law to this effect—which allows for important exceptions—is creating a new problem situation. The issue is very controversial, and it will be some time before there is much wisdom as to how justice can be done to both older and younger people, and as to how best to preserve for the community contributions from older people who are near the peak of their capacities, without imposing rules that might discourage innovations and fresh approaches. Certainly the contributions of experienced and able people should not be recklessly discarded as is often the case today; arbitrary absolutes about retirement age should be abandoned.

One fact that has been uncovered in recent investigations is somewhat surprising, but it does reduce the dimensions of the problem: the great majority of people *want* to retire at sixty-five or earlier. This is not to say that for any one of these people retirement is not a traumatic experience; separation from the job often means loss of prized associations. The idea of retirement, particularly if one's job is not very interesting and if commuting takes two hours a day, may seem in advance the greatest possible good. However, after one has had enough of the anticipated satisfactions of leisure, having no place to go regularly away from home, the attractions of retirement may pall.

People do not choose to retire from the most interesting and creative jobs. In political life age seems to be a very secondary factor. The list of people over sixty-five who have continued to make important contributions to art and literature, to humanistic scholarship and science and thought, and to religious leadership and statesmanship, is well known. The world would be very different today if Pope John XXIII had retired at sixty-five.

CONTINUING RESPONSIBILITIES

Whether one retires at sixty-five or in the early seventies, the following period of life should not be a long vacation from responsibility to make contributions to society. This responsibility will change, and the nature of the change will differ so much from person to person that it is difficult to generalize. Part-time work in the person's area of competence and experience or voluntary work in community and

church may fulfill a portion of the responsibilities. There will be a
wide variety of family responsibilities, many of them new, especially
if one member of a couple is ill or handicapped. There should be
more time for rest than in one's earlier years, and more time for hobbies
which may once have been crowded out.

There should be more emphasis on continuing education, whether
on one's own or as part of the many programs sponsored by schools,
colleges, churches, and other associations in the community. Keeping
the mind working and moving into new areas of intellectual activity
can help to prevent the deterioration of mental faculties often associated
with old age. For many individuals such deterioration is unavoidable
at some stage, but to assume that this must be the experience of the
majority is to perpetuate a false stereotype. Continuing education also
enables people to make new and unexpected contributions to the community, giving support to opportunities for responsible citizenship that
come with extended leisure and greater freedom of action.

At this point I want to call attention to a remarkable change in
thinking by those who specialize in the problems of the aging. In
the early 1960s it was said that it is natural for the elderly to become
more preoccupied with their inner world, more preoccupied with the
self; society tends to withdraw from them and they respond affirmatively
from within to this withdrawal. This picture of things gained the dignity
of being called "the disengagement theory." It was propounded as a
discovery that would provide major illumination for the lives of the
elderly. The theory has some truth, for disengagement from many
activities and relationships does take place. Retirement, decreased mobility, and the death of contemporaries obviously do mean disengagement. The theory did provide one important piece of advice: do not
try to hold on desperately to all your familiar activities and relationships,
identifying your sense of self-worth with them. There will be necessary
withdrawals which should be accepted without any diminution of oneself. This is good advice both psychologically and ethically. Compulsive
interference with the world of one's previous responsibilities can be
destructive both for oneself and for one's successors.

However, the truth in this theory does not make it a self-sufficient source of ethical guidance. Greater attention to one's inner world is good; it may deepen one's self-understanding and sense of the meaning of life in a religious context. But this need not be the same thing as egoism or self-preoccupation. Disengagement should be selective, and should be accompanied by or followed by *re-engagement*. The serenity that comes from accepting necessary disengagement need not become apathy or complacency.

Older people have important responsibilities as citizens. When this is mentioned, often the first thought is about the "senior power" being used to achieve more just conditions for older people themselves. I believe that the use of the power of the elderly as citizens should not be limited to the goals that have importance only for their welfare. They have broader responsibilities, and more discrimination is needed in thinking about the aging as a group with considerable political power. The aging are not a social class. Their children are among "the others," among those who are not yet elderly. Everyone in the nation who lives long enough will be elderly and will benefit from the political achievements of those who are now in that age bracket.

It is not selfish to organize a group of people in order to gain advantages, if those advantages can be defended as just—especially if they are remedies for poverty, exploitation, or injurious neglect. An organized group usually consists of people who have had the most vivid experiences of conditions which should be the concern of society as a whole. People best know where the shoe pinches when they are the victims. Our understanding is limited when we have not experienced what other people suffer. Statistics help us to learn the range of need or the results of injustice and neglect, but it takes more than that to enter into the intensity of a wrong that society continues to permit. Political pressure from organized older citizens should be a creative element in American politics.

The aging will need to pay close attention to details of legislation that directly affect them. They obviously have a great stake in all the changes that will come about as efforts are made to provide a more secure financial base for Social Security. They should carefully watch the struggle to enact new legislation to make medical care more available to all. For example, will the legislation encourage alternatives to expensive and often depersonalizing institutional care rather than discourage as do the existing laws governing Medicare and Medicaid. They have a great stake in more effective regulation of nursing homes, more adequate provision for inspection of nursing homes, and for the enforcement of those laws. There are various kinds of organizations that can help keep the elderly informed about legislation as it is moving through Congress, and can help organize them as voters to bring pressure on the decision-makers in government. The Gray Panthers, the National Council of Senior Citizens, and the American Association of Retired Persons, for example, have different roles, and respond to different preferences, but all will inform older people as legislation is enacted or policies formed.

Older people have a special contribution to make on broader public issues in our national life and in international relations; some of which, as we know, involve human survival. They may have a better chance to have more independent judgments and freedom to choose and act than many people who live under the immediate pressures in business, politics, or other forms of institutional life. The combination of pension and leisure should free one to take positions on controversial issues which might be difficult to take if one feared they might reflect on one's institutions or hinder advancement or security. In spite of the legally supported freedoms that we have in this country, there are millions of people who are inhibited in their freedom by what is expected by "the company." Thus, stereotypes of older people as generally holding rigidly to the views of another time, are mistaken.

"THE RIGHT TO DIE" AND "DEATH WITH DIGNITY"

The ethics of aging includes complex and controversial questions about actions that directly or indirectly hasten death. The question continually arises in cases of a terminal illness that condemns a person to a future of long unconscious existence or unrelieved pain. Few subjects related to death are more discussed in both medical ethics and ethics informing legal policy.

The moral tradition of the West, with its origins in Christian moral theology, has been adamant in its opposition to suicide and euthanasia. Positive euthanasia, or mercy killing, is called "murder" by the compassionate moral theologian Bernard Häring.[8] It is said to be taking an innocent life, and that is the end of the argument. However, liberal Protestants long ago broke the taboo about euthanasia. A petition addressed to the New York legislature in the 1940s asked that the law be amended "to permit voluntary euthanasia for incurable sufferers." Remarkably, it was signed by fifty-five Episcopal and thirty-three Baptist ministers, along with ministers from a number of other denominations.[9]

The traditional Christian attitude toward suicide has been cruel, and it is a blot on the history of the Church. Some churches have denied Christian burial to suicides, though today there is a growing tendency to deal in an understanding and pastoral way with suicides and their families.

A decisive development occurred when authorities and moral theologians in the Roman Catholic Church accepted the principle that it is permissible to withhold life supports from some patients who are incurable, unconscious, or in hopeless pain. In 1957 Pope Pius XII gave the signal for this, and today negative euthanasia, or the withholding of "extraordinary means" for keeping persons alive, has come to be widely accepted both in churches and in secular society. There was the beginning of legal acceptance in the very sad Quinlan case. Significantly, the priests who were advising the Quinlan family supported the parents' decision to turn off life-support systems.

The high courts in at least two states, New Jersey and Massachusetts, have given permission for withholding life-supports under some circumstances. In 1976 the California legislature passed "The Natural Death Act," which provided for the right of a patient to refuse treatment, and authorized a directive by a patient to physicians against life-sustaining procedures.[10] This law is too limited because the directive has legal force only if it is signed by persons *after* they are informed that they have a terminal illness. This means that the law would not apply if a patient is incompetent and therefore unable to be informed about the illness. Since 1976 seven other states have passed similar laws, and they are under consideration in many others.

The so-called "living will," which gives a directive to physicians to withhold life-supports under appropriate circumstances, has been in use for some time. It is signed when one is competent and its directive applies to later situations, whether or not one is competent. It does not have legal force, but it may help physicians decide whether to initiate or withdraw life-supports. Physicians have often made these decisions quite apart from the legal situation. There is a problem in using the words "extraordinary" or "heroic" to describe the means to be withheld (i.e., the extraordinary may soon become ordinary). A further development of thought and practice includes the idea that where all remedy is in vain, therapy should be withheld while at the same time doing whatever is possible for the patient's comfort. This has been stated as the policy of the prestigious Massachusetts General Hospital.[11]

Moral authority has also developed for giving drugs to people in great pain, even though the drugs are known to shorten life. Such a policy should be regarded as a step toward positive euthanasia, although the shortening of life is a secondary effect, not the intention. This is a familiar distinction in Catholic moral theology. (Reference is made here to Catholic thinking because Catholic moral theologians have tended to be more precise in this area than Protestant students of Christian ethics. Since they have started with a strongly negative position on euthanasia, every move they make toward greater flexibility becomes extremely important for students of ethics in general.)

Moral permission for indirect euthanasia has wide support. What can be said about positive euthanasia? Not only has traditional Christian teaching been adamant against it, but so have the legal and the medical traditions. Because mercy killing is deliberate and premeditated, in the U.S. it is legally classified as first-degree murder. Since malice is involved in first-degree murder, while mercy killing is not malicious in intent, it is not possible to deal with it fairly under the present law. When cases have arisen, juries have sometimes refused to convict, and judges may give minimal sentences. Yet, anyone who feels driven to engage in mercy killing, perhaps as an accomplice of suicide, runs a considerable legal risk.

Careful, still quite limited movement is being made toward the acceptance of direct euthanasia. Charles Curran, one of the most influential Roman Catholic moral theologians, suggests that he has some doubt about the distinction between indirect and direct euthanasia since both have the same intent. This makes him more flexible about positive euthanasia.[12] Especially notable is the very cautious movement in the thought of Paul Ramsey, who has always been reluctant to admit the moral permissibility of positive euthanasia. He does now admit that in extreme cases of hopeless suffering, or when a person is permanently in a comatose condition, direct euthanasia may be permitted.[13]

A much more decisive opening up of ethical thinking to the acceptance of positive euthanasia are the thoughts of Daniel Maguire, who presents the ethical and legal aspects of the subject very helpfully.[14] A lay theologian and moralist, his roots are in Catholic moral theology, and he moves very carefully into new territory. I take for granted the more decisive support for positive euthanasia that has been present for a long time in many liberal religious circles of which Joseph Fletcher is the most articulate representative.[15]

Three objections are commonly raised to any movement in this direction. One is the sanctity of all life. Those who take these reluctant steps toward accepting positive euthanasia believe that mere physical life may lose all the qualities that justify our regarding it as either human or sacred. In a theological context, another objection is that this is to assume a prerogative that belongs only to God. However, using medical science to prolong life beyond the point at which its human quality justifies efforts to preserve it, can itself be seen as an example of human agency assuming a divine prerogative. In both cases, there is the tendency to see the action of God as present only when we let nature take its course. Can we not see God as active in medical science and in the human caring that seeks to counteract some of the results of medical prolongation of life? There is no end to the puzzles when we try to relate divine action and human freedom, but these should not cause us to deny either of them.

Even those who have responded to the first two objections are troubled by the danger that direct action to take a life may have a "domino effect," leading to other practices on a larger scale, perhaps to eliminate people for social or political purposes. I recognize the dangers of this possibility. When it is discussed, the practices of the Nazis are always used as an illustration. Negative euthanasia, it seems to me, lends itself less than positive euthanasia to schemes of this sort. I believe, however, that ethical thinking and law should guard against these dangers. If we are convinced that there are situations in which positive euthanasia is justified, we should not sacrifice persons to our ideas about a remote danger against which there are many steps that can be taken to protect society.

I have mentioned cruel treatment of suicides by the Church and the law. It seems to me that suicide committed by the dying may at times be the most defensible form of positive euthanasia; it is based on the consent of the person involved and often the motive is concern for others. The suicide of the dying, who objectively have no future in this world, is entirely different from the suicide of those who are in despair only at the moment—especially the young who for a time may see only dark clouds over their future. It might be well if we could qualify this particular kind of suicide as the suicide of dying, or find another name, perhaps *terminal suicide*.

Such terminal suicide should never be contemplated without regard to objective knowledge about medical and legal aspects of a person's situation. Where possible, it should be undertaken in an atmosphere of support and open communication with those who are most loved and trusted. In any event, it should never be an example for persons in other situations. Suicide without any such justification is far too common in our society.

In what I have written about this difficult subject—the purposeful hastening of death—I have seemed to argue in terms of trends, although we well know that the latest trends are not always the best. In this case, however, I believe that the traditional positions in Christian morality and in Western law have been too much separated from concrete human experience, imposing abstract and absolute laws. One of the tendencies in the current development of ethical thinking is to pay greater attention to living and changing experience, to the exceptional situations which produce exceptional hardship and suffering. There is now less tendency to sacrifice individual persons to an abstraction. I believe that this humanizing of ethics is a better expression of love and compassion than is the absolutism of the ethical and legal tradition, and it is, therefore, more in harmony with the ethic of love itself, which is at the heart of the Judeo-Christian tradition and the humane secular ethic that has been influenced by it.

NOTES

1. Robert N. Butler, *Why Survive? Being Old in America* (New York: Harper & Row, 1975), p. 11.
2. Robert Atchley, *The Social Forces in Later Life—An Introduction to Social Gerontology*, 2nd ed. (Belmont, Calif.: Wadsworth Publishing Co., 1977), p. 125.
3. Butler, *Why Survive*, pp. 24–25.
4. Donald Marquis, "Ethics and the Elderly: Some Problems" in *Aging and the Elderly*, ed. Spicker, Woodward, and Van Tassel (Atlantic Highlands, N.J.: Humanities Press), pp. 341–355. Professor Marquis does not find the kind of confirmation he wants in either Kantianism or Utilitarianism. I suspect Kantians might find that treating older people as ends in themselves would point to more beneficent policies. Utilitarians, who are systematic ethicists, might rationalize some degree of sacrifice of the elderly for the sake of the happiness of the majority, but they would be unhappy about it, and perhaps the majority would be unhappy, too.
5. The relation between love and justice is much discussed in Christian ethics. Most often there is an emphasis on the idea that while they are not identical, they should interpenetrate each other. In this context justice is raised to a new level of sensitivity by love, and in other contexts justice may keep love from taking the form of oppressive paternalism. Paul Tillich used the adjectives "creative," "dynamic," and "transforming" to describe the justice that is so influenced by love in *Love, Power, and Justice* (New York and London: Oxford University Press, 1954), chap. 4.
6. Robert N. Butler and Myrna L. Lewis, *Aging and Mental Health*, 2nd ed. (St. Louis: C. V. Mosby Co., 1977), p. 244.
7. The laws governing nursing homes and the problems of enforcement are discussed in *The Rights of Older People*, ed. Brown, Allo, Freeman, and Netzorg (New York: Avon Books, 1979), especially chap. 8.
8. Bernard Häring, *The Law of Christ*, vol. 3 (Cork, Ireland: The Mercier Press, 1967), p. 214. Father Häring in many ways bridges the gap between traditional and recent postconciliar moral theology. This statement is fully traditional.
9. This petition says: "We no longer believe that God wills the prolongation of physical torture for the benefit of the soul of the sufferer . . . We believe that such a

sufferer has the right to die, and that Society should grant that right." The petition was initiated by a letter signed by five of the most distinguished Protestant liberals of that period: W. Russell Bowie, Henry Sloane Coffin, Harry Emerson Fosdick, John Howard Lathrop, and Guy Emery Shipler.

10. For the facts about recent legislation see *The Rights of Older People*, Chap. 10, and an article by Robert M. Veatch, "Death and Dying and the Legislative Options" in *The Hastings Center Report*, October 1977.

11. William F. May, "The Right to Die and the Obligation to Care: Allowing to Die, Killing for Mercy, and Suicide" in *No Rush to Judgment*, ed. David H. Smith and Linda M. Bernstein (Bloomington, Ind.: Poynter Center, University of Indiana, 1979).

12. Charles E. Curran, *Politics, Medicine and Christian Ethics: A Dialogue with Paul Ramsey* (Philadelphia: Fortress Press, 1973), pp. 161–162. Curran shows in the context that he has become more flexible about direct euthanasia than Father Häring, with whose spirit he has much in common. This contrast is most interesting as an illustration of a developing moral theology.

13. Paul Ramsey, *The Patient as Person* (New Haven: Yale University Press, 1970), pp. 161–162. Ramsey may have difficulty admitting that there has been as much movement in his thought as others detect, but he has opened a door that needed opening and because of his history no one could have done it with more effect.

14. Daniel C. Maguire, *Death by Choice* (New York: Schocken Books, 1974), see especially chap. 2.

15. See Joseph Fletcher, *Morals and Medicine* (Princeton, N.J.: Princeton University Press, 1954), chap. 6. Fletcher opened up discussion of the subject in this book and he has dealt with it in many contexts in subsequent writings.

10

Religion and the Elderly in Today's World

Barbara Payne

This chapter is a sociological look at religion and aging. It is concerned with the social aspects of religion from the individual and the group perspective, the factors that determine the religious patterns and participation of the aged, and the implications for religious organizations of the age structure in society.

Since 1900 the age structure of American society has undergone three dramatic changes: the baby boom of post–World War II; the fertility rate decline of the 1960s to 1970s; and the growth in size and proportion of the population over 65 years of age. The older population has increased at a greater rate than the general population, rising from 3 million in 1900 (4 percent) to 23 million (10.9 percent) in 1977. Furthermore, the fastest-growing age group is 80 years of age and older, which in 1977 comprised 20 percent of the older population. These changes are reflected in the current projections that by the year 2030, 18 percent of the population, or 55 million persons, will be over 65. The growth in the older population—the consequence of lower infant mortality rates, fertility rates, and medical technology—has been accompanied by increasing life expectancy. During this century life expectancy at birth has increased 26 years, from 42.9 years to 73 years in 1976. This growth in life expectancy has not been uniform for the total population: for white females it is 77.7 and for white males 70.0; for black females 76.6 and black males 64.6. Since the average woman lives longer than the average male, the majority of older persons are women (146 women for 100 men), comprising approximately 60 percent of the older population. America is changing from a youth to an adult population, a fact that is reflected in changes in societal orientation. Business leaders noting these changes are shifting to an emphasis on the middle-aged and older consumer (persons 45 and older). Other institutions—including churches and synagogues— are also reflecting the transition from a youth- to an adult-oriented society.

RELIGIOUS PARTICIPATION OF THE ELDERLY

The religious participation or nonparticipation of the elderly can be expected to reflect the patterns and practices of the local community and society. Variations in participation reflect period effects such as the religious "boom" of the 1950s, the sharp decline in religious interest of the 1960s and the leveling off of the 1970s. Furthermore, the older people of today were members of the children and youth cohorts that joined a church at the height of membership and participation in churches—1900–1940. (Cohort here encompasses all individuals born in the same time interval, e.g., 1915–24, 1925–34.) They have retained the memberships, and the importance they had attached to them, throughout their lives.[1] It may well be that society and the religious roles in it have changed, and not that people become more or less religious as they age.[2]

Even with all the fluctuations in religious interest, the Gallup Global Study (which covered most of the free world) found Americans to be the most religious people in the world.[3] It reports that 94 percent of Americans believe in God, 71 percent hold church or synagogue memberships, 40 percent attend a church or synagogue in a typical week, and 68 percent have confidence in organized religion. Further- more, these indicants of religious life have remained constant over the past twenty-five years. The 1976 Gallup data are remarkably consistent with the 1958 U.S. Census report that 97 percent of persons in every age category over four years of age reported a religious affiliation (see Table 1).

Table 1. RELIGION REPORTED* BY AGE, UNITED STATES,
MARCH 1957 (PERCENTAGE DISTRIBUTION)

Religion	Total (Age 14+)	Ages 14–19	Ages 20–24	Ages 25–34	Ages 35–44	Ages 45–64	Age 65+
Total	100.0	100.0	100.0	100.0	100.0	100.0	100.0
Protestant	66.2	66.9	65.0	64.8	64.5	66.6	70.0
White	57.4	56.2	54.3	55.1	55.8	58.7	63.6
Nonwhite	8.8	10.6	10.7	9.7	8.7	7.9	6.3
Roman Catholic	25.7	26.6	27.5	28.0	27.7	24.0	20.8
Jewish	3.2	2.5	2.4	2.8	3.2	4.0	3.4
Other Religion and Not Reported	2.2	2.0	2.1	1.8	2.1	2.5	2.8
No Religion	2.7	2.1	3.0	2.6	2.5	2.9	3.0

* In answer to the question: What is your religion?
SOURCE: *Current Population Reports,* 1958, P-20, no. 79, p. 7.

Like most Americans, the elderly identify with some religious group. Their predominant affiliation is Protestant (70%, which is slightly higher than for the total population, 66.2%). The decline in membership by age shown in Tables 1 and 2 is among the Roman Catholic and Jewish groups. The National Council on the Aging study, the most recent extensive analysis by age of frequency of church attendance, indicates attendance neither significantly increases nor declines with age (see Table 3).

Howard M. Bahr interprets these variations in attendance through four different models. In the traditional model there is a sharp decline in religious activity between ages eighteen and thirty, with the lowest point being between thirty and thirty-five, followed by a steady increase

Table 2.   RELIGION OF PUBLIC BY AGE
(PERCENTAGE DISTRIBUTION)

Religion	Public 18–64	Public 65 and Over
Protestant	60	70
Catholic	28	24
Jewish	3	2
Other	7	2
Not Sure	*	*

* Less than 0.5 percent

SOURCE: *The Myth and Reality of Aging in America.* A study prepared by Lou Harris Associates, Inc., for the National Council on the Aging (Washington, D.C., 1975), p. 182.

Table 3.   ATTENDANCE AT A CHURCH OR SYNAGOGUE
IN LAST YEAR OR SO

		When Attended Last				
	Attended in Last Year %	Within Last Week or Two %	A Month Ago %	2–3 Months Ago %	More Than 3 Months Ago %	Not Sure %
Total						
Public	75	71	13	7	9	*
18–64	74	70	14	7	9	*
65–Over	77	79	9	5	7	*
18–24	67	60	18	8	14	*
25–39	73	72	11	7	10	*
40–54	78	70	15	8	7	–
55–64	81	79	11	4	6	–
65–69	80	79	9	5	6	1
70–79	78	79	10	4	7	*
80–Over	68	76	10	6	8	*

* Less than 0.5%

SOURCE: *The Myth and Reality of Aging in America.* A study prepared by Lou Harris Associates, Inc., for the National Council on the Aging (Washington, D.C., 1975), p. 181.

until old age. The stability model views church attendance as constant throughout the individual's lifetime and therefore not related to age; while the family life cycle model interprets the stage of the life cycle as related to church participation. The final model, progressive disengagement, is used as additional support of the disengagement theory that there is inevitable mutual withdrawal or disengagement resulting in decreased interaction between the aging person and others in society.[4]

Regardless of which model specific research seems to support, there is agreement that attendance declines at a much older age than formerly assumed—probably well into their nineties. The National Council on the Aging study found that 68 percent of persons over 80 years attend a church or synagogue sometime during the year. These conclusions question the appropriateness of using church attendance rates as the sole evidence of participation in worship, withdrawal, or disaffiliation with the church. Decreases in church participation rates by the elderly from weekly to bimonthly or even annually do not necessarily indicate a loss of identification with or commitment to the church. A closer examination of factors affecting participation will explain the variations more satisfactorily than does the disaffiliation, or disengagement, model.

FACTORS AFFECTING RELIGIOUS PARTICIPATION

To understand the religious behavior of the elderly, it is necessary to separate church attendance from church membership, and from other, nonassociational forms of religion, viewing church attendance as an indication of religiosity for some but not all older people. This section will survey the patterns of church attendance and their relation, if any, to the process of aging, and identify and discuss factors supporting the religious participation of the elderly in church and synagogue activities.

CHURCH ATTENDANCE

One of the continuing contradictions about the relationship of religiosity and aging is that religious participation declines with age, but that people become more religious as they age. The use of church attendance as one of the better indicants of religiosity adds to the confusion of the issue. Church attendance may be a reliable measure of the religiosity of younger age groups, but for the elderly it can be deceptive. Furthermore, there is little agreement among sociologists concerning the relation between church attendance and the process of aging. Some studies report attendance increases with age, others that it decreases, and still others that age makes no difference in attendance.[5]

From the longitudinal analysis of church attendance (1939–1969) using Gallup Poll data, C. Ray Wingrove and Jon P. Alston report a pattern that does not fit any of Bahr's models.[6] While they found that church attendance seems to vary by age, there was no consistent pattern in this relationship. Each cohort has its own particular profile.[7] For example, attendance peaked during their mid-twenties for persons born in 1925–1934. This pattern was atypical of other cohorts, whose attendance peaked just before age fifty or after age fifty-five, contradicting the stability model. These age differences, along with the observation that all cohorts had their peak or near peak attendance between 1950–1960 and that they all experienced a decline in attendance after 1965 (regardless of age at that date), indicate that there are forces affecting attendance other than the aging process. Robert Wuthnow has recently attributed the decline in the 1960s to the youth counterculture, which sought alternatives to established religion.[8] Wingrove and Alston conclude that church attendance appears to be related to the mood of the times; if it is fashionable to attend church during a particular time, people are more likely to attend regardless of age.

HEALTH

Older people have health problems, but the assumption that decreases in church participation by the elderly is due to ill health is also misleading. It is true, however, that older people have more chronic illnesses (39%) than younger adults (7%), and that those illnesses limit major activities such as working and home maintenance.[9] Approximately 80 percent of the elderly have one or more chronic illnesses, but only a small number (about 14%) are severely limited by these illnesses. Although acute conditions such as pneumonia, influenza, and injuries decline with age, the number of days of restricted activity increases. Older people take longer than younger adults to recover from incidences of acute illness, which frequently trigger major "attacks" of their chronic conditions.

Health may be one of several significant factors affecting frequency of church attendance and participation in other church-related activities. However, the more important issues are how age affects functional health, and how handicapping conditions are related to participation in church activities.[10] For example, church buildings and facilities may have major structural barriers to attendance for many older adults— such as steps, slick floors, and absence of ramps, elevators, hand rails, or toilet facilities to accommodate wheelchairs.

One study has found the major reason that older volunteers dropped out of a church-sponsored Senior Center program was a change in health—theirs or a close family member's.[11] Over a five-year period, many of the active volunteers reported no change in their own "good health," but these older volunteers frequently became caretakers of a family member. This study and others report health as the major factor affecting participation in voluntary organizations. They further suggest that old people who are the "healthiest" do participate, and that they seem to remain healthy for a sustained period.[12]

We may conclude that although health is a factor in decreased participation for many older persons, most older persons are functionally healthy enough to continue church involvement.

SEX

A double standard of church attendance persists for all age groups. At all ages females have maintained higher church attendance than males. Furthermore, this trend persists into old age and advanced old age.[13] Even when regular attendance declines for those over seventy-five, the decline is less for females than for males.[14] Wingrove and Alston report exceptions to this pattern in their cohort analysis. For one cohort, attendance for the sexes is equal between ages forty and fifty—which is accounted for by an increase in male attendance and a decline in female attendance. For another cohort the male-female differences are almost erased after age sixty-five.[15] These cohort variations suggest intergenerational differences and some changes in male-female participation patterns. The fact that men may increase participation in the church after retirement has important implications for churches. At a time of declining income and membership, but increasing numbers of persons over age sixty-five, churches need to plan programming in response to the increasing elderly population.

MARITAL STATUS

Although most religious organizations are nuclear family-oriented, being a part of a couple is less likely to influence the church participation of older adults than of younger adults. Widowhood has an adverse effect on social participation only when it places a person in a position different from that of most age-sex peers.[16] The number of widowed persons is greatest for the age group over sixty-five. Over one-third of the men are widowers and over half of the women are widows. This disproportion of widows to widowers increases with each decade after age sixty-five. Older women, then, are most likely to be widowed, and can be expected to be "socially comfortable" in continued church participation.

INCOME

For most adults, income declines with age. In 1976 the median income for couples with a husband sixty-five and over was $8,020; for elderly persons living alone (mostly women) the median income was $3,495. Many older adults experience severe economic problems for the first time. Although poverty has been decreasing for older people over the past fifteen years, nearly one in six older persons lives in official poverty, and the rate is much greater for older blacks. Obviously, inflation—especially in utilities, health care, and food—affects older people on fixed incomes more than adults still in the labor force.

The cost of church attendance, then, could be a significant factor affecting the participation of older persons. The reduction in income decreases elderly church members' ability to contribute financially.

Some of the older persons interviewed by David O. Moberg reported they would stay away from church if they could not contribute financially.[17] Others who would not stay away said that they would be embarrassed. Moberg also suggests that another economic factor affecting church attendance may be the inability of many older people to dress as well as they did when they were younger, which is both an economic and a mobility problem.

TRANSPORTATION

Researchers consistently report that transportation is an important factor influencing the participation of older people in a variety of social activities, including participation in voluntary associations such as the church.[18] Many older people no longer drive or own a car—particularly in advanced old age. They are, therefore, dependent on public transportation or friends and family for transportation. The distance the member lives from the church is a critical factor in participation. In fact, two studies found that for use of a house of worship, the critical distance was three blocks from the older person's residence.[19]

RELIGION AND THE EVERYDAY LIFE OF THE ELDERLY

Frequency of church attendance is only one indicant of religiosity or commitment and tells us little about the nature and *meaning* (or value) of attendance and participation to the elderly member. In other words, frequency alone does not tell us whether attendance is a social habit or a religious act, whether it is the result of peer pressure, for business or political contacts, or to fill a void in the family for the elderly women.[20] In any event, frequency of attendance measures do not account for the actual factors affecting attendance or nonattendance, and are therefore less sensitive to changes in those forces which may explain the social participation of the elderly.

Decline in church attendance is too often dismissed as additional evidence of the disengagement process accompanying aging. This theory holds that as a result of the aging process, people inevitably and voluntarily withdraw, and that society (and its organizations) withdraw support from the individual, ceasing to seek commitment from him or her.

Disengagement is not merely giving up membership or becoming a dormant member in a formal organization, but is the surrendering of one's social roles.[21] Religious roles, however, do not have to be relinquished at any specified age. There is no retirement age for religious roles. Furthermore, the religious role encompasses more than participation in the church; it includes private and everyday religious behavior, as well as the feeling that religion has meaning. Through nonorganizational or daily religious practices, the religious role is a salient factor in the lives of the elderly. For example, the older person whose church attendance is limited by physical and/or social factors associated with the aging process, may at the same time be highly committed—cognitively, emotionally, and morally—to their church. Their faith may be strong, their personal decisions may be made in relationship to the "faith of the church," and their feelings of self-identity with and love and loyalty for the church may remain.

It is the thesis of this chapter that the decline in church attendance or in participation in other church-related activities by older members is not sufficient evidence of a decline in religiosity or commitment to the church. The new conditions of the aging stage of life stimulate new patterns of everyday religious expression that are not reflected in social gerontological research. This section, then, examines other dimensions of religiosity in light of available evidence in three areas of research: age differences in beliefs, informal or nonassociational religioning, and life satisfaction and spiritual well-being.

AGE DIFFERENCES IN RELIGIOUS BELIEFS

There is no significant age-based difference in beliefs held by American adults about God and life after death. Most adults (94%), whatever age range, believe in God, and this belief pattern has remained fairly constant over the last quarter of a century. The meaning of these beliefs does vary by age, however; for example, persons over fifty are more likely than young adults to believe that God or a universal spirit observes their actions and rewards or punishes them for their actions.

Belief in life after death has also remained fairly constant with very little difference due to age. Gallup reports that 69 percent of all adults believe in immortality, with only a one percent difference between those over fifty and those adults thirty to thirty-nine. Younger people (under age thirty) are less likely to believe in immortality.[22] Studies of commitment to orthodox beliefs reveal no apparent relationship to the process of aging, but belief in survival beyond the grave does increase. The tendency seems to be that older people adhere to more orthodox or conservative religious viewpoints than younger people.[23]

Another age difference is found in the importance placed on religion (beliefs, faith, and practices). Most researchers report that older people say religion is very important to them, and the importance seems to increase with each decade (see Table 4).[24]

In the only study of centenarians' religion, Belle Boone Beard interviewed 700 persons over 100 years of age. She reports that over 90 percent of them said religion was very important to them and that they feel they are more religious than they were in their earlier life.[25] Many of these centenarians were still actively participating in their churches, including service activities. Beard also reports that unusual religious experiences and the desire for personal experiences with the supernatural are more frequent among these persons in late life than among younger adults.

Although these studies indicate some age differences in beliefs and feelings about religion, they are cross-sectional studies and can only tell us about the beliefs of particular age groups and the differences between them at a specific point in time. Until we have more longitudinal studies that study the same persons or the same age group in different time periods, the questions of the increase in the importance of religion and church participation with age will remain unanswered.

NONASSOCIATIONAL ACTIVITIES

Individual and privatized forms of religious life are not restricted to the frail elderly, but have been a significant aspect of most major religions. Nonassociational religious participation—Bible reading; prayer; meditation; small informal Bible and prayer groups; discussing

Table 4. IMPORTANCE OF RELIGION IN YOUR LIFE

	Total Public						Total Public			
	18–64 %	65–Over %	18–24 %	25–39 %	40–54 %	55–64 %	65–69 %	70–79 %	80–Over %
Very Important	49	71	34	45	58	65	69	71	73
Somewhat Important	33	21	40	35	29	25	22	21	19
Hardly Important at All	17	7	25	20	12	10	8	8	6
Not Sure	1	1	1	*	1	*	1	*	2

* Less than 0.5%

SOURCE: *The Myth and Reality of Aging in America.* A study prepared by Lou Harris Associates, Inc., for the National Council on the Aging (Washington, D.C., 1975), p. 181.

religion with neighbors, co-workers, and friends; and giving helping service to individuals and the community—has always been a part of the religious behavior of most Americans. However, devotional practices such as private prayer, reading the Bible and religious literature, and using religious media apparently increase with age. For example, ninety-year-olds studied by Michael Argyle and by Dan Blazer and Erdman Palmore listened to religious programs and prayed more frequently than people in their sixties.[26] The increase in the devotional aspects of religioning may be attributed to the increased interiority of personality that accompanies aging.[27] Whether this increase is in addition to church participation or whether it replaces church attendance, is not clear.

From the results of the American Piety Study, R. Stark has concluded that personal devotional activities provide the primary outlet for the anxieties and deprivation of old age and that the increasing piety of the elderly is manifested through prayer.[28] The widespread notion that people become increasingly pious as they age is true only if piety is carefully defined as private devotionalism and belief in an immortal soul.

The Georgia State University longitudinal study of older volunteers supports these conclusions about private religious practices.[29] A majority of the 250 older volunteers studied (55%) read the Bible daily and one-third (34%), once or twice a week. Almost one-fifth (18%) never read it. Most volunteers prayed daily or almost daily and only a few (6%) said never. The study sought the meaning and content of these practices, and found that older volunteers usually read from the New Testament and Psalms, especially the 23rd Psalm. They pray for themselves or others, mostly for intervention or help in daily situations, for guidance, inspiration, health, peace, about depression, and in thanksgiving. None mentioned death. Discussion of the nonassociational forms of religious participation by the elderly is limited to the "passive devotional, subjective practices" and omits any active informal group or collective religious behaviors.

Maggie Kuhn founded the Gray Panthers after her retirement as a staff member of a national board of the Presbyterian Church. She has spent her "retired" years raising the social conscience of Americans and showing thousands of other older and younger adults how to be active reformers, questioning the practices of business, industry, medical and health practices, gerontologists, politicians, government agencies, and public policy. It was the youth in the 1960s whose active nonassociational practices raised our collective religious consciousness. It may be that the next groups to do so will come from the emerging elderly subculture.[30] These active informal groups may form in neighborhoods, high-rise apartments for the elderly, retirement villages, senior centers, nursing homes, and clusters of neighbors. Bible study and prayer groups already exist in many of these settings and may provide the network for new active religious practices and roles for the elderly.

EVERYDAY FUNCTIONS OF RELIGION

Early efforts of gerontologists to relate religion to aging, focused on the expected positive function of religion in personal adjustment to old age.[31] The Chicago Inventory of attitudes and activities developed by University of Chicago researchers remains the most frequently used measure of religion and aging.[32] Using the Inventory on a variety of populations in the 1950s, some investigators found church participation and religious interests to be significantly correlated with old age adjustment, while others found only a slight relationship between attitudes toward religion and personal adjustment.[33] More recently, the adjustment scales were administered nine times to the longitudinal panel of the Duke University study of aging over an eighteen-year period. This study by Dan Blazer and Erdman Palmore indicated that religious attitudes remained stable. Religious activities and religious attitudes had strong relationships to happiness, feelings of usefulness, and personal adjustment—especially among men and among those persons over seventy. Blazer and Palmore conclude that "despite declines in religious activities, religion plays a significant role in the personal adjustment of many older persons."[34]

Twenty years ago Barron identified four gerontologic functions of religion which are the bases for increased religious activity of older people: to help face impending death, to help find and maintain a meaning in life, to help accept the inevitable losses of old age, and to help discover and utilize compensatory values that are potential in old age.[35] As yet there are few sytematic studies to test these assumptions.

Interest and participation in religious activities does not protect persons of any age from loneliness or fear of death.[36] Some very "religious" persons have been most disturbed and anxious about death. From her work with dying persons of all ages, Elisabeth Kübler-Ross reports the "true believers"—those who are "authentic and internalized in their faith (whether religious or atheist)"—show more serenity and less fear of death than those adults who are "uncertain."[37]

Knowledge about the function of religion in the lives of old people is limited by the low priority that has been given to research in this area. For example, the 1960 *Handbook of Social Gerontology* devotes less than one page to reporting on religion and aging, and one survey of research on religion and aging concludes that data on religious roles contribute less than data on other roles, such as the political, to understanding aging as a process.[38]

RELIGIOUS INSTITUTIONAL RESPONSES TO THE ELDERLY

Most religious organizations are experiencing a proportional increase of members who are over sixty-five years of age. The proportion is much higher for all religious institutions than the 10 percent for the general population. Estimates from several of the major denominations vary from 30 to 50 percent of the membership. The growth of the aging population, however, is sufficient to affect the churches and elicit some programmatic responses.

Religious institutions have not responded uniformly to these increasing numbers of older people. In the 1960s Jewish congregations responded with more responsible and creative programs than did Catholics or Protestants.[39] The 1960 White House Conference on Aging recommended that churches make a concerted effort to provide services

and educational programs which would integrate older people into the
mainstream of the congregational church. The conference suggested
that churches assist people in making happy and orderly transitions
to retirement and old age.

The early response of churches, then, was integration of its older
members. Robert M. Gray and David O. Moberg provide the first
social science data on age integration in the churches.[40] From his
research, Gray concluded, "The welcoming of all people into the church
often helps integrate older and younger persons in a common fellowship
like that of an extended family. . . . [W]hen the aging are treated
as individuals . . . and not categorically as old people, the morale of
the older member is greatly built up." Moberg later found no difference
in the adjustment of older persons in churches with special programs
and without special programs.[41] Contrary to this research evidence,
and to the "national policy," in the 1960s many churches began to
develop special programming for older members.

Response to the graying of the churches has generally been slow,
and research on that response is limited to a few studies on the clergy
and theological education. We do know that the religious institutions
have responded to the needs of the elderly by founding retirement
homes and nursing homes. According to Robert M. Butler and Myrna
I. Lewis, religious institutions provide 44 percent of all nonprofit homes
and 14 percent of all nursing homes.[42]

Butler and Lewis identified other significant functions of religious
institutions: to provide a practical ecumenicity through which churches
can protect their identities but yet pool their resources in a planned
effort to help the elderly in a quasi health and welfare function; to
provide trained clergy as professionals to serve as counselors for the
elderly in areas of special problems; and to use their power and influence
in advocacy roles to improve the economic conditions of the elderly.

ECUMENICAL HEALTH AND WELFARE RESPONSES

One of the most successful and most publicized health and welfare
responses was by The Shepherd's Center in Kansas City, Missouri.
It is a multipurpose ecumenical center planned and operated by older

persons, most of whom are volunteers. Organized in 1972, it has developed into a national noninstitutional project of the United Methodist Church's Health and Welfare Division. There are now eighteen model projects. The original center and two centers in Atlanta, Georgia, based on the same model, have been a part of the Georgia State University Longitudinal Study of the Older Volunteer (1972–1979). Older volunteers in these "peer centers" have found new social roles that have meaning to them and the community. These new social roles compensate for some of the work, friendship, church, and family roles older people have either lost or relinquished. New intergenerational relationships are forming, and these older volunteers are helping their own peers (and themselves) to avoid unnecessary or early institutionalization. These volunteer roles represent new religious leadership roles and suggest that an elderly lay ministry is emerging in the churches.

RESPONSES OF THE CLERGY

As "head" of the local congregation, ministers and parish clergy play significant roles in the organization's response to older people. A popular assumption about the clergy is that they are more comfortable with parishioners their own age or younger. In line with these popular beliefs, clergy do share some of society's negative attitudes toward the elderly—but to a lesser degree.[43] They frequently evaluate the elderly as forgetful, traditional, slow, lonely, noncontemporary, worried, dependent, nonsexual. Ministers do not have an aversion to ministering to older people, in fact clergy enjoy ministerial contacts with older people, but they prefer teaching youth and middle age adults.[44]

An explanation for the attitudes of the clergy toward the elderly and their ministry to them may be found in seminary training. In 1976 the curricula of most seminaries offered no special courses in gerontology. The National Interfaith Coalition on Aging's survey of seminary training of the clergy in aging shows that of 137 seminaries responding, 37 had one course in aging, 285 courses with some aging content were identified, and no seminary students were reported as completing an internship in a placement setting related to aging. The report concludes:

In view of the fact that the respondent schools collectively place about 10,000 graduates every year in positions of influence and responsibility among more than 100,000,000 people, it is important that every effort in the future be made to infuse the learning experience of future clergy with the realistic needs and characteristics of older persons in their constituency.[45]

ADVOCACY AND POLICY RESPONSE

There is some evidence that clergy and laity serve as advocates for their members in nursing homes and in federal and state legislation, but there is no known systematic data about the advocacy role of religious organizations. In the future, the National Interfaith Coalition on Aging can be expected to perform this role—and to collect the much-needed data.

In the late 1970s many denominations were preparing policy statements on aging which will guide the programming, advocacy, and ministry of these groups for the next decade.

THE FUTURE OF RELIGION AND AGING

The prospects for religion and the church look brighter than in the past several decades. Some denominations have suffered membership losses, but for the nation as a whole, membership has changed very little in forty years. The declines in religious interest of the 1960s were levelling by the 1970s. Being "very religious" may now simply be less related to the church or organized religion—especially for young adults. Gallup concludes that "while some observers contend that we are entering a post-Christian era, the data . . . would seem to portend just the opposite—that we may be in the first stages of a spiritual renewal in this country.[46] These period events will affect each age cohort, and become a part of the function of religion for those who will be the aged in the future.

Seminary training will include gerontological curricula and internships which will provide neighborhood leadership to develop social and psychological supports for an increasing aging population. The future response will include specialized ministeries to the elderly.

The elderly of the future will be more numerous, healthier, fill more work and volunteer roles, seek more educational and artistic opportunities, and more will live in "natural" communities. Post-industrial societies will plan and inaugurate a set of "social transformations" that integrate work, leisure, education, and employment as lifelong activities, and the age of aging as a social problem will end.[47]

NOTES

1. Barbara Payne, "Religious Life of the Elderly: Myth or Reality?" in *Spiritual Well-Being of the Elderly*, ed. James A. Thorson and Thomas C. Cook, Jr. (Springfield, Ill.: Charles C. Thomas, 1980).

2. Louis Harris Associates, *The Myth and Reality of Aging in America* (Washington, D.C.: National Council on the Aging, 1975).

3. *Religion in America 1976*, Gallup Opinion Index, no. 130, Part 1, pp. 7–21.

4. Howard M. Bahr, "Aging and Religious Disaffiliation," *Social Forces* 49 (1970): 59–71. The classic presentation of progressive disengagement is Elaine Cumming and William E. Henry, *Growing Old* (New York: Basic Books, 1961). Bahr himself favors this model; see also, *Old Men Drunk and Sober* (New York: New York University Press, 1973). This is supported by other researchers such as Paul Maves, "Aging, Religion and the Church," in *Social Gerontology*, ed. Clark Tibbitts (Chicago: University of Chicago Press, 1960); and Milton L. Barron, *The Aging American* (New York: Thomas Y. Crowell, 1961). The traditional model, on the other hand, finds support in the work of researchers such as Joseph H. Fichter, *Social Relations in the Urban Parish* (Chicago: University of Chicago Press, 1954); and Charles Y. Glock, Benjamin Ringer, and Earl Barbee, *To Comfort and to Challenge: A Dilemma of the Contemporary Church* (Berkeley, Calif.: University of California Press, 1967).
Elements in the research of Bernard Lagerwitz lend support to both the stability model and the family life cycle model; see his "Some Factors Associated with Variations in Church Attendance," *Social Forces* 39 (1961): 301–309. Ruth Albrecht leans toward the family life cycle model; see her "The Meaning of Religion to Older Adults—the Social Aspect," in *Organized Religion and the Older Person*, ed. Delton Scudder (Gainesville, Fla.: University of Florida Press, 1958). For additional information on the stability model, see H. L. Wilensky, "Life Cycle, Work Situation, and Participation in Formal Associations," in *Aging and Leisure*, ed. Robert W. Kleemeier (New York: Oxford University Press, 1961); and Marjorie Lowenthal and Betsy Robinson, "Social Networks and Isolation," in *Handbook of Aging and the Social Sciences*, ed. Robert Binstock and Ethel Shanas (New York: Van Nostrand, 1976).

5. Louis Harris Associates and the Gallup Poll report increases. Matilda W. Riley

and Anne Foner report decreases, in *Aging and Society* (New York: Russell Sage, 1968). Among those who report no difference is Harold L. Orbach in "Aging and Religion: A Study of Church Attendance in the Detroit Metropolitan Area," *Geriatrics* 16 (1961): 530–540.

6. C. Ray Wingrove and Jon P. Alston, "Cohort Analysis of Church Attendance, 1939–1969," *Social Forces* 53 (1974): 324–331.

7. The disengagement model receives some support from a study of those born 1915–1924 and 1905–1914, but is contradicted by the cohort born 1895–1904 which had a high percentage of attendance (52%) for ages 61–70 (supporting the traditional model). High attendance into later age categories also casts doubts on the disengagement model.

8. Robert Wuthnow, "The New Religion in Social Context," in *The New Religious Consciousness*, ed. Charles Y. Glock and Robert N. Bellah (Berkeley, Calif.: University of California Press, 1976).

9. United States Department of Health, Education, and Welfare, *Facts about Older Americans, 1978* (Washington, D.C.: Superintendent of Documents, 1978).

10. Russell A. Ward, *The Aging Experience* (New York: J. B. Lippincott Co., 1979).

11. Barbara Payne and C. Neil Bull, "Report to the Andrus Foundation on the Longitudinal Study of the Older Volunteer" (paper for the Andrus Foundation, Atlanta, Ga., 1979).

12. Stephen J. Cutler, "Age Differences in Voluntary Association Memberships," *Social Forces* 55 (1976): 43–58.

13. Albrecht, "The Meaning of Religion to Older Adults," and Bahr, "Aging and Religious Disaffiliation."

14. This trend is supported by research in the 1950s, 1960s, and 1970s. See Philip Taietz and Olaf F. Larson, "Social Participation and Old Age," *Rural Sociology* 21 (1956): 229–238; Cumming and Henry, *Growing Old*; Orbach, "Aging and Religion"; Joffre Dumazedier, *Sociology of Leisure* (New York: The Free Press, 1974), and Barbara Payne and F. J. Whittington, "Aged Women: Variables Unique to Women and Common to the Sexes" (paper delivered to the Southern Sociological Society, Atlanta, Ga., 1974).

15. Wingrove and Alston, "Cohort Analysis."

16. Barbara Payne and F. J. Whittington, "Older Women: An Examination of Popular Stereotypes and Research Evidence," *Social Problems* 23 (1976): 488–504.

17. David O. Moberg, *The Church as a Social Institution* (Englewood Cliffs, N.J.: Prentice-Hall, 1962).

18. Stephen J. Cutler, "The Effects of Transportation and Distance on Voluntary Association Participation Among the Aged," *International Journal of Aging and Human Development* 5 (1974): 81–94; M. P. Lawton and T. Bagerts, *Community Planning for the Elderly* (Washington, D.C.: U.S. Dept. of Housing and Urban Development, 1973); and Victor Regnier, "Neighborhood Planning for the Urban Elderly," in *Aging: Scientific Perspectives and Issues*, ed. Diana S. Woodruff and James E. Birren (New York: Van Nostrand, 1975).

19. M. P. Lawton and L. Nahemow, "Toward an Ecological Theory of Adaptation in Aging," in *Environmental Design and Research*, ed. W. Prieser, vol. 1 (Stroudsburg,

Penn.: Dowden, Hutchinson, and Ross, 1973); and R. Newcomber, "Group Housing for the Elderly: Defining Neighborhood Service Convenience for Public Housing and Section 202 Project Residents" (Ph.D. diss., University of Southern California, 1975).

20. Payne, "Religious Life of the Elderly."

21. Charles H. Mindel and C. Edwin Vaughan, "A Multidimensional Approach to Religiosity and Disengagement," *Journal of Gerontology* 33 (1978): 103–108.

22. Researchers through the years have noted this phenomenon. In addition to the 1976 Gallup study, see Robert J. Havighurst and Ruth E. Albrecht, *Older People* (New York: Longmans Green, 1953); and David O. Moberg, "Religion in the Later Years," in *The Daily Needs and Interests of Older People*, ed. Adeline M. Hoffman, 1st ed. (Springfield, Ill.: Charles C. Thomas, 1970).

23. See, for example, Yoshio Fukuyama, "The Major Dimensions of Church Membership," *Review of Religious Research* 2 (1961): 154–161.

24. Louis Harris Associates, *Myth and Reality of Aging*. Earlier research also emphasizes the importance older people attribute to religion. See Frances C. Jeffers and Claude R. Nichols, "The Relationship of Activities and Attitudes to Physical Well-Being in Older People," *Journal of Gerontology* 16 (1961): 67–70.

25. Belle Boone Beard, "Religion at 100," *Modern Maturity* 12 (1969): 1–4.

26. Michael Argyle and Benjamin Beit-Hallahmi, *The Social Psychology of Religion* (London: Routledge and Kegan Paul, 1975); Dan Blazer and Erdman Palmore, "Religion and Aging in a Longitudinal Panel," *The Gerontologist* 16 (1976): 82–85.

27. Douglas Kimmel, *Adulthood and Aging* (New York: John Wiley and Sons, 1974).

28. R. Stark, "Age and Faith: A Changing Outlook as an Old Process," *Sociological Analysis* 29 (1968): 1–10.

29. Payne and Bull, "Report to the Andrus Foundation."

30. Barbara Payne, "Non-Associational Religious Participation," in *Informal Social Participation: The Determinants of Political Participation, Leisure Activity and Altruistic Behavior*, ed. Jacqueline Macauly and David Horton Smith (San Francisco: Jossey-Bass, forthcoming).

31. Ruth S. Cavan et al., *Personal Adjustment in Old Age* (Chicago: Science Research Associates, 1949).

32. The inventory includes eight scales to measure adjustment in the specific areas of health, friends, economic security, religion, feelings of usefulness, happiness, and family. A composite score is used for overall adjustment and scores for each scale indicate adjustment in specific areas. The religion index includes measures of church attendance, listening to services on radio and TV, reading the Bible and/or devotional books, and feelings about religion. These scores appear in the "Handbook of Research Instruments in Social Gerontology," University of Minnesota Press, 1979.

33. For significant correlation, see especially the work of David O. Moberg, "Church Membership and Personal Adjustment in Old Age," *Journal of Gerontology* 8 (1953): 207–211, and "Religious Activities and Personal Adjustment in Old Age," *Journal of Social Psychology* 43 (1956): 261–267. See also Havighurst and Albrecht, *Older People;* this study is representative of those who found little correlation.

34. Blazer and Palmore, "Religion and Aging," pp. 34–35.
35. Milton L. Barron, "The Role of Religion and Religious Institutions in Creating the Milieu of Older People," in *Organized Religion and the Older Person,* ed. Scudder.
36. C. T. O'Reilly, "Religious Practice and Personal Adjustment of Older People," *Sociology and Social Research* 42 (1957): 119–121.
37. Elisabeth Kübler-Ross, *Questions and Answers on Death and Dying* (New York: Macmillan, 1974). See also Richard A. Kalish, "Death and Dying in a Social Context," *Handbook of Aging and the Social Sciences,* ed. Binstock and Shanas.
38. Riley and Foner, *Aging and Society.*
39. Robert Atchley, *Social Forces in Later Life* (Belmont, Calif.: Wadsworth Publishing Co., 1977).
40. Robert M. Gray and David O. Moberg, *The Church and the Older Person* (Grand Rapids, Mich.: Wm. B. Eerdmans, 1962).
41. David O. Moberg, "The Integration of Older Members in the Church Congregation," in *Older People and Their Social World,* ed. Arnold M. Rose and Warren A. Peterson (Philadelphia, 1965), pp. 125–142.
42. Robert M. Butler and Myrna I. Lewis, *Aging and Mental Health: Positive Psychosocial Approaches,* 2nd ed. (St. Louis: C. V. Mosby, 1977).
43. David O. Moberg, "Needs Felt by the Clergy for Ministries to the Aging," *The Gerontologist* 15 (1975): 170–175.
44. Charles F. Longino and Gay C. Kitson, "Parish Clergy and the Aged: Examining Stereotypes," *Journal of Gerontology* 31 (1976): 340–345.
45. Derrel Watkins, "Seminary Instruction in Gerontology," *NICA INFORM* no. 1 (August, 1975): 2–3.
46. Gallup, *Religion in America.*
47. Sanford A. Lakoff, "The Future of Social Intervention," *Handbook of Aging and the Social Sciences.*

II

The Family Relations of Older Persons

Allen J. Moore

The church in recent decades, in spite of its vision as an inclusive community, has generally reflected the family values of society as a whole. With the value that our society has placed upon youth, it has become commonplace to view aging, in all of its social forms, as a "problem." Thus, when the family is conceived as a married couple with children, those persons who are beyond the childbearing years or whose marital relation has been disrupted by death are viewed as atypical or at least no longer in a "normal" relationship. The nuclear family has been assumed to be the norm and many churches have organized their basic programs of nurture around the needs of a husband, wife, and dependent children. Although never intentional, the older family members were either neglected or were segregated into separate program groups.

The "life stage approach" to people has dominated Christian education for the past two decades. Attention has focused on the needs and experiences of each separate age group rather than on common human experiences shared through the whole life span. This has served to enhance age segregation and the idiosyncratic aspects of personality rather than affirm the family as a whole life of mutual needs and relationships.

The historical Christian understanding of the "household of faith" provides a vision of family relationships compatible with current family social theory. The relationship was not limited to marriage but was the covenant community in which all were understood as children of God—brothers and sisters in their shared experience of faith. The "family of God" was made up of people of all ages and represented a variety of marital and familial relationships.

FAMILY DEFINITION

What is at issue is the definition that we are to give to that unit of relationships that is to be called "family." For example, the classical sociological view is that the family is a product of marital interaction.[1] In this understanding, marriage is the "precondition" to the family. Having children establishes a set of relationships—with prescribed social roles and functions—that is normally known as a family. In short, the family is established through procreation.

Social statisticians make a distinction between a *household* and a *family*. A household refers to all people living within a given residential unit and a family refers to two or more people living together who are related either by blood or marriage. Persons living alone are considered members of a household, but not a family.

Although it is important for social science language to be precise in describing the patterns through which persons live their lives, an adequate definition of "family" has proven to be elusive in our time. The growing number of older individuals in our society has created a need to reexamine those norms which have prescribed how persons relate in family-like living. Many of the normative definitions emerged in an era when the young were the dominant age group and many of the studies of family living used the convenience of this available young-adult age population to study. Not only are people now living longer, but the number of older adults in society will soon be a population group as large as the group that formerly made up the young marrieds.

Family studies are dramatically demonstrating that not all people live in a family unit; that not all marriages produce children; that there are a significant number of people who live alone; and that, even among older people, there is a great deal of variation in how marital relations are organized. The preoccupation with the normal, childbearing family concept stigmatizes those whose life style or social situation leads to a variation in familial living.

Some recent work in anthropology has deemphasized biological lines as a basis for identifying family members and defining the network of relationships known as the family. In some societies, a distinction has to be made between the biological parent and the nurturing parent. Erik Erikson, in his work on generativity, seeks to suggest that not all adults must become biological parents in order to enter into the larger social responsibility for parenting a new generation.[2]

Kin relations can include more than blood and marital relations. For example, in some societies adoption and godparenting are not only very meaningful but also a significant part of the family network. Increasingly, grandparents and even great-grandparents play a variety of roles which are not limited to blood lineage. These and other kinship relationships may have had their origins in biological concepts of the family, but now have symbolic meanings representing some of the qualities of love, trust, and solidarity that are inherent in family living. These are the kinds of relations that humans require for survival in an increasingly complex world: "They symbolize trust. . . . They stand for the fact that birth survives death, and that solidarity is enduring."[3] People in modern social movements seek to emulate these qualities when they refer to themselves as a "family." These are also the kinship qualities picked up by religious groups when they refer to themselves as "brothers" and "sisters."[4]

EXTENDED FAMILY

There are two basic family models frequently utilized by social theorists to describe the modern family. The first, which many feel is more dominant in modern urban society, is the *nuclear* family (or the *conjugal* family). The marital relation is of primary importance in a family composed of a husband and a wife and their immediate children. It is generally assumed that this pattern of family life emerged as the result of industrialization. Urbanization caused high mobility and the need for people to live near the factories in which they worked. With modern technology and transportation, suburban communities emerged which allowed for greater isolation of the "marital" family.

These social developments during the past 100 years or so are believed to be the major causes for the predominance of the nuclear family form in our society. This has also contributed to separating the generations, both in housing patterns and in spatial distance. After their adult children established their own marital relations, the elderly became increasingly isolated and unable to participate in family living.

Today family sociologists disagree as to what extent the nuclear family does indeed exist and to what degree it has contributed to the isolation of the generations—and the loss of value that aging had held in more traditional society. One can at least agree that housing has become much more age-oriented; older people do to a large degree live segregated from typical family life. At the same time, modern transportation and communication do make possible frequent interaction between the age groups and provide the means for families to transcend social barriers and spatial distance in order to continue a shared kin identity and emotional ties. These social constrictions make any clear generalization on family life difficult today.

Partly in an attempt to overcome the social isolation resulting from nuclear family life, and partly in recognition that the isolation of older family members has not been very satisfying to either generation, some family theorists have taken another look at a traditional family organization or what has been called the *extended* family. Although this model is described in a variety of ways, its basic intent is to place less emphasis upon the marital bond and more upon the kinship relations or the line of descent. Generally, this form of family life is organized around several generations within one family unit. They either share a common residential home, live in close proximity to one another, or function together as a unit in spite of spatial distance.

It is likely that at this time in our social history the "extended" family has been overly idealized and the "nuclear" family has been unjustly criticized. Betty Yorburg points out that the extended family has always been "most pronounced among the very rich and the very poor."[5] The rich could afford to remain together; the kinship network functions to ensure the continuation of power and position in each new generation. Older persons retained their positions as heads of the family and performed important roles in preserving the family solidarity, holding in trust wealth and social position for the younger family members.

Among the poor there was no escape from the family network because few could afford to leave and go out on their own. Generations clustered together, often living in the crowded household of middle-aged parents. Both sets of parents served economic needs by caring for children while young members sought work. When illness and increasing age fell upon them, older parents became more and more dependent upon the family.

On the other hand, there is evidence that the nuclear family may not have been as free of kinship influences as some have proposed. Michael Gordon suggests that the isolation may have been exaggerated and that kinship patterns actually have much durability even in modern society.[6] At the same time, he reminds us that generational issues are not new; as late as the eighteenth century older people were considered a nuisance and a family liability.[7]

What might be concluded is that there is great variation in how people organize their familial lives today. Neither of the two family models seem to adequately describe either the growing value which older family members are beginning to enjoy in our society, or the relationship which they may have to the contemporary family network. Some may choose to remain in a close relationship with adult children and grandchildren, while others are choosing the freedom of retirement to explore new life styles and new forms of familial expression.

There is no single pattern of behavior today that defines the relationship between middle-aged children and aging parents. Not only are there unrecognized psychological motivations—such as guilt—which operate in these relationships, but family members also approach each other out of a variety of values and life experiences.[8] In addition, we are living in a time when most traditional roles are under examination. There is still much confusion as to what is expected of a person in the various stages of life. For example, there is presently little research on the traditional role of a grandparent and almost none on the fourth generation role of the great-grandparent.[9] What we do know is that for some people these roles have little meaning and may even be rejected. For others, the roles are not clearly understood and defined. How, for example, does one function as a forty-year-old grandmother and what impact will this have when this same woman tries to find a useful family function at sixty-five? The stereotypes of a grandparent provide little help in fulfilling roles when the relationship between the various parts of the family are as yet unclarified.

The shift in life styles is not limited to the young adult. Older persons are also forced to explore alternative ways for organizing their life, especially in relation to their place in marriage and the family. At least a quarter of the older population are living alone today. In addition, the traditional value attached to "couples" can severely limit the social interactions of many people when they find their marital relations disrupted by death or other forms of separation. Present Social Security laws work against remarriage of older persons. Many, like their grandchildren, have turned to a variety of "living arrangements" which will allow for companionship and for conjugal relations while at the same time permiting both partners to retain the financial security which may be derived from dual Social Security benefits.

A DYNAMIC VIEW OF THE FAMILY

What may be called for is a model of family life that is not static and that does emphasize the "normal" to the exclusion of those older persons who are beyond the marital and procreative stages of life. Any view of the family that functions to exclude older people from the basic institutions of society, such as the church, needs to be carefully reevaluated.

To a large extent social theories of the family have lagged behind the facts of social life and people's changing expectations. Older persons have a continued need for significant relationships that will sustain their lives. They have much to give to others, especially to the younger generation. They continue to have the ability and the desire to express themselves sexually and to make and maintain sexual relations. And they continue to have significant and socially useful roles to play in society and in the family.

Among the recent family theorists who have sought to avoid the limits of a biological and institutional approach to family studies is Roy H. Rodgers. Although not specifically addressing the older person within the family unit, he does attempt to find a more comprehensive view that allows for changes in social status and for a continuous redefinition of family roles.

Rather than emphasizing the organizational characteristics of the family—kinship lines and the biological dimensions such as mating and procreation—Rodgers' orientation is on the dynamic and the behavior characteristics of persons through the life span (or history) of a family. Using what he calls a developmental and interactional view, he sees the family as a system of relationships in which the roles and positions of each individual are changing in relation to the actions of other family members upon them. They in turn act upon other members of the family, each changing as the family situation changes and as each member progresses through the family life cycle.[10]

An analogy is an actor on the stage, who is both acting out a role and responding to the acting of the other actors. The content of the role depends upon the scene, the other actors, and the demands of the role in that one situation of the play. The older person participating in this family life scene brings expectations to the role, but also interacts with the expectations that others may have. The script is available but one is never limited by a script. Each player brings a unique interpretation to the part and no two players will play the part the same way. Neither will any two performances of the identical scene be done the same way. Analogously, within the lifetime of any one person, that person's role will be defined by family setting, particular life situation (such as aging), and the individual's unique interpretation of the part within the family stage of life.

As is well- known, the family is undergoing many changes today. Change is inevitable even within the life span of any one family, as people are born and people die. Family relations have always been complex and are becoming even more demanding under the influence of today's society. This new social matrix contains a growing number of older adults who continue to have much to contribute as well as to receive within a variety of familial relations. Any theory of the family that is to serve our current understanding must include a place for the older family members.

INTERGENERATIONAL RELATIONS

A dynamic approach to the family must also take into consideration the fact that an "average" family is now composed of four generations. It is now estimated that in the United States more than forty percent of the persons aged sixty-five or over have great-grandchildren. Peter Townsend writes that this is a "new phenomenon in the history of human societies" and a major factor causing changes in family patterns and the experiences of aging.[11] He believes that the increasing number of older family members in our society has had a greater impact upon family organization and relationships than the economic and social changes discussed earlier.[12]

The issue of intergenerational relations has become a concern of social scientists in recent years. It was in the 1960s that the term "generation gap" was formulated to describe what some felt was a disjunction in moral values and life styles between young adults and their middle-age parents. The generation gap concept also refers to the breakdown in communication structures between the generations, the strain placed upon continuity due to rapid social change, the segregation of age groups leading to social barriers to interaction, the emergence of age-oriented subcultures, and the struggle to define the social character of a people.[13]

There are those who now believe that a similar generational problem has emerged between the second and third and fourth generations.[14] It is this same middle generation of adults, caught in the 1960s with a young adult generation that they did not fully understand, who are now having to come to terms with aging parents.

Two demographic factors have contributed to this new generational strain. The first is what has become apparent: the longer life span has resulted in a population of older persons who are increasing numerically two and a half times faster than the remainder of the population. The second is that this same population of older persons contributed to the sharp decline in the birth rate several decades ago. This resulted in fewer adult children to care for and interact with aging parents. Both of these demographic factors have probably been heightened by changes in social and family styles brought about by new housing patterns and spatial distances.

Empirical studies suggest that, regardless of the reason, most families at one time or another experience differences and even conflicts between the generations.[15] Rather than formulate a generation gap concept with its emphasis upon discontinuity between the generations, it might be more appropriate to see that in any interaction between age groups differences will emerge. A dynamic and interactive view of family relations will allow us to accept these differences as a natural element in any system of relationships. Individuals stand at different levels of maturation and experience, they have been influenced by a different history (they each stand in a different point in the stream of history), and each must constantly cope with the changes in their role and status in the family system.

It may be too much to expect that differences and conflict between family members can be eliminated. What can be expected is that people come to use conflict creatively to further the common life of the family and to recognize the need which each generation has for the other. Actually, there is evidence that young marrieds require more help than older persons. Mutual dependency is the nature of good family life—"each generation needs a teacher for life and each generation is a teacher for life." For example, the older generation is the bearer of culture and tradition, as the younger generation is the bearer of change and newness. The family needs both of these perspectives.

FAMILY LIFE CYCLE

Evelyn Duvall and others who have written about the developmental cycle of the family assert that there is a relationship between individual growth and maturation, and the patterns of family interaction.[16] Individuals develop in relation to social expectations which must be reconciled with their own internal physiological and psychological needs. Although there is variation in the rate of growth, there are commonly shared times in life in which human transitions are required. Such transitions, or points of human growth and change, are made in relation to socially defined behavior and cultural norms. For example, it is generally agreed that the late teens and early twenties is a time when persons "normally" come to sexual maturity. Society indicates that marriage is the best way to satisfy this sexual urge. The numerous courtship and marriage rites and norms are society's way of directing the maturity of personal sexuality.

The family life cycle is the sequence of events that bring about changes in the family structure and shifts in family roles and obligation. Beginning in marriage and continuing through the birth of children, the major cycles of the family include the launching of the young into adulthood, the retirement from work, the death of a partner, and the establishment of a grandparental role with a family of an offspring.[17]

Each phase of the family life cycle is marked by several factors:

1. A time in life that is described by chronological age and is marked by social and biological characteristics.

2. A role that has been socially defined and that carries social value. At each stage new roles must be learned and old ones discarded.

3. An event that marks the transformation from one place in the life cycle to another, such as one's sixty-fifth birthday. It may also be

an historical event, such as the death of a father, that forces one to take leadership in the extended family before one's time.

Although other stages of the family life cycle have received much attention, there is a dearth of research on the older person's place in the family. Irwin Deutscher has suggested that with increasing longevity and the reduction in the birth rate, a new phase of the family life cycle can be identified. He calls this the post-parental phase.[18]

A couple in their early to mid-fifties can usually expect that the last child will leave home, grandchildren will be born, and they will have another twenty-five years to live together before separation by death. It is popularly believed that this is a time of marital crisis and dissolution. Husbands and wives do find that, following the withdrawal of the last child from home, their roles must be redefined. The wife especially may find it necessary to shift from a parental role to concentrating again on a marital partner. For some this becomes a time of marital crisis but for others it is an opportunity to heighten marital satisfaction. Deutscher concludes that most studies show recovering conjugal relationships is generally a positive experience.[19]

The marital satisfaction of retirement couples has been studied by Harold Feldman. A majority of the couples reported that marital satisfaction improved as parenting responsibilities ended, although retirement itself was sometimes a problem. Older couples tended to find increased marital satisfaction and experience a deeper companionship and an enhancement of loyalty to one another.[20]

Since work is so central to the social experience of most people, retirement often results in a loss of self esteem for the man. For the woman, a husband's retirement often causes her to feel a loss of freedom and mobility (the "husband is underfoot"; "I have to be home with my husband"). Unfortunately most studies of retirement still stereotype sex roles. The growing number of women in the work force, however, will change the ritual of retirement and the pattern of couple interaction.

For the majority, retirement becomes an opportunity to explore new dimensions of human intimacy and to develop new patterns of communication. Many couples experience a new cohesiveness and closeness, and even though some report a growing decline of passion, there is at the same time a greater sense of caring for each other and the experience of comfort and strength.[21]

Although the research is limited, observations would suggest that instability and divorce have increased in this age group as in others. Most persons of all ages now accept divorce as an option, and in the over sixty-five age group, there are annually 10,000 persons who divorce.

A major factor in the marital relations of older couples is their expectations. In other words, marital socialization is a lifelong process and indirectly older persons have been taught the roles they are to take in old age, the patterns by which they will relate as husband and wife, the appropriate retirement behavior, and the sexual expectations they should have. For those who have come to expect the best from their marital relations, they will probably continue to have what they have had in the past, and to improve upon it.

Most studies of marital interaction among older persons find health is a major concern. Much money and energy is invested in either preserving good health or in responding to the health problems of old age. This can become a dominant factor in the marriage and cause much anxiety. It can also become the motivation for extreme caring between the marriage partners.

There are some theorists who see old age—especially when health is a problem—as a time of social disengagement (withdrawal from social roles and family interaction). An example might be a grandmother who decides no longer to exchange gifts at the family Christmas tree, or a father who decides he is too old to visit his adult children in a nearby community. There are some theorists who believe that withdrawal is related either to an experience of social exclusion (such as the dropping of one's name from the Men's Club upon retirement) or the fear that one might be excluded because one is now too old (the Annual Church Family Camp). Happily, disengagement does not seem universal among all older people, and studies suggest that people are happier when they remain involved to the degree that they are able. It seems especially positive for older individuals to participate actively in their family and to continue to fulfill familial roles.

SEX AND OLDER ADULTS

It is sometimes erroneously believed that sex belongs to the young and that with the coming of middle- and old-age, sex is gone forever. One of the reasons for this belief is that sex research has been preoccupied with the sexual functioning of the young, especially with the orgasmic goal of sexual relations. Until the studies of Masters and Johnson, we knew almost nothing about the sexual behavior of older adults. Likewise, until very recently there have been almost no educational programs and resources designed to aid the older person in coping with sexual functioning in later life. For far too many persons, the socialization process has led them to believe sex comes to an end at mid-life and they should cease to have any sexual expectations. One observer commenting on this suggests that "if sexuality in aging humans has no place or meaning, then our nature as sexual beings is called into serious question."[22]

Actually, old age is for many people an opportunity to explore new and creative forms of sexual expression, and to become free from the performance forms of sexuality that early marriage seems to require. For many couples, the urgency and explosiveness of young sexuality is replaced with a deeper sense of relatedness and with the eroticism of the total body. Rather than orgasm as the goal of every sexual contact, total intimacy of the two persons becomes the central concern.

There is truth in the common knowledge that the male does experience some gradual loss in sexual desire as he grows older, and that the woman's decline is somewhat less and comes rather late. And yet, research has now confirmed that for both men and women, sexual expression can and does continue well into later years. For some persons it may actually expand. The important information coming from most recent studies is that use contributes more than anything else to the continuation of sexual functioning. It is time to become honest with

older adults about their sexual potentiality, and to allow them freedom
to find fresh forms of sexual expression.

A NEW STAGE OF FAMILY LIFE

Marital and familial relations do not end with the coming of old
age. New understandings of older adulthood are contributing to a new
stage in the family life cycle, sometimes referred to as the post-parental
and retirement stage. There are clearly defined family roles appropriate
for older people, including those who have never married or have remained childless. These roles are still in the process of being clarified.
Older people are whole individuals, capable of providing for one another
and for the young generations relationships of familial quality and solidarity. Especially important is the awareness that older people are fully
sexual humans, and we must aid them in clarifying the nature of their
sexual expression in old age. It may be that in the future the models
of healthy sexuality will come from the old rather than from the young.

To fully understand the place of the older adult within the family
unit, a new model of the family is needed. This model should take
into consideration both development and interaction in family life and
should allow for changes in family roles and patterns. This means
especially that those social institutions wishing to understand and serve
older adults within the context of family life, must reexamine their
assumptions and value judgments, not limiting their view of the family
to procreative and nurturing roles.

The church today can become a value-advocating and value-forming
community. Rather than accepting uncritically social views of "normal"
family life, its programs should liberate and bring wholeness to human
life, including the older family member.

NOTES

1. Harold T. Christensen, ed. *Handbook of Marriage and the Family* (Chicago: Rand
   McNally, 1964), p. 3.

2. Erik H. Erikson, "Identity and the Life-Cycle," *Psychological Issues*, vol. 1 (New York: International Universities Press, 1959). See also, *Adulthood* (New York: Norton, 1978).

3. Cited in Arlene Skolnick, *The Intimate Environment* (Boston: Little, Brown, 1973), p. 21.

4. Ibid., pp. 20–22.

5. Betty Yorburg, *The Changing Family* (New York: Columbia University Press, 1973), p. 108.

6. Michael Gordon, ed., *The Nuclear Family in Crisis: The Search for an Alternative* (New York: Harper & Row, 1972), p. 5.

7. Ibid., p. 14; see also Philippe Aries, *Centuries of Childhood* (New York: Vintage Books, 1963), p. 31. Just as children who were not wanted were in the past discarded, so old people were sent to poor farms to die. The growing value that our society is presently giving to older persons is actually a revolutionary concept.

8. Lillian E. Troll, Sheila J. Miller, and Robert J. Atchley, *Families in Later Life* (Belmont, Calif.: Wadsworth Publishing Co., 1979), pp. 83–107. See also, James A. Peterson, "The Relationships of Middle-Aged Children and Their Parents," in *Aging Parents*, ed. Pauline K. Ragan (Los Angeles: University of Southern California Press, 1979), pp. 27–36.

9. Vivian Wood and Joan F. Robertson, "The Significance of Grandparenthood," in *Time Roles and Self in Old Age*, ed. Jaber F. Gubrium (New York: Human Science Press, 1976), pp. 278–304. This is one of the rare studies on this aspect of the family.

10. Roy H. Rodgers, *Family Interaction and Transaction: The Developmental Approach* (Englewood Cliffs, New Jersey: Prentice-Hall, 1973). Rodgers provides a basic new theory for family studies. A good review of theoretical issues related to the family and older persons can be found in Leopold Rosenmayr, "Family Relations of the Elderly," *Journal of Marriage and the Family* (November, 1968), pp. 672–680.

11. Peter Townsend, "The Emergence of the Four-Generation Family in Industrial Society," in *Middle Age and Aging*, ed. Bernice L. Neugarten (Chicago: University of Chicago Press, 1968), pp. 255–257.

12. Ibid., p. 257.

13. Allen J. Moore, *The Young Adult Generation* (Nashville: Abingdon Press, 1969).

14. Stephen Z. Cohen and Bruce Michael Gans, *The Other Generation Gap* (Chicago: Follett, 1978). A popular treatment of the issue.

15. Vern Bengtson et al., "The Generation Gap and Aging Family Members: Toward a Conceptual Model" in Gubrium, *Time Roles*, pp. 237–263.

16. Evelyn Duvall, *Family Development* (Philadelphia: J. B. Lippincott, 1957). Also, Reuben Hill, *Family Development in Three Generations* (Cambridge, Mass.: Schenkman, 1970); and Hill and Rodgers, "The Developmental Approach," in Christensen, *Handbook of Marriage and the Family*, pp. 171–211.

17. Irwin Deutscher, "The Quality of Postparental Life" in Neugarten, *Middle Age and Aging*, pp. 263.

18. Ibid.

19. Ibid.

20. Cited in Troll et al., *Families in Later Life*, p. 49.
21. Ibid., pp. 39–67. See also, Harold Feldman and Margaret Feldman, "The Family Life Cycle: Some Suggestions for Recycling," *Journal of Marriage and the Family* (May, 1975), pp. 277–284.
22. Charles Meridenhall, "Sex and Aging," unpublished manuscript, 1979. A good review of the current research in sexuality and the later years is found in Troll, et al., *Families in Later Life*, pp. 62–64. See also, William H. Masters and Virginia Johnson, *Human Sexual Response* (Boston: Little, Brown, 1966). A summary of Masters and Johnson is found in "Human Sexual Response: The Aging Female and Aging Male," in Neugarten, *Middle Age and Aging*.

III

DESIGNS

Adults with Parents in Crisis: A Personal Account

James W. Ewing

Thou turnest man back to the dust and
sayest, "Turn back, O children of men!"
For a thousand years in thy sight
are but as yesterday when it is past,
or as a watch in the night.

Let the favor of the Lord our God be upon us,
and establish thou the work of our hands upon us.
Ps. 90:3–4, 17 (RSV)

NARRATIVE

"Jim," the husky voice spoke, betraying my laryngectomee father at the other end of the line, "you had better come." The broken voice filled with overwhelming emotion meant that Mother had had a relapse and she was in the hospital again. The pastor, who had stood by Mother and Dad during these past years, then spoke, filling out the details of the crisis.

This was Mother's third hospitalization in the past six months. Although I did not want to believe that we are really "turned back to the dust," the reality of this call finally penetrated what I had been denying: parents do become weak and deteriorate in health. Certainly I realized that they were getting older and one day they would die, but deep in the unconscious assumptions of my life lingered the belief that my parents had never been helpless, and would never be helpless like children. But this lingering infantilism inside my vigorous, self-preoccupied, mid-adult life style was challenged by this phone call from 750 miles away, and quickly as a flash in the night, I became a parent to my weakening, deteriorating parents.

In retrospect I should have detected the signs of their declining health with more precision. Except for my father's major cancer surgery 20 years earlier, they had been healthy for their entire lives. Both of them are ministers, and through their fifty-seven years of married life they had developed deep care and support for each other, teaming as a couple in their ministry. Following the cancer surgery, they retired and took up residence in the four-roomed frame house in the small town in Minnesota where they had previously lived. This was a good choice, since the people in the town had known them in their younger years, which allowed their aging to be informed by the memory of their strength, vigor, and vitality. Their pride during the retirement years revolved around their good health, their capacity to continue to work and to take care of themselves, and their meager dependence on anyone, especially their children.

This capacity gradually began to change, especially during the hard winters. Their activity gradually decreased and vulnerability to colds increased, but as children we paid little attention to these frailties, unaware that bit by bit their bodies were wearing out and their capacity to resist viral and bacterial infection was lessening. They encouraged such inattention by convincing us that they needed no help, except occasional visits in the summers. For years they had annual physical examinations and the reports were always positive "for their age." Blind to their aging, we refused to probe beneath the verbal reports for they were determined to take care of themselves.

Such motivation, pride, and independence activated their will to remain healthy and to deny their emerging frailty. But others knew differently, for friends and pastor who watched over them in quiet and unassuming ways observed the gradual decline in their strength and vigor. In silence, friends and pastor tended to little needs like dropping by the house with small amounts of food and making sure that basic living needs were being met. They noticed the increasing struggle that my parents were having with keeping up the chores of the house and the large garden. The friends said nothing, but only cared for them, waiting for the adult children to become aware of the increasing difficulty the parents were having in managing themselves at ages eighty-six and eighty-eight.

Such unawareness is not unusual, for as children we were proud of our parents' self-sufficiency and financial independence. With myself 750 miles away and my sister, 2,000 miles away, we were insulated from their day by day struggle. One visit a year stimulated them to be alert, active, and to put on the appearance that life continued as usual. We were shielded from the awareness of the emerging signs of deterioration.

The serious alert began, however, during the last winter they lived in their house. The usual colds did not go away quickly. Then, toward spring while raking in the garden, Mother fell and crushed a disc in the spine, placing her in the hospital for three weeks. Neither my sister nor myself traveled to tend to them at the time. While Mother recuperated at home, Dad proceeded to plant his usual oversized garden. However, Dad began to press for a visit, speaking hints of dying. Such hints sounded manipulative, for it seemed to me that he was prone to stretch the truth when he wanted something for himself.

My sister, following her annual early summer visit, reported the declining condition of their health. By mid-summer Mother, who was almost recovered from the injury to her spine, was hospitalized again, this time with pneumonia aggravated by her heart condition. This signal demanded direct response.

I was not fully prepared for what I found. Mother, whose usual 140 pound body was now under 100 pounds, was severely weakened, unable to walk even to the toilet. Dad's usual brisk walk was now a shuffle. Neighbors, friends, and the pastor had been the sustaining agents for them during the past three months. A beloved neighbor lady had been coming to the house daily to bring food, clean house, and tend to their physical and emotional needs. The pastor had visited regularly, offering emotional support and providing friendship.

The pastor had offered to meet me at the airport in the neighboring town and transport me to the hospital. The forty-five minutes spent in the car together provided a fortuitous visit, for in his sensitive but clear way, he was able to forewarn me of my parents' physical condition. But more significantly, he pointed to my responsibility to take charge of their care—the limit of resources and authority had been reached by friends, neighbors, and the church. Decisions about their continuing care had to be made by a member of the family. I was selected. The time for decisive action had arrived, for the reality of my parents' declining situation no longer could be ignored.

My parents were caught in an ambivalent world. On the one hand their life was helplessly falling apart, and on the other hand they were fighting hard to maintain the hope that they were going to be all right. The ambivalence of knowing their own situation, yet not knowing the outcome of the crisis, exposed their confused emotions of fear, hope, anger, and affection. Not only was the external situation in rapid change, but their internal worlds were also up against forces which pushed them to the brink of helplessness. Clearly, the authority of the children was needed to guide them through the turmoil of this new ambivalence. But for me to take on a parental role to them for emotional support, interpretation of reality, and management of decisions, was a new and uncharted path.

A new relationship was emerging between us, centering around my leadership role. Two immediate decisions had to be made. The first decision was to nurse Mother back to health in whatever way was possible. Her condition was precarious, so we visited her two and three times a day, sometimes finding her bright and hopeful and at other times bitter, angry, and filled with crazy thoughts. Her weakness and the dependency upon medications and hospitalization were leading her back to infantile memories and fears. This called for a confrontation with her about her condition and the reality of her life. Crazy thoughts had to be called crazy thoughts. Unrealistic planning had to be labeled unrealistic planning. Moments of anger and bitterness arose between us as we dealt with these realities. Memories of our conflicts and frustrations over the years arose and had to be handled straightforwardly. No longer could she as the parent shield me. Relating to her helplessness, encouraging her in her fight for recovery, formed a quality of relationship never experienced between us before, exposing the raw emotions unprotected by rationalization and intellectualization.

The second decision was to rearrange the living patterns and housekeeping routines so they could continue, if possible, to live in their home. Immediately, I took the driving chores from Dad, for clearly he should not be driving anymore. He was not a cook or one to keep the house clean, so I took over the chores of meal preparation and house upkeep. While the beloved neighbor had kept the house livable for them the past months, it was obvious that it had not had a thorough cleaning for several years. The old refrigerators and the broken beds had to be replaced. Carpeting had to be cleaned and repaired or replaced. This flurry of activity and exercise of my authority alerted Dad to the realization that we were in a new day together. Old personality conflicts resurfaced, and for the first time in our lives we had to become clear about our angers and affections for each other.

In the two weeks spent in the intensity of crisis and management of daily routine, my new authority with them became clear, and I could not abdicate my parental role. I was clearly in charge of the situation, and watchful care had to be taken that I not be seduced out of it for fear of hurting them, or be excessive in my authority by stripping them of more power and position than was necessary.

Mother's strength returned sufficiently to allow her to be released from the hospital. With the house thoroughly cleaned and rearranged, the freezer filled with food for a month, and an agreement with the neighbor to tend to their needs, it seemed possible that they could continue to manage in their own home. Buoyed by the support of family, friends, pastor, and church, I returned to my own home with the hope that my parents might manage for themselves through the next winter.

They attempted the readjusted life style, but recovery of strength and capacity to manage was very difficult. Barely able to walk around the house, Mother was unable to cook or clean. Dad became very anxious and prematurely cashed some bonds in a frenzied hope to move to Arizona to live with my sister. The strain on the neighbor pushed her strength to the limit. The full situation was again shielded from me, for they desperately wanted to prove that they could manage for themselves. But within four weeks the call came, "Jim, you had better come!" Mother's heartbeat was racing to a fatal degree.

What we had accomplished between us the previous month was now under a severe test. On this trip, I prepared myself for Mother's burial. The pastor again met me at the airport, but this time he was very clear about the inability of the beloved nieghbor lady, the friends, and the church to manage the care of my parents. It was clear to him and to the others close to my parents, that should they survive this current crisis, they needed the convalescent care of the nursing home. But I, as the son, had the only authority to make this decision.

The next two days Mother wavered in serious condition in the intensive care unit. She was in good spirits, and although her mind was clear, she had a hard time eating. She was relieved to see me. Dad and I visited and talked about the plans we would need to make, including admittance to the nursing home.

Dad's primary preoccupation, however, was with a driving test the license bureau had requested he take. In preparation for the test, he had scheduled an examination with his physician, and a serious irregularity in his heartbeat had been disclosed. An immediate consultation by phone was made with a specialist in the cardiac center a hundred miles away, and the next day Dad and I were on our way to the center to have a pacemaker installed in his heart. Though he had undergone serious surgery twenty years before, this was a critical time for him, precipitating awareness of his death as well as the death of my mother.

Leaving Mother in the intensive care unit of the local hospital, while traveling 100 miles to admit Dad to the cardiac center, called for a series of logistics which would have been impossible to manage without the help of the pastor. He agreed to be the mediator and communicator with Mother, but more importantly he had now become my pastor. The situation demanded that I be in charge and demonstrate strong, decisive, and unambivalent action. However, the strain upon me was beginning to take its toll, and the pastor recognized my suffering and emotional turmoil, allowing my weakness to surface in brief conversations. He was now standing by me, not taking over, but offering that quiet, unassuming presence that assisted me in keeping my thinking and actions focused and efficient.

Dad and I were not prepared for the elaborate procedure in the cardiac center. We had been led to believe that the installation of the pacemaker was a simple procedure taking two or three days, but as it turned out the experience took seven days. However, the environment in the cardiac unit was superb in that the sophisticated technology of the surgery and monitoring devices was softened by the friendly yet competent care of the nurses and physicians. The procedures of the surgery, the after-care, and the instructions in the use of the pacemaker were carefully explained and reinforced by those assigned to the cardiac unit. This, at least temporarily, helped dispel the fear, anxiety, and confusion which was occurring all around us.

The special role of the chaplaincy staff in the hospital quickly came into play. The minister, with special training in caring for heart disease patients, turned out to be a colleague and friend of thirty years with whom Dad and I both had lost contact. The renewal of friendship, as well as the understanding care of his professional relationship, was a special bright light in the experience.

The logistics of handling the arrangements and tending to the welfare of my parents in intensive care units in hospitals more than one hundred miles apart began to draw my attention to what was happening to me. I was beginning to lose a sense of my own identity under the consuming forces of the critical situation. I felt I had to do some things purely and simply for myself. Five activities came into play.

The first was eating. I had already started a calorie-counting diet in an effort to lose weight. Maintaining this discipline gave me a point of contact with myself. The second was exercise, a routine of walking each day which I had started a few months earlier. Maintaining these disciplined routines, particularly under the intensity of the crisis, were the only reminders that I still had a grasp on my sense of myself.

Three other activities were important to me in maintaining a sense of reality outside of the crisis. Managing time became vital, for the situation changed so rapidly from day to day that I chose to live only with the units of time over which I had some control. During the height of the crisis this meant only one half-day at a time. I could not allow the anticipation of the afternoon to interfere with the necessary activity of the morning. This served to modify the sense of helplessness generated by the insecurity and uncertainty of the constantly changing situation.

Maintaining close contact with others who were away from the situation became an immeasurable source of help in managing a balanced perspective of myself. One, sometimes two, telephone calls a day to my own family 700 miles away was the means of expressing my need to reflect, to laugh, to escape, to cry, to curse. My wife and daughters were there to listen, to support, to console, to confront me. This kept alive a clear sense of who I was apart from the immediacy of my involvement.

Relating to the chaplaincy staff in the hospital complex provided a reminder of my own professional identity. One noon was spent having lunch in a restaurant several miles from the hospital with the cardiac unit chaplain, visiting about a range of subjects in our respective lives and interests over the years. Another afternoon was spent with the director of the chaplaincy service sharing ideas about recent developments in pastoral education. The important dimension other than renewing personal friendships, was the internal awareness that in spite of the crisis my professional identity was still intact.

While I did these things for myself, the forces of disintegration were at work in my parents. They were being stripped of their life style and the integrating myths of their personal lives. Their pride in their good health, self-sufficiency, and emotional and financial independence was disappearing. In two short months the myths or core ideas which kept their lives integrated had changed. They were in between worlds, and both needed to talk, to grieve, and to sense a guiding support toward the next phase of their life.

Such movement was not philosophical, but came through simple activities. For Dad it started as he began to walk and speak in a friendly and joking way to other patients in the cardiac unit. For Mother it started as she began to eat her meals again.

Should my parents survive this immediate crisis, I had made the decision, in consultation with the physician, that both of them would be admitted to the nursing home, a new facility attached to the hospital in their hometown. Dad had already seen the wisdom of this possibility, but Mother was adamant in her resistance to the idea, thinking that residence in a nursing home was tantamount to death. No space was immediately available and the length of time before they could be admitted was uncertain. Fortunately, their applications were next on the waiting list. With both of them beginning to respond favorably to medical treatment, it was time to inform them of the decision to admit them to the nursing home.

The day following Dad's pacemaker surgery, I left him to travel back to the hometown hospital to visit Mother. Dad did not want me to leave him, for he feared loneliness. But as I left, we recognized together the pain of separation, almost like a rehearsal of our final separation in death. Throughout the experience of the crisis, it was the brief moments like this parting which carried the intensity of deep feelings between us.

I arrived at Mother's bedside just as her meal was delivered, and she immediately complained that she was not hungry. She had hardly eaten anything the past few days, claiming that the food was too bland and too much. As I listened to her complaints, I rearranged the food on her plate, separating out a few spoonfuls of each selection. I encouraged her to attempt only these few spoonfuls, and, as if not to embarrass herself, she took a bite. After fiddling awhile she took another bite, and by the third bite she went on to finish the portions I had attractively rearranged for her. Somehow this simple exchange began another level of relationship between us.

As I helped her get comfortable in her bed, we began to talk, for the physician had told her about the decision to admit her to the nursing home. She talked at length about her dread and negative images of nursing homes. She did not want to be old nor treated as an old person for she felt she had so much she yet wanted to do. As I recognized her fear, I offered two suggestions. The first one concerned the reasoning behind the decision—at this stage in her recovery she needed constant surveillance of her physical well being and medications. She was not strong enough to manage herself at her house, and of all the options available to us this was the most adequate. The decision was based upon the next six months of her convalescence, and in the spring we could reconsider the decision.

The second suggestion concerned her attitude toward the life style of the nursing home. She had a choice, not of whether she would be admitted, but whether she would use the nursing home for her recovery and resuming the activities which she wanted to do. She could use the nursing home as a place to be angry, bitter, and die, or she could use the home as a place to gain strength and readapt her life. No one could make that choice for her. Using the home was like eating her food. She could use it as a means to be angry and resistant about the reality of her current life, or she could use it as a means to nourish herself back to strength. In the nursing home—freed from responsibilities of cooking, housekeeping, and management of her medications—she could, as her strength permitted, concentrate on her writing, something she had longed to do for many years.

As we continued to talk our conversation focused upon our relationship and the times of closeness and conflict between us over the past forty-seven years. Distorted images, secret feelings, concern over my life decisions were reviewed. We had reached another level of relationship with an openness and candor never before experienced between us. That simple meal in her hospital room has since become a symbol for us, particularly at times when tough decisions have had to be made.

When I returned to the cardiac center, I found Dad had moved from intensive care to the intermediate care unit. He was not in his room, but I soon found him walking the hall, visiting other patients, sharing the stories of their lives. He had shaved himself, had been

eating well, and had begun to tease the nurses. The pallid color of
his face was replaced with his normal reddish complexion, indicating
that the pacemaker was now doing its work. He told me with some
pride about the pacemaker and wanted me to read the instructions
in the booklet that had been given him. He was beginning the process
of incorporating the pacemaker as part of his identity. Resuming his
normal activity of talking and joking with other people and listening
to their stories was his way of doing ministry as well as gaining gratifica-
tion for himself. In my absence of a day and a half he was beginning
to adapt to his new situation and to reassert his energy and pride.

We talked of the decision about the nursing home, the conversation
with Mother, and alternate plans for his care. We planned the closing
of the house for the winter and the management of the finances.
We agreed that I would take over the financial record keeping, payment
of bills, and arrangements with the property and bonds. He was now
placing in my hands an important part of his self-sufficiency, the management of his financial affairs.

Three days later he was released from the cardiac center and we
returned to his home town with the help of a friend who had come
to transport us. We found that Mother had been already moved to
the nursing home residence, and a place in the same room awaited
Dad. Such fortune was totally unanticipated. Mother had already begun
to make friends with other residents who had come to welcome her.
While the new situation seemed strange to all three of us, the change
of life style had already begun, with its mixture of joy and grief.

In the next few days, relationships began to form with the nursing
staff and other residents in the home. However, the signal which actually
sounded the beginning of their adaptation to their new life was the
interpretation which they were placing on the change. The nursing
home was not only for their convalescent care, but also for a new
phase of ministry. They began recounting each period of change in
their lives, starting with their first ministry in the foreign mission field
in India. They had begun to incorporate their new situation into that
primary thread of meaning that had tied life together over the years—
mission and ministry.

ANALYSIS

This personal experience of one family of course cannot be general-
ized for all situations. A dynamic process with five identifiable steps
does appear in the experience, however, and provides a way to understand the progressive flow through which such experiences of change
proceed.

The first step is the *precipitating event(s)*. Critical illness signaling
irreversible deterioration of health often begins the crises. This signal
comes in both sudden and gradual ways. In our family situation the
hospitalizations which finally centered upon the heart disease in both
parents were the events that brought about the change of residence
to the nursing home. Behind the sudden crisis, however, was the gradual
decline of health, particularly in the preceding three years. This had
been monitored by the physician so that, in the health care procedure
of the hospitalizations, he could make more precise judgments about
my parents' capacity to continue managing themselves in their own
house, especially with their children living so far away. The physician
became a pivotal person in the changing situation, for a trust and
almost godlike confidence had been placed in him. When he was clear
about the need for the nursing home, his recommendation was accepted
without challenge. The humane and competent way in which the physician and hospital staffs responded to the critical illnesses set a tone
and context for the entire process of change.

The second step involves the *management of life routines*. The ordinary routines of life, such as food preparation and management of
the household, could no longer be maintained. Accepting this reality
meant both parents and children had to undergo permanent psychological, as well as physical, change. The pastor became the pivotal person
in confronting this reality, for he could appreciate the need to resist
such change and, at the same time, he could be clear about the limitations of friends and neighbors in taking over the management of the
life routines of my parents. While the responsibility for developing a
new system for maintaining life routines was within the family, trust
and confidence in him allowed his influence to be accepted with a

minimum of defensiveness, overreaction, and avoidance. His support and assistance in exploring alternative possibilities allowed the family eventually to choose the nursing home as the most viable option.

The reality of deteriorating health and the inability to manage life routines led to the most painful step in the process, *the internal crises.* These crises centered on feelings of loss, confusion, helplessness—in short, depression. These feelings were manifested in a decline in motivation for living, withdrawal from social contacts, and burdensomeness of eating and sleeping. In his book *Childhood and Society* Erik Erikson has offered a way to understand the struggle of internal crises. In his description of the eighth developmental stage of life, he speaks of the polarity continuum of integrity versus despair. Directly confronting our feelings of the loss of life's meaning eventuated in an affirmation of a new integrity, but this would not have happened without the presence of friends, neighbors, and pastor. This presence, manifested in the concrete offers of help, provided a context which affirmed continued living in the midst of life's disintegration. It kept active a sense of reality which was coming from outside of our family's own resources, stimulating the drive to seek the meaning of the change. Faith was active in times of despair, not through pious words, but through the presence of others who without panic continued to assist our family in the day by day arrangements, thus maintaining a sense of normalcy in the situation.

The depression of the internal crises was worked out through *transitional factors.* This fourth step in the process revealed the dynamics of transition as regaining a sense of control over the decisions and options demanded by the new reality. This meant that we had to do much sorting out of meanings, values, and attachments. The factors through which the transitional dynamics took place were in the change of relationships between the children and parents, the meaning and use of money and possessions, the concepts of time, and the choice of attitude toward the new situation.

The narrative has described the change of dynamics in the relationship between parents and children. Systems of relating to each other and the emotional patterns of expressing feelings were opened for review and change. Resistance to the risks of such new relationships would have seriously hampered the transition to the new life style in the nursing home. Taking these risks created opportunities for growth for each family member.

Money and possessions took on new and different meanings in the transition period. Rather than a reserve to be inherited by the children, financial and property resources were now to be used for the care of parents in their new situation. The substance of the parent-child relationship in the decisions about money and possessions became that of mutual trust and affirmation.

A change in concepts of time encompassed another factor in the dynamics of transition. Residence in the nursing home did not need to be for the rest of their lives, but could be reevaluated given the particular needs and wishes of my parents. They could still exercise some choice about the future, allowing for some control over decisions for their own care and welfare. Time in the nursing home could be used for multiple purposes to enhance their lives.

The key transitional factor was the choice of attitude toward the changing situation. This attitude depended to a great extent on the image which parents, children, and friends had of the nursing home. What ultimately had to be sorted out was the internalized meanings of their lives, and how these meanings could be preserved and reevaluated in light of this next period.

Gaining a sense of a *new vision of life* as residents of the nursing home is the fifth step in the process. The new vision depended upon the stories and images which had tied their lives together and the capacity to adapt these to the new life condition. The basic image was that of ministry and mission in service to others. As my parents found new ways of living out this image in the relationships in the nursing home, they began to reestablish daily routines and patterns of living. While the nursing home had its own schedule to which all residents needed to conform, private routines allowing for personal satisfaction also emerged. Daily routines—dressing, eating, visiting, reading, writing, watching television, getting mail, napping, taking medication—became a blend of the schedule of the nursing home and personal choice. Weekly routines evolved, such as trips to the town, going to church, visits from friends, telephone calls to family. Many long established routines were easily adapted to the new residence in the nursing home.

In short, becoming aware of the gains as well as the losses in a new life style, allowed for a new vision of life to emerge within the limitations and capacities of their physical and mental health.

The five steps through which the experience of change flows is a cyclical process. The steps are closely associated with all human experiences which encompass loss and recovery. This dynamic flow is not only a process through which the total scope of the change passes, but it also repeats itself many times around many of the concrete issues of the change. For instance, the cycle is experienced in the specific decision to sell home property or in recurrence of critical illness. Some factors in the change never do fully resolve themselves, remaining irritants which get in the way of a full transition to the new life style.

None of the steps can be avoided, although specific ones may not be felt with the same intensity each time the cycle is experienced. It is important to understand that adequate recovery and resolution to the new life situation cannot be accomplished apart from confronting the moments of depression and despair. As in any loss there is hurt, and most of us seek to avoid experiencing hurt, whether it be physical, emotional, or spiritual. To dwell on the hurt impedes recovery and leads to despair, but to avoid the hurt prevents recovery and leads to disintegration and death. Consider these words of Psalm 23:

> Even though I walk through the
>   the valley of the shadow of death,
> I fear no evil:
> for thou art with me;
>   thy rod and thy staff,
>   they comfort me.

This insight points to the profound spiritual task involved in any change which confronts us with our human limitations.

CONCLUSION

This personal account of the experience with my parents at a time of critical change gathers together many of the dimensions discussed in this volume. It is but one concrete statement representing hundreds of thousands of families who live through similar critical change. But whether it be my experience or the experience of others, the significant presence of friends, pastors, and churches demands a concluding comment. Our most meaningful help came when others assisted and encouraged the dynamic process of change to proceed through its steps. The reliable presence of others functioned particularly in four important ways.

First, "outside" assistance was invaluable in helping us to maintain a realistic perspective on the day by day happenings. The shock and unpredictable developments in the situation often resulted in distorted perception and overreaction. To have reliable people—like the pastor—intervene with a realistic perspective, provided for balanced decisions under the intensity of emotional stress.

Second, friends provided timely intervention. To have others detect our exhaustion and be willing to take over specific tasks or to insist on moments of rest and withdrawal enabled us to regain our strength.

Third, others were willing to share the burden when the demands felt utterly overwhelming. Sharing the burden meant both that they were available to talk through plans and solutions, and to take on specific limited tasks when it was impossible for one person to do everything.

Fourth, the consciousness that the home church and specific persons were praying with and for us provided a feeling that we did indeed belong to a wider company of caring persons. Such a spiritual context of encouragement and sustenance provided important resources at times when all our energy seemed to be depleted.

Despite pain, suffering, and confusion, then, others played a vital part in helping us keep alive the faith that the realities of life had a substance, quality, constancy, and tangibility that could be grasped and affirmed.

13

Education for Ministry with the Aging

Melvin A. Kimble

Any examination of ministry and aging evokes both surprise at what the church has done and disappointment and dismay at what it has left undone. Clearly the church is called to speak the Word of God and to provide a vision of society in which there is justice for the aged. Participation in the political realm on behalf of the aged can easily be seen as part of the Christian's vocation and response. There is, in fact, a special urgency for Christians to be involved in any constructive change of public attitudes and values about aging and the aged. The social statements of many of the denominations underscore the importance of understanding the church as a prophetic community and as an advocate for the elderly.[1]

The responsibility of the institutional church to be a caring community and an agent of positive change can best be carried out through the local congregation. Indeed, the parish is emerging as the natural context for a rich and variegated ministry with older adults. Pastors are obviously in a strategic position to respond to developmental changes and life-cycle crises of the aged and their families. Pastors also have a unique opportunity to be facilitators and enablers of congregational programs involving the entire community.

Unfortunately, pastors sometimes prove to be ill-equipped or apathetic in responding to opportunities for individual and congregational ministering. Their inadequacy appears to be rooted, in part, in the pastors' own attitudes and anxieties about the aging process, a problem shared with most people in our society. Pastors are no more likely than anyone else to be comfortable with aging or to be well-informed on gerontological issues.

Not surprisingly, theological educators, like the rest of society, have tended to give more attention to earlier stages of the life cycle. Few seminaries lack courses that examine developmental crises of childhood and youth, but many seminaries have only recently considered adding courses that have the aged as their primary focus. Moreover, the gerontological content of existing courses has often not been comprehensive enough to equip pastors to minister effectively with older adults.

As interest in and concern about aging spread, improvements are being made in seminary curricula. A number of successful experimental courses have been developed recently as part of the Gerontology in Seminary Training (GIST) project of the National Interfaith Coalition on Aging, Inc.[2] This is all well and good for future pastors, but what can current pastors do about their shortcomings in the area of ministry with the aging? More than that, what can pastors do for congregations and laypeople who want to learn more about the process of aging and older people—either as a basis for some kind of lay ministry or for their own enrichment? These are valid questions, and this chapter will attempt to suggest some practical approaches that can be taken in the development of gerontologically oriented programs.

Seminarians naturally tend to be drawn more to formal courses. To a limited extent, this is true for participants in pastors' continuing education programs as well, but pastors are also interested in possibilities for self-enrichment and in training and enrichment programs for laypeople. While it is impossible to be all things to all people, it is, I hope, possible to provide some ideas and resources for individual study and for program development for long- or short-term "professional" and lay groups.

BASES FOR PROGRAM DEVELOPMENT

A bewildering accumulation of theories and concepts, facts and falla-cies, myths and realities about aging exists in our culture. No program, be it information- or action-oriented, can afford to ignore this plethora of ideas and feelings. The development of programs directed toward either individuals or groups should take into account certain gerontologi-cal basics.

First of all, aging is a multidimensional reality that demands an interdisciplinary approach. A segmental approach to the aging process would result in a reductionistic, one-dimensional caricature of the aged person. Any examination of aging and the aged should reflect an under-standing that it is a *whole person* who is aging and is aged. This wholeness requires the interfacing of spiritual, social, physical, mental, and emotional dimensions of human growth and development. Insights of medicine, sociology, psychology, and theology need to be brought into dynamic dialogue if an integrated understanding of the older adult is to emerge.

If the enormity of such a task frightens you, be assured that this integration is a natural and commonsensical thing to do. It is, after all, the practice of specialists to break things apart for investigation and scrutiny. Then we must decide which subjects and issues need an interdisciplinary approach to pull them back together again. Geron-tology is one such subject, and its students, at whatever level, should recognize that it is as broadly based and as specialized as the varied backgrounds of its experts.

Anyone who takes an interdisciplinary approach tends to be biased in favor of a particular point of view, and integrates the subject accord-ingly. For example, I have indicated that we who have a religious orientation are inclined to view gerontology as something we need to grasp in order to be more effective ministers and ministering congrega-tions. We tend to feel that the spiritual dimension is the inclusive dimension for understanding and integrating theories and concepts of human development with techniques and programs for ministry with older adults. Theology, we believe, encompasses that which is not comprehensible in biology, psychology, and other disciplines—that is, ultimate meaning, ultimate concern. What is not allowed for in other disciplines is that which is answered in faith.

An interdisciplinary approach to aging that includes a theological or spiritual perspective recognizes the spiritual core of a person as capable of taking a positive stand toward negative and painful external circumstances. By stressing that a human being is not simply a psychosomatic organism, this perspective affirms the defiant power of the human spirit and its capacity to find meaning in suffering. This unique spiritual capacity conveys a renewed awareness of self-worth and human dignity and helps persons comprehend themselves as fashioned in the image of God.[3]

We interpret aging from the perspective of God's gracious purpose in creation and redemption. God's love is not determined by a person's age or productivity, but is unconditional and external. The wholeness of existence is undergirded by an understanding of spiritual well-being that is an "affirmation of life in a relationship with God, self, community and environment that nurtures and celebrates wholeness."[4]

DESIGNING A SELF-ENRICHMENT PROGRAM

Whether you are embarking on a self-directed learning program on the subject of aging and the aged or are just looking into it, ask yourself *why* you are interested. Are there very personal reasons involved—your coming to grips with your own aging, perhaps, or with your parents' increasing frailty? Or do you realize that if you knew more, you could do a better job of ministering to an often-neglected segment of your congregation? Or are you simply curious about the present high level of interest in aging? Based on your answer, you should give some thought to the kinds of information you need. Are you more interested in nursing homes, retirement, day-to-day living problems of the elderly, terminal illness, psychosocial issues, or ethical and/or theological questions?

Regardless of the reasons for your interest and the kinds of information required, you will probably find that you reflect an almost universal uneasiness with the aging process. Most of us betray in subtle ways our acceptance, or rather nonacceptance, of our own aging. We find it difficult to acknowledge the process until we are hit with a brickbat—a birthday, becoming a grandparent, or the death of a contemporary, for example. Our discomfort may affect the quality of our relationships with persons who are already aged. Are pastoral visits with the elderly in the congregation too easily postponed? Are conversations with elderly parishioners superficial or patronizing?

If you are not willing to become aware of these problems in yourself, then all the information in the world about nursing homes, retirement opportunities, and the pros and cons of "death with dignity" cannot help you be a better minister. The price of information is involvement.

So where do you begin your search for enlightenment? Where there was once a dearth there is now a spate of information. Listed below are some easily obtainable books you might find useful. They touch various areas of interest, though there is an emphasis on ministry. Other choices, equally useful, are cited in other chapters.

Baer, Louis. *Let the Patient Decide: A Doctor's Advice to Older Persons.* Philadelphia: Westminster, 1978.

Beauvoir, Simone de. *The Coming of Age.* New York: Warner Books, 1975.

Butler, Robert N., and Lewis, Myrna I. *Aging and Mental Health: Positive Psychosocial Approaches.* St. Louis: C. V. Mosby, 1977.

Butler, Robert N. *Why Survive? Being Old in America.* New York: Harper & Row, 1975, paperback 1977.

Clements, William M. *Care and Counseling of the Aging.* Philadelphia: Fortress Press, 1979.

Heinecken, Martin J., and Hellerich, Ralph. *The Church's Ministry with Adults: A Theological Basis.* New York: Lutheran Church in America, Division for Mission in North America, 1976.

Kart, Cary S., and Manard, Barbara. *Aging in America: Readings in Social Gerontology.* Sherman Oaks, Ca.: Alfred Publishing Co., 1976.

McClellan, Robert W. *Claiming a Frontier: Ministry and Old People.*
Los Angeles: University of Southern California, Andrus Gerontol-
ogy Center, 1977.
Tournier, Paul. *Learn to Grow Old.* New York: Harper & Row,
1973.
Wolf, Betty, and Wolf, Umhau. *Ten to Get Ready: Preparing for
Retirement.* Philadelphia: Parish Life Press, 1979.

As you work through the resources you have gathered and become
more aware of the needs of aged persons and their families, you may
realize that you need to polish up certain professional skills. You may
want to review appropriate techniques of crisis intervention or expand
your knowledge of bereavement, for example. Several of the books
suggested above stress the importance of listening to the older person's
concerns and reminiscences. Listening appreciatively to an older person
reminisce about days gone by is a most significant ministry, though
too often we think of this activity as tedious at best. If you really
want to improve your ministry with the aging, do not neglect enhancement of your listening skills. Pastors need to realize, and help families
realize, that by reminiscing a person is able to review and evaluate
the past and to introduce new perceptions and meanings of the past.[5]
Robert Butler's research has been instrumental in indicating the importance of reminiscence. His clinical observations and work with the
aging have provided data for his theory that reminiscence is "part of
a normal life review process brought about by realization of approaching
dissolution and death. It is characterized by the progressive return to
consciousness of past experiences and particularly the resurgence of
unresolved conflicts which can be looked at again and reintegrated.
If the reintegration is successful it can give new significance and meaning to one's life and prepare one for death, by mitigating fear and
anxiety."[6]

The life review process described by Butler can be aided by a listener
who cares. At appropriate moments gently probing questions can delve
into significant relationships, personal histories, and unfinished business.
Spending time listening to and talking with an aged person is an enrich-

ing experience. More often than not the listener comes away with respect and admiration for the manner in which the person has coped with losses, surmounted illnesses and disappointment, moved through radical changes in life style and environment, maintained self-esteem, contributed to church and society, and approached dying and death.

Close attention to what aged persons are really saying can help you understand not only their past but also their evaluation of their present circumstances and their hopes and concerns for the future. You may find it helpful to be aware of practical referrals in your area—community agencies, services for the elderly, professionals who are adept at working with older people, etc. Is there a "Meals on Wheels" or "Congregate Meals" program, for example? Is there a physician who is particularly experienced with elderly patients? Do any community agencies have a geriatric social worker, a day-care program? Are there agencies or organizations who would appreciate elderly volunteers?

You may well find that there is precious little practical help or understanding available to your elderly parishioners and friends. This can be a depressing discovery, but it can also inspire action. An intellectual understanding of aging and the needs of aged persons is not enough. Reading about conditions is an important part of learning, whether on a group or individual, self-directed level, but it is no substitute for personal observation and experience.

DESIGNING PROGRAMS FOR GROUPS

Working with groups generally takes a little more planning than designing a program for yourself. The kind of group you are working with and the kind of goals you have will, of course, dictate your choices of format and materials. For example, your group may be a formally organized course for seminarians or a continuing education workshop for pastors. It may be a loosely organized church school class or a one- or two-session event (such as a program for a particular church group or for "family night"). It may be inner-directed—for enrichment, problem-solving, and practical service. You may want to concentrate on one aspect of aging, such as becoming acquainted with public policy

and community resources or understanding the uses and value of reminiscence and the life-review process. Or, if you have a longer time
period in which to work, you may want to explore the sociological,
psychological, physiological, and spiritual dimensions of aging or the
relationship of the aged to the life and mission of the church. Once
you have determined your time-frame, your "audience," and your goals,
you can plan your approach and outline specific program components.

Because participants in your education group will generally feel a
certain discomfort with the subject of aging regardless of their motivation for participation, a good place to begin is with what I call "awareness techniques." Interaction about their uneasiness, usually best
introduced by sharing feelings and experiences, can do much to enhance
self-awareness and ease the need for defense mechanisms (such as denial) that can block effective learning.

There are a number of fine audiovisual materials available to stimulate
strong feelings and creative thinking in a group. The following films,
and others like them, can prime group members for sharing personal
and family concerns and dilemmas: *Peege, Portrait of Grandpa Doc,
The Wild Goose, The Detour, Wild Strawberries, Harry and Tonto,
Going in Style,* and *I Never Sang for My Father.* More information
about films and their availability can be obtained from an audiovisual
rental catalogue.

Viewing such a film under the right circumstances can be a powerful
experience. It can provide an opportunity not only for significant personal sharing but also for discussion of such issues as the intergenerational alienation that conflicting value systems and life styles all too
often produce.

Another very effective "awareness exercise," particularly suitable for
smaller groups, allows participants to experience a sequence of problems
resulting from normal sensory loss in aging. Restrictive devices of various
types simulate auditory, visual, tactile, coordination, and mobility losses.
A physician, nurse, or occupational therapist would probably be familiar
with such simulations, although simple ear plugs, wax paper taped
over eyeglass lenses, and gloves worn on the hands will do an adequate
job. Most people find that participation in sensory loss simulation results

in an increase in empathy and a new understanding of the debilitating conditions suffered by so many elderly people.

As you develop the program for your group, you will want to consider utilizing the skills and experience of various resource persons. If there is a "gerontologist" available, you are indeed fortunate. However, any "geriatric professionals"—people whose specific jobs within their fields of expertise have brought them into close contact with the elderly— would be appropriate guest speakers or panel members: nursing home administrators and nurses, oncology unit nurses, hospice program personnel, recreational therapists, welfare workers, etc. If you are preparing a long-term program such as a seminary course, you might want to require that students interview some of these professionals.

Of course, older people themselves are the best resources and should not be overlooked in either planning or staffing the event. Too few younger people interact with elderly people sufficiently to break down cultural stereotypes of what it means to be old. Structured opportunities for talking with and listening to elderly people can be a significant means of intergenerational exchange and provide positive models for growing older.

A formally organized group, such as a seminary or other long-term class, would benefit from focused interviews with older persons, following the life review technique discussed earlier. These interviews may be recorded on tape and shared with the group, with the interviewee's permission or even direct participation. (Using such a recording is a good way to give a taste of the technique to a group whose members do not have the time or opportunity to conduct their own interviews.) My experience is that the interviewers (listeners) gain considerable insight into such matters as how various individuals at this stage of life cope with grief and depression resulting from personal losses and arrive at some psychological and spiritual integrity and meaning.

As your program progresses, group members realize that they need more understanding of such matters as health and emotional problems common to the aged, anticipatory grief, and the symptoms of unresolved grief. Inclusion of related material may be planned/scheduled for seminary and continuing education groups, and for certain lay groups. Other groups may prefer to explore these matters as they occur. Although research papers are obviously unsuitable for most groups, systematic research into some facet of the aging process can encourage independent inquiry in seminary or college students. Where research is appropriate, a wide variety of individual topics can considerably broaden the students' learning experience. My own students have chosen such subjects as "Meaningful Existence and Ultimate Values," "Sexuality in the Elderly," "The Elderly Alcoholic," "Housing for the Elderly," and "Long-term Care Ministry."

More innovative, perhaps, and certainly more widely applicable, is the technique of role playing. It gives participants a good opportunity to refine skills in active listening, evaluating, responding, affirming, clarifying, and comforting. Role playing also reinforces the feelings of empathy tapped by sensory loss exercises and audiovisual materials. The variety of roles and situations is limited only by your imagination. Possibilities include: (1) Adult son or daughter tells elderly parent of a decision to move away to a distant city; (2) Pastor/chaplain talks with family of elderly patient who is terminally ill; (3) Group of nursing home residents converses together during a craft session/bridge game; (4) Newly retired man (of any occupation) is at home during the day with his wife. They have been surprised at many changes in their relationship and are willing to frankly discuss them with their pastor, if asked; (5) Elderly person (of any previous status) goes to the welfare department to apply for food stamps. Many feelings come to the surface that need to be talked over with a close friend; (6) You, the pastor, are called to a retirement home by a ninety-two-year-old man who was formerly active in parish life. You fear the worst. However, when you arrive, you discover that he wants you to meet another resident, whom he plans to marry.

SOME IMPACTS OF A PROGRAM ON AGING

Obviously, no program should be seen as a panacea for the perplexing and increasingly prevalent problems of aging and the aged. Certainly no program, however long-term or multifaceted, can hope to transform its participants into omniscient gerontological practitioners. However, a well-planned event can be a stimulus for creative response to the growing challenge and opportunity of developing new ministries with the aging. An understanding of the changes and crises experienced in the aging process should undergird lay and professional ministry. People of all ages who are informed and sensitized to the experience of growing old can provide a supportive atmosphere in which the elderly can share their concerns, strengths, and abilities and can develop their resources.

I have found that participants in education programs struggle to develop and articulate a theological perspective that refracts knowledge and theory about aging and the aged through theological and biblical concepts relevant to the human condition. They see God's gracious purpose in creation and redemption as confirming the intrinsic dignity and value of each person regardless of age. They realize that the context for a Christian understanding of aging is the life of the church. It is here that theological resources for ministry and for the expression of the caring community are made visible.

NOTES

1. See, for example, Lutheran Church in America, "Aging and the Older Adult," *Social Statements* (New York: Lutheran Church in America, 1978), p. 2.
2. Many of the ideas set forth in this chapter evolved from a model course developed as part of the Gerontology in Seminary Training (GIST) project of the National Interfaith Coalition on Aging, Inc., and taught by the author at Luther Northwestern Seminaries in St. Paul, Minnesota.
3. Melvin A. Kimble, "Applications of Logotherapy in Pastoral Psychology," *The International Forum for Logotherapy* 2, no. 2 (1979), pp. 31–34.
4. T. C. Cook, Jr., *Spiritual Well-Being—A Definition* (Athens, Ga.: National Interfaith Coalition on Aging, 1975).
5. William M. Clements, *Care and Counseling of the Aging* (Philadelphia: Fortress Press, 1979), pp. 44–56.
6. Robert N. Butler and Myrna I. Lewis, *Aging and Mental Health: Positive Psychosocial Approaches*, 2nd ed. (St. Louis: C. V. Mosby, 1977), p. 49. Butler's original research is reported in his article "The Life Review: An Interpretation of Reminiscence in the Aged," *Psychiatry* 26 (1963), pp. 65–76.

14

Death, Dying, and the Elderly

George Paterson

Older people have no monopoly on dying. Death comes to children, to young adults, and to persons in middle age. Nevertheless, the conquest of infectious diseases in the past half century has made death increasingly a phenomenon of later life. While the young may realistically view death as far in the future, those over sixty-five live with the inescapable knowledge that the end of their life is drawing near. Thus, anyone who would minister effectively to the elderly must have some understanding of the characteristic thoughts, feelings, attitudes, and behavior of those people who are facing death.

THE DYING PROCESS

One of the most widely read and influential studies of the dying is *On Death and Dying*, by Elisabeth Kübler-Ross, which appeared a decade ago.[1] She described the psychological dimensions of the dying process as a series of five stages: denial, anger, bargaining, depression, and acceptance. Her account proved to be enormously popular, no doubt in part because of the warm and humane attitude she exhibited toward her patient-subjects. It also gained acceptance, I believe, because it introduced a semblance of order into a realm that had heretofore seemed mysterious and chaotic, and because it suggested that the process moved rather naturally to a positive conclusion, that the final stage might bring peaceful surrender rather than agonizing struggle. However, some readers, including a few in the helping professions overliteralized her account. They took the model for reality itself, and overlooked the fact that her stages are simply a conceptual framework—and not the only possible one—for understanding the feelings and behavior of those who are terminally ill.

It is important to realize that not all thanatologists agree with Kübler-Ross's conclusions. Edwin Shneidman, for example, sees the dying process not as a series of stages, but as a constant flow of negative and positive feelings, similar to the movement of bees in a hive, with an alternation of denial and fear, rage and surrender, hope and despair.[2] E. Mansell Pattison finds no evidence for specific stages in the emotional reactions of those who are dying, but prefers rather to divide the living-dying interval into three phases—acute, chronic, and terminal—each with its own characteristic emotional tone.[3]

Although the stages outlined by Kübler-Ross are an extremely useful guide to the person who seeks to help the dying, they should never lead one to overlook the enormous amount of individual diversity in the way people traverse the final phase of their life's journey. The five stages do describe the most common reactions people display toward impending death, but they are by no means universal. Not everyone goes through all five, and few persons move through them sequentially, in neat, orderly fashion. In *The Death of Ivan Ilych*, Leo Tolstoy has drawn a convincing and accurate picture of the way an individual may shift back and forth between denial, anger, and depression, between hope and despair, until finally acceptance is reached at the very end of the struggle.[4] The value of the stages lies in the fact that one who is acquainted with them will seldom be completely surprised by any response from a dying person. Yet we should never use the concept of stages as a norm to judge the rightness or wrongness of an individual's responses. Each dying person should be respected in his or her uniqueness, and allowed—even helped—to manage the process in the manner that seems most appropriate to him or her.

Older persons in particular may deviate from the typical path described by Kübler-Ross. Denial, for example, may play a less prominent role for the elderly than for those in mid-life. The person who has lived for some years with the expectation of death is not likely to be shocked at the discovery of a fatal illness. I often invite participants in workshops on death and dying to imagine how they would feel if they had just been told that they had cancer, and then to share their reactions with the total group. In one such group, a physician looking toward his own retirement said, "I felt relief. I realized that I've been expecting something like this for a long time."

I knew a lady in her mid-nineties who lived with her daughter and son-in-law. Until a stroke physically disabled her, she had slept in an upstairs bedroom. After the stroke her bed was moved to a room on the first floor, but she was unhappy about the empty bedroom upstairs and talked about it continuously. Finally a new bed was bought, and the lady was content. Only then did her family think to ask her why it had been so important to her to have a bed in the empty room. She answered, "When the whole family comes home for my funeral, I want them all to have a place to sleep here in the house. But I knew if I told you that, you'd just say, 'Oh, Grandma, you're not going to die!' "

As denial may be a less significant response to dying for some older persons than for those who are younger, so the anger and depression which the elderly exhibit may not center so much on death itself as on the circumstances of living in a state of continual decline. A patient in his seventies with cancer of the rectum said, "It's not death I fear so much as all that I may have to go through before I get there." Weakness, pain, physical disability, loss of control over bowels and bladder, financial dependence, and the deterioration of mental abilities are just a few of the things that many older people fear more than the cessation of life.

Indeed, for some older persons death may come to be viewed not as an enemy but as a long-awaited friend. Joseph Rheingold has shown that death bears a variety of personal meanings for individuals, both positive and negative. On the one hand, it may signify separation, loss, pain, and punishment, but it may also signify deliverance, rest, reunion, rebirth, and loving self-sacrifice.[5] For the person in the final phase of the life cycle who has experienced considerable suffering, the positive meanings may come to outweigh the negative ones. A widow in her seventies was admitted to the hospital numerous times for treatment of congestive heart failure. Each time she was treated successfully and sent home with the instruction that she must continue to follow a strict low-salt diet. Within a short time she would be back with an accumulation of body fluids and shortness of breath, having totally ignored the physician's advice. On one admission she was even discovered hiding salt in her suitcase! Since the medical and nursing staff were at a loss in securing her cooperation, and since religious faith appeared to be very important to her, the chaplain was asked to see her. He found her a very lonely, wistful person. Her husband had died several years earlier. She had a number of grown children, all married, and though she claimed that she "got along" with all of them, it appeared that she was close to none of them. Frequently she would sigh deeply and remark, "All I have left now is my Lord." When the chaplain would reflect, "You must feel very lonely," she would quickly reply, "Oh, no! I'm never lonely." (How could she be lonely when she had her Lord as a constant companion?) Yet it was clear that she did feel very much alone in the world, however strongly she denied it. Eventually, shortly after her last discharge from the hospital, she died at home.

In retrospect, I am convinced that this woman both desired her own death and indirectly sought it. Her particular faith would not allow her even to consider actively taking her own life, but it did not require that she adhere to the diet her doctor prescribed. It is likely that, for her, death had come to represent deliverance from an intolerable burden of loneliness, and perhaps a reunion with both her husband and her Lord as well.

SIGNIFICANT LOSSES

The stages described by Elisabeth Kübler-Ross can help us become aware of still another aspect of dying that is especially significant among older people. I sometimes ask students to think of all the events and circumstances other than death to which a person might respond with feelings of denial, anger, bargaining, depression, and finally acceptance. Some of the most frequently given answers include the death of a loved one, separation or divorce from one's spouse, a physical disability such as those resulting from a stroke or an amputation, the loss of a job, failing an examination, and having to give up one's home. (One person claimed she had seen her neighbor go through all five stages in the space of twenty minutes after she drove her car into the corner of her garage!) All these experiences have one thing in common: they represent significant losses. This suggests that denial, anger, bargaining, depression, and acceptance may not only be a way people deal with the threat of impending death, but a way in which we respond to the loss of *anyone* or *anything* that is important to us. Death is not the only loss we experience in the course of our lives; it is simply the final and ultimate loss.

We must recognize that most older people experience many important losses prior to death. The thinning or graying of their hair, vision or hearing losses, weakened muscle tone, diminished sexual potency, degenerative changes in bones and joints, the departure of children from home, retirement from work, restrictions in income, the necessity of moving to a retirement or nursing home, the death of friends, family members, or spouse—all of these are losses that are common to persons in the last stage of life. Martin Berezin has coined the term "partial grief" to describe the reaction to such losses not only by the older person but also by his or her family members.[6] Keeping these losses in mind may help us to understand why death is not always dreaded by the older person, and may sometimes be viewed with actual longing.

Dying itself can usefully be viewed as an experience of progressive and multidimensional loss, a loss that affects individuals in the physical, social, emotional, and spiritual dimensions of their being. I well remember a conversation with a married woman in her sixties who was dying after an illness of several years. She began by remarking that the chemotherapy she took to control her cancer had made her lovely red hair fall out: "It was always my best feature, and it seemed so unfair that I should have to lose it." She and her husband had operated a small antique business in their home; she loved old furniture, and enjoyed meeting others who shared her enthusiasm. This too they had had to give up as her disease progressed. Although she was not an active church-goer, she had always felt close to God while walking in her garden in the cool of evening; now she realized that she would never be able to do this again. For many years she had prayed that she might live long enough to raise her daughter; the daughter was now grown and had children of her own. It seems clear that this lady was reviewing the many losses which dying represented to her: physical (her hair, her beauty), social (her family and business), emotional (her sense of fulfillment in nature), and spiritual (her sense of being close to God).

COPING WITH LOSS: FAITH, HOPE, LOVE

How can the minister be of help to the dying older person?[7] From studies of bereavement it is clear that three things must be done if a person is to cope successfully with loss. First, the reality of the loss must be recognized and acknowledged. We cannot adapt to or overcome loss by pretending that it isn't real or that it isn't really important. What has been or is being lost must be identified and its value assessed before it can be given up. Second, the painful feelings which accompany the loss must be shared with another person or persons. These may include anger, guilt, sadness, dejection, fear, and despair. Finally, one's remaining resources must be reassessed and reinvested in other goals, activities, and relationships so that the experience of loss may result in growth. As Lily Pincus says of grief in *Death and the Family*,

> There is no growth without pain and conflict; there is no loss which cannot lead to gain. . . . We all know that we grow through overcoming difficulties

and pain, yet our aim, quite rightly, is to eliminate pain and suffering. Nevertheless, whatever our medical and social successes may be, there does not seem to be any prospect of dispensing with death and the pain of loss. Instead, we have to increase our recognition of death and use the unavoidable pain of loss to help us grow.[8]

The importance of religious faith is that it provides a framework of meaning in which loss is not the final reality of human existence, and thus helps to point toward and mobilize those forces within and beyond the individual which make growth a genuine possibility, even through loss. This possibility is described by Paul:

> We are afflicted in every way, but not crushed; perplexed, but not driven to despair; persecuted, but not forsaken; struck down, but not destroyed. . . . So we do not lose heart. Though our outer nature is wasting away, our inner nature is being renewed every day. [II Cor. 4:8–9, 16]

The minister stands as a symbolic representative of such growth, and of the forces that make it possible. As an empathic listener, she or he can assist the dying person in recognizing the reality and significance of the losses that are being sustained, and expressing the painful feelings which this recognition evokes. But the minister can do more than this: as a person who symbolizes the dying individual's faith, the community of believers, and the presence of God, he or she can help to mediate the grace and strength which enable one to be renewed inwardly, even though familiar supports and treasured possessions are being gradually stripped away.

That such renewal is not empty rhetoric but a genuine possibility was demonstrated by an eighty-five-year-old man in a congregation I served many years ago. He was frail in body and his hearing and eyesight were almost gone, yet he had a sturdy faith and a delightful sense of humor. When we visited I had to shout to make him hear, but he seemed to enjoy my coming, and I found myself refreshed by his spirit. Hearing that he had become very sick, even near to death, I went to see him in the nursing home. His family was gathered round. At first they had difficulty making him understand who had come to see him; but when he realized it was the preacher, he turned his face in my direction and with a wry smile asked, "Did you come here looking for a job?" Although he had almost nothing left except his trust in God and the sense of dignity that it gave him, he could still face death, as he had faced life, with courage and humor.

"So faith, hope, love abide, these three" (I Cor. 13:13a). These are the forces that make growth through loss a possibility, and the minister can be one who helps the dying person get or stay in touch with these forces. *Faith* should be understood not as a kind of magical formula that enables one to put God to work for oneself, nor as the recipe for a successful bargain with the Almighty for a miraculous cure. Rather it is to be viewed, in Erik Erikson's famous phrase, as an attitude of "basic trust," an attitude that arises from the conviction that whatever may come—whether strength or weakness, renewed health or continued illness, comfort or sorrow, extended life or imminent death—one will be given the courage and insight to face it, and that in spite of death the purpose of one's life will be graciously fulfilled and brought to completion. As the ancient Hebrew poet put it:

> God is our refuge and strength,
>   a very present help in trouble.
> Therefore we will not fear though the earth
>   should change,
>   though the mountains shake in the heart
>   of the sea. [Ps. 46:1–2]

The importance of *hope* has been stressed not only by Elisabeth Kübler-Ross, who found that it persisted throughout the dying process until very near the end, but also by Viktor Frankl in his autobiographical study of the feelings and behavior of prisoners in concentration camps.[9] According to Frankl, those who managed to survive the camps were those who were able to hold on to some hope for the future, while those who lost hope succumbed to exhaustion, starvation, or disease.

Of course, there are many different forms in which hope may be expressed by persons who are terminally ill, and these forms may undergo considerable change during the course of a progressively fatal illness. The task of the minister is both to sustain and nurture hope through the dying process, and to help the person who is dying surrender the unrealistic forms of hope in favor of more appropriate forms as death draws near.

At the outset of the illness, persons who are dying may hope that their disease can be cured or at least controlled by appropriate medical treatment, and their lives extended by months or even years. If this expectation proves unfounded, they may still hope for adequate time and strength to set their affairs in order, or for time to spend at home with members of their family, as well as for some pain-free days and enough mental alertness to continue to relate to friends and loved ones. As their disease progresses, they may focus on the hope that they will be able to meet death in a dignified way, with courage, composure, and a measure of self-respect. But hope extends beyond the event of death: dying persons may also hope that after death they will be remembered with affection and respect by those with whom they have lived, or that their work will be carried on by others, or that their family members will be cared for adequately, or that they will inherit eternal life in the presence of God.

Another kind of hope which does not depend on cure or extension of life can be seen in the case of a Protestant minister who, only a few months before his scheduled retirement, was found to have cancer of the liver. He and his wife had been looking forward to some years of leisure together. Now his future seemed very short. His doctors had no effective treatment for his disease. They did, however, offer him a highly experimental form of chemotherapy, which they advised might not help him, and might even add significantly to his discomfort. He decided to accept chemotherapy. "First of all," he said, "I figure it's better to fight than to give up. Besides that, even though it doesn't help me, the doctors may learn something from me that will enable them to help someone else later on." This man was sustained by the hope that his living and dying might ultimately benefit others unknown to him.

"But the greatest of these is *love*" (I Cor. 13:13b). I can hardly overemphasize the importance of warm and supportive relationships to the dying person. One of the most frequent consequences of illness is isolation. The sick person is significantly cut off from others by the need to be in a hospital or nursing home, or by being shut in at home. Further, the attitude of others toward the sick person often seems to change because of illness. Cancer patients sometimes say, "You'd think what I have is contagious, the way people avoid me." This avoidance may result partly from the discomfort friends and neighbors feel over not knowing what to say to or do for a person who is terminally ill. Finally, debility, discomfort, and pain are themselves very private experiences; no one can feel them with or for you. Not only is isolation a very common consequence of serious illness, it also represents one of the greatest fears of those who are facing death. An elderly woman in the end-stages of leukemia kept repeating, over and over again like a litany, "I'm not afraid to die, but I don't want to be alone."

There is increasing evidence that those who have someone to live for, someone who cares about them and for whom they care, actually do survive longer and resist the effects of illness better than those who are isolated and lonely.[10] The importance of religion here lies in that it not only provides a belief system which nurtures hope and trust, but it also makes available a network of significant relationships, it gives access to a community of faith. The minister serves as a symbol of a community which cares for and about the elderly, the sick, and the dying. One who knows that he or she belongs to such a community does not live or die in isolation, but rather as a fellow citizen "with the saints" and as a member of "the household of God" (Eph. 2:19). By being present with the dying person the minister can serve as a reminder of this reality.

But love is a more-than-human phenomenon according to the teachings of Judaism and Christianity. It furnishes a dynamic and direction for the whole creation: "He who abides in love abides in God, and God abides in him" (I John 4:16). People who have learned how to receive and give love may experience growth and fulfillment even when death draws near, because their existence is empowered and directed by this fundamental force. A devout Catholic woman dying of metastatic cancer said, "I believe in heaven, and I expect to go there. But

I can't imagine how it can be any more beautiful than the love I've experienced during these past few months."

CARING

How can the minister help to mediate and mobilize the power of faith, hope, and love for the dying older person? In my own work with seriously ill and dying persons I try to adhere to four principles. The more closely I am able to follow these, the more effective I feel I am in helping others. The first is simply to *be there*. The most valuable thing we have to offer the older person facing death is our own caring presence. What we say or don't say is not nearly so important as the fact that we are there. Yet it is easy for us to find reasons to avoid the dying person, for we are apt to feel anxious, uncomfortable, and inadequate in his or her presence. How many times have those of us who are pastors or chaplains looked in a hospital room to find the patient lying in bed with eyes closed, and tiptoed by, saying to ourselves (with some relief!), "Mrs. Wilson needs her rest more than she needs a visit from me today." Over the years I have learned at least to walk up to the bedside and call the patient's name gently, for that "sleep" may be the drowsiness that comes from boredom, depression, or loneliness rather than a genuine need for rest. (In fact, many hospitalized patients have difficulty sleeping at night and need help to stay awake during the day.)

"Being there" doesn't necessarily mean spending large blocks of time with the person who is dying. Few pastors can afford to sit with a seriously ill parishioner for hours at a time, several times a week. But it does mean being *all there* while we are there, being fully present and giving our entire attention to the person before us, if only for five minutes at a time. When possible, it means sitting down to show that we have time to listen, and to put ourselves on approximately the same level as the other person. It means resisting the temptation to allow a part of our mind to think about the letters we have to write or the other persons we have to see before the day is over. "Being there" means concentrating on the unique, irreplaceable individual who is before us. It also means being with the dying person in a dependable and consistent way, following through in the relationship. The individual who is facing death needs to be able to count on us to keep coming back as long as we are needed.

The second principle I try to follow is to *be myself.* Orville Kelly, a cancer patient who founded the organization "Make Today Count" for people suffering from life-threatening illness, was once asked by a group of student nurses, "What should we say to a dying patient?" His answer was, "How about starting with 'Good morning'?" He understands how important it is for people who are trying to help to be themselves. I am convinced I am most helpful to others when I don't feel it necessary to put up a front or wear a professional mask, when I don't pretend to have an answer to every question or solutions to all problems, when I am not afraid to let some of my own vulnerability show through. I believe I am most helpful to others when I am most aware of my own feelings—not only the negative feelings such as anxiety, anger, or helplessness, but also such positive feelings as warmth, caring, and competence.

My third principle is to *listen.* Dr. Cicely Saunders, a pioneer in the hospice movement for the care of the terminally ill, tells physicians that what they say to their dying patients is not as important as what they allow their patients to say to them.[11] This principle is equally true for ministers. The story is told that the wife of a famous writer was distressed by his constant use of profanity. Hoping to break him of the habit she decided to show him how he sounded when he swore. One day when something went amiss in the kitchen she let out a string of oaths. He chuckled at her language. "What are you laughing about?" she demanded. "My dear," he replied, "you know the words but you don't know the tune!"

Listening involves paying attention not only to the words, but to the music as well. It means being sensitive to the feelings contained in the other person's statements as well as to the verbal content. It is more than waiting for the conversational ball to fall in one's own court, or rehearsing one's own lines until there is an opportunity to speak them. Active listening involves the whole self of the listener;

it is a way of saying, "I am *with* you and *for* you."

The final principle I follow is to *try to understand*, to perceive as fully as possible the ideas, attitudes, and feelings of the other person. This task involves not just the mind but the imagination, the emotions, and at times the viscera as well. Often we are so anxious to change the dying person that we don't take time to try to understand him or her. We may want to cheer the person out of a gloomy, depressed mood; to moderate angry, unreasonable attitudes; or to help the person realize how serious the illness is. Ironically, the attempt to understand how the other person really perceives the situation may be the only thing that can make change possible. Take depression, for example. Our first impulse in talking to a depressed person is generally to cheer the person up by reviewing all the reasons he or she has to feel good: "You have excellent doctors . . . a loving family . . . many friends . . . you're able to be on your feet . . . you're not in intolerable pain. . . ." This tactic is seldom successful. In fact it usually has the opposite result: the person is left feeling even more depressed than before! This is not surprising, for now he has one more thing to be depressed about; someone he trusted cannot understand or accept his feelings, and he is now alone in his dark mood. Understanding and accepting unpleasant feelings without trying to change them *may* help to relieve them. At least one other person is able to share the feeling, and it is no longer an isolating factor.

Understanding may sometimes be communicated by the counselor's technique of reflecting the other person's feelings; at other times by a simple, "I see"; and at still other times by a nod, a smile, a touch of the hand, or even a respectful silence. Understanding means respecting the separateness of the other person, and the right of the other to feel lonely, sad, angry, anxious, or hopeful. It also means recognizing that these feelings do not belong to oneself, but to the other who displays them. Further, it means inviting the other person to share as many of these feelings as he or she cares to share, but it does *not* mean forcing, intruding, or invading the other person's privacy.

Many seriously ill and dying persons derive considerable comfort, reassurance and support from specifically religious aspects of ministry to the dying, such as reading from the Scriptures, offering prayer, or administering the sacraments. Others may feel uncomfortable with them, however, and not a few clergy express uncertainty over the appropriateness of such rites in the sick room. Ideally these rites should emerge from the pastoral relationship rather than being imposed upon it. Their specific content and timing should be related to the individual needs, expectations, and spiritual history of the sick person. The sensitive pastor will be guided both by prior knowledge of the parishioner's life and by any significant clues that may appear during the course of the interview itself—present attitudes, feelings, and felt needs. Scripture reading or prayer should never become routine ways of ending every pastoral visit to a seriously ill person; neither should they be used as a convenient device for closing a conversation that has aroused feelings of discomfort in the pastor or patient, or for telling the dying person indirectly how he or she ought to feel or act. The content of religious rites will be most helpful when the language is able to incorporate both the painful and distressing feelings of the patient, and a realistic hope for relief, renewal and transcendence. There may well be occasions when the most appropriate prayer is for a gentle and peaceful death.

Much of what has been said about the emotional and spiritual needs of dying persons could also be said of the family members of such persons. The spouse and adult children of the older person who is dying are also experiencing a painful and progressive loss in their relationship with their loved one. They too need to discover sources of inner strength which will enable them to endure and grow from their loss. They constitute the primary support system for the dying individual; often the most effective pastoral care can be in sustaining and enabling the members of the family to carry out their demanding but indispensable care-giving role.

Nothing I have said in this chapter should be taken to imply that the death of an older person is always a peaceful or fulfilling experience. It can be, but it is not always so. I have seen older people die with dignity, grace, and composure. I have also known some who—because of excessive pain, fear, dependence, isolation, or underlying personality disturbance—were emotionally and spiritually devastated by the approach of death. No minister, no matter how conscientious, sensitive or well-informed, can ever guarantee that death will be graceful. Nevertheless, thoughtful pastoral care can enhance the possibility that the ending of life not be a destructive negation of its meaning, but rather become its consummation and fulfillment.

NOTES

1. Elisabeth Kübler-Ross, *On Death and Dying* (New York: Macmillan, 1969).
2. Edwin Shneidman, *Deaths of Man* (New York: Quadrangle, 1973); reprinted in *Death: Current Perspectives*, ed. Edwin S. Shneidman (Palo Alto, Calif.: Mayfield Publishing Co., 1976), pp. 443–451.
3. E. Mansell Pattison, "The Experience of Dying" and "The Dying Experience— Retrospective Analyses," in *The Experience of Dying*, ed. E. Mansell Pattison (Englewood Cliffs, N.J.: Prentice-Hall, 1977), pp. 43–60, 303–306.
4. Leo Tolstoy, *The Death of Ivan Ilych and Other Stories* (New York: New American Library, 1960), pp. 95–156.
5. Joseph Rheingold, *The Mother, Anxiety, and Death* (Boston: Little, Brown, 1967), pp. 1–23. Evidence from studies on the fear of death among various age-groups suggests that it is not particularly strong among older adults. For a review of these studies see Robert Kastenbaum and Ruth Aisenberg, *The Psychology of Death* (New York: Springer Publishing Co., 1972), pp. 81–89.
6. Martin Berezin, "Partial Grief for the Aged and their Families," in Pattison, *The Experience of Dying*, pp. 279–286.
7. The meaning of the term "minister" in this chapter should not be restricted to persons who are ordained or offer help on a professional basis. I intend for the term to refer to any person, ordained or not, professional or lay, who seeks to offer help as a representative of the faith or community of believers to which he or she is commited.
8. Lily Pincus, *Death and the Family: The Importance of Mourning* (New York: Pantheon Books, 1974), p. 278; copyright © 1974 by Lily Pincus, reprinted by permission of Pantheon Books, a Division of Random House, Inc.
9. Viktor Frankl, *Man's Search for Meaning* (New York: Simon and Schuster, 1962).
10. E. Mansell Pattison, "The Will to Live and the Expectation of Death," in Pattison, *The Experience of Dying*, pp. 61–74.
11. "The Moment of Truth: Care of the Dying Person," in *Death and Dying: Current Issues in the Treatment of the Dying Person*, ed. Leonard Pearson (Cleveland: The Press of Case Western Reserve University, 1969), p. 59.

15

Adult Religious Education and the Aging

Donald E. Miller

By *aging* I mean the awareness by an individual or community that people, including themselves, are following the normal decline in vitality that characterizes the latter part of life prior to death. With this definition I put the emphasis upon social, cultural, and psychological awareness in response to a biological process.

Since nurture, or education, has traditionally been a central function of both Jewish and Christian communities, it is appropriate to ask how adult religious education ought to function in relation to the elderly. My focus will be religious education for the aging, but I will also be concerned with the aging as an educational resource for the community, and, additionally, the importance of the aging for the religious education of the whole religious community.

THE AIMS OF RELIGIOUS EDUCATION FOR THE AGING

Any concept of education implies certain ideas of individual and/or community maturity, that is, an idea of a direction of optimal growth toward which learning aims. The issue is not whether educational procedures are derived from the idea of maturity or whether the concept of maturity is inferred from the education procedures. In either case the concept of education logically includes the idea of maturity. When religious educators raise the question of maturity, they are raising not only a profound educational question, but also equally profound theological questions. We cannot avoid raising such questions here.

Erik Erikson's work presumes that maturity is the constant and continual growth of persons toward a confidence with humility, an openness with receptivity, and the correspondence of inner feelings and discipline with outer feelings and values. Erikson has intimated that this understanding of adult maturity is adequate from a Christian standpoint as well as from the standpoint of other religious traditions: "The essential element in the Christian idea of adulthood is, the capacity for growth, which is assumed to be a potentiality of any age of life. . . . The primary experiences through which the Christian grows are social experiences. One encounters Christ and the opportunity to serve him in others; the maturity of the individual is realized only in loving unity with others."[1]

Therefore, let me suggest the following concept of maturity for the Christian education of older adults: faithful response to the love of God and growth in Christ-like grace through interaction within a responsive and responsible community in ways that are appropriate for and with persons of declining and limited vitalities. Such a conception of maturity implies characteristics of awareness, intentionality, coherence, and mutuality. These are characteristics which come from a consideration of what constitutes strength of personhood and moral agency, and each suggests an aim of education for the aging.[2]

EDUCATION FOR AWARENESS

Aging is a time of changing sensibilities and capacities. Such changes are of course radically individual. Persons of a given age will vary widely for any given physical or mental characteristic (for example, memory, visual acuity, reaction time). There is nevertheless clearly a decline in vitality from younger years, and there is a change in sensibilities. The vision of what is possible in life and the sense of the proximity of death certainly change. Aging people are treated differently, and their bodies function differently than during their earlier years.[3] To be able to speak about these changes, to be able to express one's feelings, and to accept such feelings, are what we mean by awareness.

This kind of awareness implies an inner perception of feelings and an outer perception of circumstances related to the aging process. Such awareness is not complete without some objective understanding of biological, psychological, social, and cultural processes, in terms of personal feelings and commitments. Awareness, then, is the realization that feelings, understandings, and interpersonal relationships within a living community, cannot be separated from one another. Religious awareness for the aging becomes a matter of following the feelings and commitments about the process of aging to their deepest roots. It is, finally, the awareness of God who sets the limits of all our experience.

EDUCATION FOR INTENTIONALITY

A second aim of education is intentionality—the owning, acceptance, and cognitive expression of the urges and impulses of our own personal existence. Intentionality may be lost by an inner failure to accept impulses, to give them cognitive form, or to meet the overwhelming press and pain of circumstances. Aging is often a time of declining responsibility, yet it is frequently a time of making very stressful decisions— moving one's residence or changing one's vocation—with little assurance that these decisions can be permanent. Aging persons are sometimes afraid to take the risk of deciding. A clear aim of education for the aging is to increase the range of intentional decisions people can make regarding their own circumstances.

Our own intentionality is limited and guided by the will and purposes of God. To penetrate deeply into one's own intentionality is to be faced with the way our intentions are shaped in a living community and with the way the intentions of the community are themselves shaped by God's will. Questions of intentionality inevitably raise theological questions. Karl Barth's concept of mature intentionality is that of "unique opportunity."[4] Every moment in life is an opportunity to take the risk to be willing, to will without compulsiveness, to stand in obedience to the purposes and direction of God. Aging is indeed a unique opportunity to discern and act in God's will. In that sense the aging as well as the young belong within the Kingdom of God.

EDUCATION FOR COHERENCE

A third aim of education is coherence, by which I mean accepting and bringing together our outer and inner experience to gain a clear sense of self, community, and world in spite of a wide range of experiences that have not yet been fully reconciled. At deeper levels our coherence derives from our sense of selfhood, community, and world; but in each of these realms coherence must be considered, acted upon, and responded to if it is to be maintained. Both slow and dramatic changes will occur in the lives of the aging—changes such as a decrease in appetite, death of a spouse, change in working patterns, or increased sensitivity to cold. Such changes must not only be understood, but also accepted into one's self-concept. To make sense of their lives and communities, aging persons need to engage in an ongoing process of reinterpretation.

The coherence—and the divergence—of life is sensed in the ambiguity of promise and fulfillment in the lives of the aging. The promise of life is always only partially fulfilled. All choices made along the way mean that other possibilities were cut off, and sometimes repressed. Repressed possibilities and missed opportunities may reassert themselves in the form of regret. Erikson speaks of "acceptance of one's one and only life cycle" with no basic regret that it should have been otherwise.[5]

On the other hand, the fulfillment of life need not remain only a thing of the past. In surprising ways the aging person may be helpful to others (even the hospitalized can minister to those who visit them). There is a freedom to reinterpret one's life, to find new meaning. There is an opportunity to find coherence with past and future generations. Fulfillment can come for the aging who continue to follow the promises of life.

The limit of promise and fulfillment in life is the Word of God, for in God's Word all things come to be. God's Word comes first as a promise to be fulfilled, and the fulfillment itself comes as a continuing promise. The disappointment of the unfulfilled promise is acknowledged and healed in God's Word of forgiveness, and the hope of the promised fulfillment is continually renewed for the aging as much as for the young.

EDUCATION FOR MUTUALITY

A fourth educational aim is that of mutuality, or the interaction between persons, groups, and generations through which other educational aims are also enhanced and extended. The concept of mutuality can be seen in Erikson's description of teaching: "Evolution has made man a teaching as well as learning animal, for dependency and maturity are reciprocal: mature man needs to be needed, and maturity is guided by the nature of that which must be cared for."[6]

Aging often means a declining range or associations as old friends die. Aging people sometimes long to be in touch with someone else; they may die from isolation and a loss of dignity as well as from physical illness. They need the interaction of mutuality, yet too often they are cut off from each other, from other age groups, and from the community at large.

The limits of injustice and interdependent care are God's judgment and God's love. God's judgment reestablishes community, and God's love deepens and extends the human community. The love of God is the basis and aim of all of our relationships with one another. The love of God for the aging means to be in touch, to regain dignity, to regain friendship, to reestablish dialogue.

We might summarize the aims of religious education for the aging as enabling the aging and their surrounding community to—

1. become aware of personal feelings as well as biological, psychological, social, and cultural conditions that affect aging, and which finally include an awareness of God who sets the limits of life;

2. care responsibly for themselves and one another, especially with
   reference to the conditions of aging, which finally includes an
   acceptance of the will and purpose of God;
3. develop a greater sense of fulfillment within the continuities of
   life with their own life experiences merging into previous and
   succeeding generations, which finally includes the power and
   meaning of the Word of God;
4. interact as a caring community toward the embodiment of justice
   in all relationships with the aging, which finally includes being
   judged and loved by God.

A LEARNING THEORY FOR THE AGING

Learning always involves change, and change always means that there
will be resistance. The function of learning theory is to understand
such change well enough to encourage and direct it toward maturity
and the aims of education.

Often a distinction is made between "defensive" and "coping" learning. Defensive learning is a change in behavior that shuts off inner
feelings and outer threats through some form of denial. Coping learning
is a change in behavior that relates to inner feelings and reduces outer
threat by some form of acceptance and interaction. Coping behavior
exhibits the characteristics of maturity. We need a theory of coping
learning that is appropriate for the religious education of the aging.

CAPACITIES FOR LEARNING

Learning depends upon the capacities of the learner. Studies of learning capacity show that the peak learning abilities are during the teen
years. Aging people do not learn as quickly as they did in earlier years,
nor do they remember as much as they once did.

These observations should be balanced, however, by studies in the
psychology of aging, such as that of James Birren.[7] Birren has shown
that older persons have a repertoire of paradigms, or patterns, within
which they organize their experiences. Such paradigms allow them

to process their experience in meaningful ways more quickly than a younger person can. The aging will more likely learn within an already established wide range of paradigms, while the young are expanding a narrower range of paradigms. Therefore diminished associational or memory capacities do not necessarily result in less learning by aging persons. In fact they may learn as much or more than more youthful persons in the same situation. The learning of the aging should not be judged upon a narrow scale of quantity, but upon a more discriminating scale of quality.

INTRINSIC MOTIVATION

Genuine learning—what I have called coping learning—takes place on the basis of intrinsic motivation. When natural curiosity, felt needs, and the desire to do something are stimulated, then learning occurs. Various writers have attempted a description of the basic needs of the aging, each with a slightly different emphasis or approach. David Moberg, for example, very much emphasizes what I have called coherence, including such needs as a more adequate concept of aging, relief from anxieties and fears, personality integration, personal dignity, preparation for death, and a philosophy of life.[8] Other authors appear more influenced by social factors such as the way in which a person is engaged or disengaged, the life pattern that has been followed in previous years, and the decisions about life style that each person makes.

All of these perspectives on factors affecting intrinsic motivation are useful to religious educators for designing classes and programs. Each suggests a possible direction for a particular class or for a more extended program. Many older people are eager to acquire practical information that will help them survive more easily. Special programs and classes on such subjects as consumer education, health education, estate planning, and even "cooking for one," might have great appeal. Often older people also enjoy enriching their lives with activities and skills they have not had time to pursue in the past—for example, writing, yoga, ceramics, foreign languages, or knitting. The list could go on and on, of course. The point is that while religious educators may emphasize a philosophy or theology of life and religious faith and practice, they must also take into account the religious dimensions of other activities for the individuals involved in their programs.

EXISTENTIAL LEARNING

Beyond capacities and intrinsic motivation, learning must be existential:

> Existential theories of learning focus upon being and nonbeing, meaning and meaninglessness, authenticity and inauthenticity, genuineness and phoniness. . . . The emphasis is upon openness in the interrelationships between person and person, personal and social situation, person and meaning. . . . Teaching and learning are ways of standing before meanings and events so that new significance and relationships arise.[9]

Existentialist learning theory emphasizes as significant and meaningful that which breaks into the consciousness. In a moment of confrontation with a person, an event, or a meaning, some truth impresses itself upon the learner. Such learning cannot be confined to formal classroom situations. The learning that occurs at home, at leisure, or on a trip is equally as significant as what may occur in a face-to-face group. The moments when one's faith stands out as vivid and intense, when God's truth breaks in, when the group clarifies its covenant, are all great events in existential learning.

Curriculum for the aging should allow for existential learning. Daily experience, crisis moments, or great encounters can become important parts of the curriculum. Classroom teaching is enriched when the teacher is aware of such moments, and when the participants are encouraged to bring such moments of their own into the classroom. What may appear to be mundane—difficulty climbing stairs, an argument with a neighbor, boredom with the daily routine—can become the occasion for interpretation and reflection.

DEVELOPMENTAL DIFFERENCES

Another approach to learning is that of developmental differences. The most durable learnings of life take place within a community of people with various competences and differences. The family, the neighborhood, and the church are such communities. In the family the younger siblings learn from the older, and the older are able to reinterpret their own earlier behavior as they relate to those who are younger.

The learning that occurs between different behavioral levels is partly a matter of "needing to be needed" in Erikson's phrase. Not only do the inexperienced need what the experienced have to offer, the more experienced also need to be able to share that experience with those who do not yet have it. In that sense all of us are both teachers and learners at heart. Not to be able to share the experience and knowledge one has gained is not to be needed.

In another sense the need to be needed can be fulfilled by encouraging the aging to volunteer to help other aging people. A visit from a peer, so to speak, can be of great benefit to those confined to home, nursing home, or hospital. A number of church boards and agencies, on both local and national levels, have organized such volunteer programs. Project Compassion of the Lutheran Church—Missouri Synod Board of Social Ministry and World Relief has, for example, trained twelve thousand older volunteers to visit nursing home patients, shut-ins, long-term hospital patients, and correctional inmates.[10] Telephone reassurance networks among the aged represent another form of poor volunteer work.[11]

Learning between behavioral levels may also rest upon the cognitive principle that we learn only that which is immediately beyond our own level of understanding.[12] A mixture of various levels of experience and understanding may allow a larger number of people to find some expression that reaches them at their own level.

Learning from developmental differences leads to a number of teaching procedures. Methods which feature life stories and experiences may appeal to various participants, each at his or her own level. Discussion and planning can use a variety of experiences. Intergenerational events are designed to allow persons of different ages to be together.[13]

Designers of such events can take a cue from the great celebrative events of church (Easter, Christmas) which have always been intergenerational in the sense that singing, drama, and games which delight all ages are a part of the tradition. For example, musicals produced by the congregation can include all ages. Bible simulations have been developed that can take advantage of intergenerational interest in both drama and Biblical themes.[14] Such events have enormous educational potential and can help build a strong sense of unity.

FACE-TO-FACE COMMUNITY GROUPS

If the face-to-face relationships within a community are understood to be the place where faith is formed, then Christian education for the aging will be planned in face-to-face groups. Such groups never isolate relationships from content. Learning occurs as much in the interaction between the intentions and commitments of persons, as in their ideas. Not only expressed promises, but also the implicit network of promises becomes the setting of learning.

In recent writing about religious education, Gwen Neville, John H. Westerhoff, and C. Ellis Nelson have emphasized the importance of the community. Nelson argues that faith begins in the interactive process, while Neville and Westerhoff insist that faith is born and expressed in community events.[15] This means that participation in face-to-face community groups is essential to learning and growth for the old as well as for the young. Bible and theological study groups can offer opportunities for such face-to-face experiences. Such groups can meet for prayer, sharing meaningful experiences or fears of becoming helpless, and help in facing death with dignity or coping with the problem of dislocation. One method of meeting is in cottage groups that come together in the place of residence of the aging, something that is especially important for many older people who cannot get out on their own.

Face-to-face groups can be used effectively as ongoing intergenerational events. Topics of special interest to intergenerational study or church school groups might include death and dying, a leisure ethic, spiritual renewal, or retirement planning. A special use of the face-to-face concept is family understanding. Margaret Sawin has developed a plan in which groups of several families and singles of various ages form a covenant together for a period of time to meet for study, fellowship, and worship.[16] An approach of this kind can restore a sense of extended family to aging persons who are becoming isolated.

PROBLEM-SOLVING AND LIBERATION

A final approach to learning is that of problem-solving, in which learning comes from the pressure of what needs to be done. Fulfilling basic needs leads to a series of problems to be solved. This is as true for the aging as for anyone. Study organized around problems to be solved leads to learning that is both intrinsically motivated and existentially experienced.

The steps of problem-solving may be variously described, but they should include the following: describing the situation, defining the problem, isolating the options for action, testing the consequences of various options for action, deciding upon a course of action, planning a procedure of action, collecting resources, carrying through the process, adjusting to obstacles, completing the action, and evaluating what was done. These steps may be collapsed into many fewer steps or elaborated formally into many more. Fewer steps become everyday judgments, and more formal elaboration becomes the scientific method.

Every step in the problem-solving process may involve study and discussion. A task force for action may at the same time be a study group. When the specific problems being solved are those that particularly affect the aging, the study group will become of keen interest to older people. For example, many public policies adversely affect the aging when they result in rising health and energy costs, or in inferior conditions in nursing homes. A task group of older people studying public policy can have an influence far beyond its own members.

Advocacy programs utilize a more active form of the problem-solving technique by bringing the aging together to develop community action aimed at bettering their social circumstances. Project HEAD (Help Elderly Adults Direct) was started by Vicky Peralta of Catholic Social Services in Philadelphia and revised by the National Interfaith Coalition on Aging.[17] Scores of such projects are now helping the aging direct their own community action programs in housing, income, nutrition, transporation, employment, social/cultural opportunities, and better health.

Paulo Freire has been most courageous in developing a model of education for justice.[18] He has study groups isolate basic "generative themes" that affect each person. The group then studies that theme to see the ways in which each member is being oppressed. They study the political, economic, and other forces which keep such oppressive themes intact, and then organize new groups to change their life style. Freire understands this process to be a form of religious education. Liberationists believe that we must begin with a religious understanding of ways in which we are responsible for situations in which we find ourselves. Certainly there is no doubt that problem-solving and "daily bread" are at the heart of the Scriptures and belong in a program of religious education for the aging.

If the curriculum and teaching of the aging is to be based upon an adequate learning theory, it must take into account capacities, intrinsic motivation, existential moments, developmental differences, face-to-face community groups, problem-solving, and education for liberation. The aging have their unique learning capacities, their own motivation, their own life situations and developmental differences. They learn in communities of challenge and support, according to problems that must be solved, and in common action against injustice.

CHURCH EDUCATION AND THE AGING

In my presentation of the most important considerations in a learning theory for the aging, I pointed out some examples of educational strategies which put the theory into practice. While some of the programs mentioned are not directly religious in nature, religious educators can be instrumental in bringing together various programs for an evening club or for an ongoing day center. A national survey of activities available for the aging shows that churches are frequently the sponsoring groups.[19] Clearly, the significance of churches and religious educators in meeting the varied needs of the increasing population of aging people can be very great.

I have largely concerned myself with educational aims and learning theories specifically relevant to the aging. Without question, any religious education program has to consider program needs and opportunities for the aging themselves. On the other hand, the attitudes of the congregation toward the aging process should also be a matter of concern.

Educational strategies aimed at the total congregation are very much needed among most church bodies. Congregations must break out of the tendency of American society to segment the aging as a group apart from the rest of society.

Sensitive, perhaps re-educated congregations will find ways in which the aging can be included in the ongoing activities of the church.[20] Many church buildings could be redesigned to facilitate such participation by enabling aged members to hear, see, and move around easily. Above all, churches ought not to automatically retire the aging from public responsibilities. Public prayer, Bible reading, preaching, teaching, and secretarial and counseling work are but some of the areas in which the aging can participate. Various boards, committees, and planning groups can also benefit from the experience and expertise of older members.

CONCLUSION

It is essential that we recover the religious attitude in caring for the aging. The field of religious education can make a significant contribution here through developing educational theory, resources, and programs for local congregations as well as denominational and interdenominational support resources.

The variety of religious educational programs already existing for the aging is impressive. Yet there are remarkably few religious education materials that take into account important aspects of education for the aging. Most church agencies have considered it too expensive to produce such specialized materials. An increasing awareness of the needs of the aging, and their growing numbers, will probably change that attitude, however. In the meantime, it is not too soon to give serious thought to what educational aims, theories, and strategies of learning should be considered in the further development of adequate religious educational resources and programs for the aging.

NOTES

1. Erik H. Erikson, *Adulthood* (New York: W. W. Norton, 1978), pp. 87, 92.
2. I have developed this argument in *The Wing-Footed Wanderer* (Nashville: Abingdon, 1977).
3. Merril F. Elias, Penelope Kelly Elias, and Jeffrey W. Elias, *Basic Processes in Adult Developmental Psychology* (St. Louis: C. V. Mosby, 1977).
4. Karl Barth, *Church Dogmatics* III/4, "The Doctrine of Creation," (Edinburgh: T. and T. Clark, 1961), pp. 656–694.
5. Erik H. Erikson, *Identity, Youth and Crisis* (New York: W. W. Norton, 1968), p. 139.
6. Ibid., p. 138.
7. James E. Birren, *The Psychology of Aging* (Englewood Cliffs, N.J.: Prentice-Hall, 1964).
8. David Moberg, "Spiritual Well-Being," paper for the White House Conference on Aging, February 1971, cited in Donald F. Clingan, *Aging Persons in the Community of Faith* (Indianapolis: Indiana Commission on Aging and Aged, 1975), p. 9.
9. Donald E. Miller, "Psychological Foundations for Christian Education," in *An Introduction to Christian Education*, ed. Marvin Taylor (Nashville: Abingdon, 1966), p. 56.
10. Clingan, *Aging Persons*, p. 38.
11. The Archdiocese of Los Angeles Commission on Aging has a booklet, "How to Organize a Telephone Reassurance Service for the Elderly." For information write to Helen Yost, 1400 West Ninth Street, Los Angeles, CA 90057; See also Clingan, *Aging Persons*, p. 37.
12. A good statement of this view is found in Lawrence Kohlberg, "From Is to Ought: How to Commit the Naturalistic Fallacy and Get Away with It in the Study of Moral Development," in *Cognitive Development and Epistemology*, ed. Theodore Mischel (New York: Academic Press, 1971).
13. The Joint Educational Development materials, obtainable through Brethren General Board, Elgin, Illinois, have a number of intergenerational resources. See also Pamela Parker, ed., *Understanding Aging* (Philadelphia: Church Press, 1974); and Donald Griggs and Patricia Griggs, *Generations Learning Together* (Richmond, Va.: Griggs Educational Service, 1976).
14. Donald E. Miller, Graydon Snyder, and Robert W. Neff, *Using Biblical Simulations*, 2 vols. (Valley Forge, Penn.: Judson Press, 1973–1975).
15. C. Ellis Nelson, *Where Faith Begins* (Richmond, Va.: John Knox Press, 1967),

and Gwen Kennedy Neville and John H. Westerhoff III, *Learning through Liturgy* (New York: Seabury Press, 1978), see especially chap. 8.

16. Margaret M. Sawin, *Family Enrichment with Family Clusters* (Valley Forge, Penn.: Judson Press, 1979). A good list of resources is included.

17. Clingan, *Aging Persons*, p. 35.

18. Paulo Freire, *Pedagogy of the Oppressed* (New York: Herder and Herder, 1971).

19. Roger Decrow, *New Learning Opportunities for Older Americans: An Overview of National Effort* (Washington, D.C.: Adult Education Association, 1977).

20. Robert M. Gray and David O. Moberg, *The Church and the Older Person* (Grand Rapids, Mich.: Eerdmans, 1977).

16

Lay Ministries with Older Adults

Elbert C. Cole

Case 1. At age eighty Lucius developed some symptoms that caused him to make an appointment with his doctor. After the usual tests and examinations, the doctor inquired how he was using his time. When he found out that Lucius was spending a good deal of time as the volunteer coordinator of a program that delivered hot meals to the homebound, he insisted that Lucius give up his responsibilities. Lucius took a month's leave of absence. When he returned to the doctor a month later, however, Lucius informed him that his work with "Meals on Wheels" was the only thing he had found worth doing since his wife died fourteen months earlier and his only child, a forty-four-year-old son, suddenly died eight months after that. Far from interfering with his health, the light but meaningful volunteer service was so important to Lucius that it was the only thing that gave him a reason for living. The doctor got the message, and quickly approved Lucius continuing his lay ministry, for it was a ministry.

Case 2. Cecilia had taught high-school English for many years, and had looked forward to her retirement when she would be free to lunch with her friends and play bridge every day. She did retire, and for a year she had a leisure fling. She was inconspicuous in a team of thirty people who were brought together to plan a new model of adult education, but then her interest and personal needs began to surface. She was invited to become the volunteer coordinator, giving a major portion of the week to taking full responsibility for the program. She later acknowledged that the invitation was timely. She had become bored with the very thing she had retired to do—lunch and bridge— and was looking for a challenge. She found it.

Case 3. Jake had a career as a paint salesman calling upon contractors. After his retirement, he was asked to head a team that would design a reliable system of providing handyman services to older people in the community who were eager to remain in their homes, but were anxiety-ridden by their inability to find anyone willing to make minor repairs around the house. Jake pulled out everything he knew from his career to put together a simple program. Jake began to see himself as a volunteer contractor with a sizeable work force of men who had indicated the kinds of repairs they would be willing to make. Some of the handymen, all of whom were retired, needed to supplement their fixed income, while others participated because they enjoyed fixing things and helping others. The handymen received a modest hourly fee, but Jake served without any financial compensation, drawing a tremendous sense of satisfaction from the many telephone calls and letters he received from people who said they didn't know how they could get along if it were not for the handyman program.

Lucius, Cecilia, and Jake had enjoyed their careers, but after a period of retirement each found that something was missing. Fortunately, they each were able to develop a new sense of vocation that has continued to shape their lives in their later years. Their sense of self-esteem was restored by the direct service of helping someone else.

DEFINED BY WORK

Retirement is often difficult for people who have drawn their sense of self-worth and well-being from their work. In fact, most people define themselves vocationally. When a retired person is asked what he or she does, the answer is usually in terms of the preretirement career: "I was a bricklayer"—or a clerk, a nurse, a barber, a teacher, or a salesman. Even naming the vocation conjures up memories of the career. This is understandable when we remember that more of a person's lifetime has been spent in the workplace than in any other waking activity.

Broadly speaking, life is divided into three sections. The years up to twenty-one or twenty-five are the years of preparation. The young person is drawing out of the gross national product but not putting anything in. These are years of schooling, of vocational selection and training, and of mate choosing; they are formative years in fashioning a life style. The years from twenty-one to sixty-five, more or less, are the years of production, with a heavy emphasis on vocation and work. Life satisfactions are largely drawn from how the job goes, peer acceptance, and recognition by superiors. Rewards are in the form of salary increases, promotions, and work accomplishments. Unfortunately, the retirement years after sixty-five mark the end of this productive process, ending the source that had nurtured good feelings about one's self and life in general. For a time there might well be a glorious holiday, but then sooner or later there is that haunting question: is there any more to life than this? A negative answer to that question can cause a person to hit bottom.

The word "retirement" is actually a negative word suggesting setting aside or laying down duties and responsibilities. For many people the retirement process is hard on a sense of self-worth, which is often diminished if not destroyed. This may soon be followed by a sense of unimportance and uselessness which can be not only discouraging, but can also call into question one's whole value structure.

The middle-years producer makes a contribution to the gross national product by investing energy and skill that can be translated into dollars. The retired person needs to make a contribution to the gross national "human situation" by caring for and helping another human being. There is a strong indication of the need to develop a sense of vocation in later years which will replace the values from productive years. This new sense of vocation would not be based on remuneration and the reward system of the productive years, but rather on such values as feeling needed, bringing joy and pleasure to another, exploring and expressing unknown and unused skills and abilities, developing a talent that had been buried, or, as one older person said, paying back some of the rent for the ground he has been using.

The wisdom and creativity that can come with a lifetime of experience have been all but crushed in our society. Benjamin Franklin, who at eighty-one helped write the Constitution of the United States, might well not have even been invited to the Convention if it were meeting today, much less have been given the opportunity to put on paper what he felt was essential to the political process.

Yet those strong winds blowing through our culture that suggest being old has little value, are now being challenged. The time has surely come for the church to take up the task of building a new value structure.

THE ROLE OF THE CHURCH

Unfortunately, the church has itself tended to incorporate societal stereotypes of older people. The aging process has been identified with disease, deterioration, and death. Getting old is bad news, even in the community of the "Good News." While society has been learning more and more about the "myths and realities of aging," the church has been slow to respond—often limiting its work to a shut-in ministry, individual pastoral care, and perhaps a Bible class, prayer groups, or a sewing circle. There have been very few models that reflect the vitality and rich diversity of human life which needs to be nurtured and encouraged in later years.

How can the church meet more responsibly, and more practically, this challenge of shaping a new value system? One way lies in the development of significant lay ministries, more specifically in the development of lay ministries by older persons. However, there is something very personal and individual about this kind of lay ministry. It has to have that quality which provides that same spark of importance the person found in a career.

Volunteer service can become a lay ministry when it represents a service or a cause that is meaningful to the volunteer. For example, Mark, who is in his seventies, finds it depressing to be among older people; he comes alive when he opens the world of an economically disadvantaged, high achieving child by tutoring as a school volunteer. John makes hospital visits his thing, but is bored with and refuses to do much of the usual hospital tasks—he feels needed only when he serves families whose loved one is terminally ill, as was his wife at the same hospital. Clearly, the kind of volunteer work that can regenerate life is that in which the volunteer can easily identify having been helpful to another person. The more dramatic the help, the more the volunteer is repaid in life satisfaction, drawing increased motivation for living.

Serving compelling causes can have the same effect. Mr. Cameron telephones for an appointment and arrives the next day on his motorcycle, gray hair sticking out of his crash helmet. He came to recruit for his cause, and when he finished, he disappeared in a burst of power, off to tilt his lance with another. Mr. Thomas gets his life satisfaction from advising small business owners how to survive; Mr. Kroog is out to find new ways to conserve energy; Mrs. Boyd comes alive helping to stem the tide of child abuse; Mrs. Fields lives and thinks "Concern Counts," a new effort in community health through mass media advertising. There are hundreds of causes just waiting for the abilities and energies of retired people. Many problems will not be helped or solved unless volunteers in their retirement years take them on and make them their own crusades. One thing for sure, crusader and cause will both be helped, and society will be the winner in the end.

Society is, in fact, fast approaching a time of hard decisions of how the already strained tax-dollar will be spent. Should it be invested in the young and all the things they need to equip them for tomorrow, or should it be spent on those in later years? There may soon come a time when there will not be enough for both. One solution will be tangible services performed by older people at low or no cost, and acknowledged as essential for all ages in society: such things as local block care for children, block handyman services, block security watches—all visible expressions of interdependent community life. Society does seem to be realizing, however slowly, that with the increasing number of older persons in America, there is no hope of providing all the services needed by older people—not to mention the rest of society—unless older people themselves accept some responsibility for creation, volunteer management, raising funds, and execution of these services.

Yet even with all of the information about older adults coming from the political and academic communities, the church has been slow to acknowledge the unique contributions it can make to what has to be thought of as a search for a new day for older adults. There has been some resistance within the church in recognizing that older adults have needs different from other age levels in the church, and thus require an intentional ministry designed for those in their later years. At the same time, a false assumption is made that older adults are not able to lead themselves and therefore need younger leadership to provide for them. Certainly there is a place for young people to assist in providing ministries with older people, but only if they are wise and capable in helping older people attain their own goals. Clergy, for example, need to see themselves as enablers and interpreters, giving support and encouragement to this new lay workforce. Older adults are quite capable of providing their own leadership. After all, who knows more about what is needed and how to go about achieving the desired goals of older adults than older adults themselves?

THE SHEPHERD'S CENTER MODEL

These ideas about lay ministries with older adults have been tested in the Shepherd's Center in Kansas City, Missouri. The Shepherd's Center focuses on people, not on programs or activities. The concept is based on a "people base" (a population base of older people living in a specific geographical area), and involves a covenant relation between center leaders and people assuring that every effort will be made to assist the people in achieving those goals needed or desired in their later years. In turn, the people provide the program leadership and participate in whatever way possible in maintaining a supportive network capable of helping themselves survive while finding some meaning and purpose in life.

The name, the Shepherd's Center, comes from the image of caring and security in the 23rd Psalm. This name is attractive to both Christians and Jews, and probably has about as good a chance as any name to hold some positive memories even for those unchurched.

The Shepherd's Center was conceived in 1972 by a small planning team from one church as an alternative to institutional care. The goal from the beginning was to utilize older people in providing those services required by other older people to remain in their own homes and to continue independent living. Other programs were to follow later which would permit the exploration of life enhancement and enrichment.

Early plans to build a retirement home were scrapped when the team realized that at any one time 95 percent of the population over sixty-five are not in sheltered care. If sheltered care was needed or attractive for only 5 percent, what kinds of supportive networks could be developed in the community which would be helpful to the 95 percent who remained in their own homes? Over those early months, two basic questions were constantly voiced, and these two questions continue to be valid: how can I get help when I need it in order to remain independent as long as possible; and what can I do in the later years to find meaning and purpose for my life?

The Center inherited a single service, "Meals on Wheels," started a short time earlier by the retired men of one church. The Meals on Wheels program grew rapidly in the early months before the Shepherd's Center was incorporated. With the requirements for volunteers greater than one church could supply, and with the recipients coming from the entire community, it was obvious that one church could not do the job alone. Thus, a working partnership of all the churches and synagogues of the community was sought. Originally there were eighteen churches who agreed to participate in the Center, and that number has now grown to twenty-five. In fact, over its seven-year history, the Shepherd's Center has grown from a single service to nineteen major services, and to about 350 volunteers helping over 4,000 people.

WHEN THE FAITH COMMUNITY BECOMES VISIBLE

The churches and synagogues working together gave stability to the original concept, supplying participants, volunteers, and security to those needing to be served. The Shepherd's Center made the care and concern of the faith community visible to older people, giving them hope and help. Its stated purposes are—

1. To sustain older people who desire to live independently in their own homes and apartments in the community;
2. To provide retired people with an opportunity to use their experience, training, and skills in significant social roles;
3. To enhance life satisfaction in later maturity and enable self-realization through artistic expression, community service, caring relationships, lifelong learning, and the discovery of inner resources;
4. To demonstrate life at its best in later maturity so as to provide attractive role models for successful aging;
5. To advocate the right of older people to a fair share of society's goods, and to assist them in gaining access to services;
6. To contribute to knowledge about what is required for successful aging and to experiment with new approaches and programs for meeting the needs of older people.

The Shepherd's Center has been incorporated, making it accountable to the community. The board of directors is composed primarily of older people, augmented by community leaders with the skills needed for a strong board. The board is responsible for goals, policy, fundraising, budget planning, staff employment, and ultimate program audit to assure older people it will maintain the covenant.

The development of programs and services is invested in the coordinators council, consisting of the chief coordinator of each service and the Center's small employed staff. The council has the responsibility of administering programs and keeping them functioning effectively. Many of the coordinators give twenty or more volunteer hours each week. Each coordinator in turn has as many committee members as are required to execute that particular service or program. Each coordinator has complete responsibility for one area, including recruiting volunteers, refining the service, and making recommendations to the council for more effective service. Motivation remains high because those serving the people are fully in charge, receiving direct feedback from the people regarding how helpful the service is to them.

The programs and services were started one at a time, with approval by the board. Some were planned for months before being launched. Others died in the planning stage when they eventually showed no promise of being helpful to older people. Ideas for new programs can start at any point: from the board, the staff, the council, or a suggestion from one of the participants. When suggestions become definitive and are verified by the coordinators council as representing something which will help an older person hold life together or find a sense of meaning, the idea is thoroughly discussed until the council identifies someone who believes in the importance of the proposed service enough to accept the job of coordinator. That person is given assistance in forming a planning team charged with closely examining the idea until all the details are worked out to make the idea manageable.

There are nine home services currently provided by Center volunteers. People qualify to receive a service simply by being over sixty-five and indicating that they cannot perform the service for themselves. Most of the home services are without charge, with the service rendered by a volunteer. Two of the services carry a small charge which is paid directly to the volunteer. Almost all of the volunteers are themselves over sixty-five, giving them a real opportunity to help others and to be useful.

HOME SERVICES

The oldest service in the intentional ministry of the Shepherd's Center is Meals on Wheels. This service has grown from five men, each helping seven people, to the present level of forty-eight men, each serving seventy to eighty people every day. The first year this program served a total of about forty people and has now grown until currently over 200 people are served some 18,000 meals each year.

The Center's Meals on Wheels program is unique because only men serve as the volunteers. This is not because anyone feels that men are better drivers or more able to get around in all kinds of weather, but rather because when men retire from the labor force, their sense of self-worth is severely threatened by a feeling of not being needed in our society. Delivering meals to people who would certainly not have eaten as well—or at all—if that meal had not been delivered, often offers sufficient reward to renew life, motivating them to discover a new role in community service. Volunteers and recipients come to know each other by name and form important ties. Errands, additional visits, caring, and interest give both volunteer and recipient hope and joy. These drivers are part of an alert system that sets off emergency procedures when a person does not respond to the driver, or follow-up procedures by others when the drivers report concern for additional needs.

The Shoppers Service began when leaders of the Shepherd's Center realized there were people in the area who could cook for themselves and therefore did not need or want Meals on Wheels, but who, because of their frailties, had a difficult time shopping. The shopper volunteers are generally younger women who shop for or take the older person on a weekly shopping trip. These usually prove to be delightful excursions with many mutual benefits. For example, a child who accompanied her mother on these trips over the years, has now entered college to major in gerontology.

The Handyman program was created to assist older homeowners in making minor repairs to their homes. The desire of older people to remain in their own homes is always threatened by the increasing number of little things that go wrong with the house. Retired skilled workmen were recruited for this program by a coordinator familiar with the contracting field. From a bank of thirty-two craftsmen, the coordinator assigns a task to the appropriate handyman. This program has been cleared with trade union leaders, who approve the idea. An agreement was made with the unions that the handymen will not do new work or major remodeling, but stick to those aggravating minor repairs and chores that are unnecessarily costly when a regular craftsman is called.

The Night Team of the Shepherd's Center is an exciting but seldom used service. After-hours telephone calls are monitored by a professional answering service, which screens the calls and refers emergencies to a select list of persons who are prepared to respond immediately. Just having this service available seems to give security and reassurance to many people who live alone.

The Care XX program refers to keeping in touch with low-income older people who qualify for some of the services provided through Title XX of the Social Security program. The Shepherd's Center staff refers those who need and qualify for those services, to the authorized public agency, and the coordinator keeps in touch to make sure their needs are being met.

The Friendly Visitors program utilizes the services of volunteers from an organization of businesswomen who make regular visits to isolated and homebound individuals in the Center area.

The Companion Aides have been screened for their ability to work in the homes of those who need extra attention. This service does not cover housecleaning or housekeeping, nor is it a nursing service, but takes on the character of duties that children might do for their parents. The Companion Aides are chosen for their personal qualities of caring for people, as well as for general competence. The volunteer coordinator tries to match the abilities of the aide and the home situation to assure pleasant mutual relations.

The Security and Protection coordinator holds sessions on maintaining personal security in the home and on the street. At various times personal property identification has been promoted through the free use of stencil machines and house markers. Neighborhood block watching has also been encouraged.

The newest home service is the Shepherd's Center Hospice Team, specially trained to give assistance to the terminally ill patient. The volunteer coordinator informs the patient and family of the availability of various Shepherd's Center services, and then designs a support program as desired by the patient and family, drawing on a bank of trained volunteers.

In the Shepherd's Center model, home services are limited to those over sixty-five living in a defined area. This is the area in which the twenty-five churches and synagogues are located and includes a population base of over 53,000 people, with nearly 12,000 over the age of sixty-five. Service has been thus limited to enable volunteers to provide a network of security and service that will serve *all* persons in that area who need some specific support.

Church people often find it hard to enforce a restriction like this; many assume that a church ought to be able to serve the "whole world." Yet too big an area of service usually results in no one really being served because people are not able to rely on the service when it is needed. It should be emphasized however, that only home services are restricted to the residents of the target area. The many programs that are provided at the churches are open to all who want to attend, regardless of their place of residence.

CENTER SERVICES

Home services are offered to help people survive in their later years, but equally important are the programs designed to deal with the question *"Why* survive?" From early in the development of the Shepherd's Center, attention has been given to life enrichment and life reconstruction programs.

Adventures in Learning is the largest of these programs. It is a full day of adult education. Participants have choices of over forty subjects that are stimulating and varied, all taught by volunteers, usually older adults themselves. Courses are offered on a four-quarter system. There is a small registration fee per quarter. Registration may run as high as 800 people, including the sixty-five required to staff the program. Courses cover such topics as budgeting, cooking for one, the Bible, Yoga, travel, books, languages, exercise, and many others. With a choice of from eight to fourteen different courses each hour, there is something for everyone in an atmosphere that conveys the idea that life is a continuing adventure in learning.

The Life Enrichment program attracts about 125 persons each year, divided into basic and advanced groups. Under the leadership of a volunteer clinical psychologist, these weekly three-hour sessions deal with life experiences. The purpose of the program is to motivate those who have led fruitful lives for a number of years but who for some reason find themselves depleted in some way.

The Health Enrichment Center is a response to the understandably high priority older people must give to their health. Health lectures, nutrition sessions, exercise classes, and nurse assistance programs are all incorporated in the Adventures in Learning schedule. In addition, the Health Center promotes health fairs, health checks with various screening services, and seasonal inoculations. The work of the Center is primarily motivational, encouraging people to take responsibility for their health, and providing education and exercise for health maintenance.

The Gadabout Tours are low-cost local bus trips to places of interest and historical significance in the area. They offer the companionship, convenience, and security that enable many older people to enjoy getting out to these places.

Defensive Driving courses are offered periodically by volunteers trained by the National Safety Council. Staying mobile is a high priority for older people. Pre-Retirement Seminars are also very popular, with an annual series of outstanding lectures offered to those on the verge of retiring. In addition, the Shepherd's Center leaders participate in pre-retirement programs in industry. A recent development at the Shepherd's Center is an employment service, organized by a group of retired professionals in personnel. The object is to find employment for those retired people who need to return to work for income supplement, or for those who want to use work to enrich life.

IMPACT ON OLDER PEOPLE

The Shepherd's Center model has had an influence on similar programs in other neighborhoods of the city, particularly the idea of accepting responsibility for a particular section of the city rather than for the entire urban area. Other communities have successfully established

Shepherd's Centers in different settings. The concept of the Center will work in any situation, because it is primarily people-oriented.

It is difficult to estimate accurately the number of people continuing to live in the community who would need to move to sheltered care if it were not for assistance from the Shepherd's Center, but that number to date may well be as many as 100. Certainly independent living is extended for a great number of persons. The Center, with its innovative program, has helped adults through what otherwise would have been a wilderness in their later years. As one older person says, "We thought life was coming to an end, only to discover we have a whole new life."

IMPACT ON THE CHURCHES

With its network of caring within the community for all older people, the Shepherd's Center has been a practical way for churches and synagogues to work together, disseminating the message that the faith community cares about older adults, and at the same time furthering the ecumenical spirit in the community. Of the twenty-five churches and synagogues participating, about fourteen are actively involved, with the rest remaining as sponsors. Most of the work done by all the churches together could not be done by any one of the churches alone.

There is now a real confidence in the reliability of the churches in helping people in the community, as the services and programs of the Shepherd's Center continue month after month and year after year. And the success of the Center has given the churches credibility in other programs. It has given a sense of reality and practicality to what might be called a marriage of faith and works.

CREATIVE LAY MINISTRIES

The point of this chapter is that helping older people to respond to the needs of other older people with creative lay ministries is a primary responsibility of the community of faith in our society. This in fact offers some hope of success in the enormously important task of fashioning a value system suitable for the "graying of America."

The experience of the Shepherd's Center suggests four objectives, or areas of direction, for these ministries—

1. Life Maintenance Ministry recognizes that basic physical needs of life must be met. Some people may need a service for some time, while others may need supportive care for only a few days or weeks. Simple, reliable caring systems can be designed so that people can count on receiving a hot meal, having someone to stay with them during a health crisis, or perhaps having transportation to whatever is needed. The planning team constantly asks the question: what do older people need in order to continue living in their situation? It then tries to fill that need in the simplest and most direct manner. Very practical needs surface which then can be met in a dependable way.

Some of the necessary services are available in many communities, but too often they fail to reach persons who need them. An intentional ministry puts people in touch with what they need to survive. It provides a network of caring volunteers, capable of undergirding an older person without destroying a sense of independence or dignity.

2. Life Enrichment Ministry fosters recurring activities and programs based on the rich variety and diversity of human life, reflecting the insatiable curiosity of people capable of learning all of their lives. These are programs of adventures, new experiences, seeking information, and exploration of new talents and interests that younger years denied.

With an abundance of weekday space available, churches are uniquely equipped to provide ministries. But more than property, the doctrine of creation would logically suggest the importance of the church taking the lead in providing programs that enhance life and reflect the fullness of the human spirit in God's creation.

3. Life Reconstruction Ministry is a continuation of a historical function of the church in society. Although our time has seen the rise of mental health organizations, the fact remains that most people continue to look to their churches for statements about life and its meaning, as well as for the resources to reconstruct life.

4. Life Transcending Ministry keeps alive a sense of wonder in a world in which wonder is rapidly vanishing. The ultimate task of all

people is to relate the events of one's life to things eternal. Hope is built on affirming a framework capable of holding all the moments of human experience in some kind of relationship.

The Shepherd's Center is not a church, but rather the expression of the love and care of the church. Therefore, participants are encouraged to return to their own religious traditions for pastoral care and religious celebrations. The residue shared in the faith community suggests the common property among all. The aging process is a part of God's plan of creation, with the good news of God's presence giving hope and purpose in life. Creative lay ministries translate this message through words and deeds, giving reality to the faith statement: God created life, and called it good.

Older people ask two questions of society, of life: how can I maintain my life, and what gives it meaning and purpose? Both questions have religious implications and the community of faith needs to be aggressive in responding.

Index

Achenbaum, W. Andrew, 58
Adolescent crises, 99–100
Adult continuing education, 144, 261–62
Adult religious education, 16, 235–49; for awareness, 236–37; for coherence, 238–39; for intentionality, 237–38; learning theory for the aging, 240–46; for mutuality, 239–40; role of the Church in, 246–47. *See also* Education for ministry with the aging
Agape, 81–82, 83
Age: differences in religious beliefs based on, 162–63; distribution in the United States, 154–55; and religious participation, 155–57
Aged, the: classified as a problem, 11, 56–61, 68, 70, 100, 175; compared to primitive humanity, 101; honesty of, 104–5; identification of, 128–29; integrated in biblical society, 27–32; physical discomforts of, 26–27, 222, 224, 229; physical incapacitation of, 29–30, 216–17; virtues of, 64, 83, 96, 106, 116–17
"Ageism," 14, 85, 137–38
Age, old: acceptance of, 34, 213; concept in the Early Church, 38; as a phase in

the life process, 25–26; transcendence of, 33–34
Aging: cultural antecedents of attitudes toward, 56–75; defined, 235; process of, 9, 118, 161–62, 211, 213, 219, 236–37, 239, 253, 265; as a technological issue, 100; value of past experiences in, 114–15
Alston, Jon P., 158, 159
American Association of Retired Persons, 146
American Piety Study, 165
Apostolic Tradition, 47
Argyle, Michael, 165
Assistance for the elderly: community action and agencies for, 215, 245–46; by the contemporary Church, 85; by the Early Church, 39–42; given with love, 83–84; by lay ministries, 255–65; national pensions for, 65; in the Old Testament, 28–29; by social workers, 50. *See also* Church; Shepherd's Center; Social Security system
Assurance of God's love, 84–85
Athenagoras, 46